In *The Cambridge Companion to Modernism*, ten eminent scholars from Britain and the United States offer timely new appraisals of the revolutionary cultural transformations of the first decades of the twentieth century. Chapters on the major literary genres, intellectual, political and institutional contexts, film and the visual arts, provide both close analyses of individual works and a broader set of interpretive narratives. A chronology and guide to further reading supply valuable orientation for the study of Modernism. Readers will be able to use the book at once as a standard work of reference and as a stimulating source of compelling new readings of works by writers and artists from Joyce and Woolf to Stein, Picasso, Chaplin, H.D. and Freud, and many others. Students will find much-needed help with the difficulties of approaching Modernism, while the chapters' original contributions will send scholars back to this volume for stimulating reevaluation.

THE CAMBRIDGE
COMPANION TO
MODERNISM

CAMBRIDGE COMPANIONS TO LITERATURE

See continuation at the back of the book

THE CAMBRIDGE
COMPANION TO
MODERNISM

EDITED BY
MICHAEL LEVENSON
University of Virginia

CAMBRIDGE
UNIVERSITY PRESS

PUBLISHED BY THE PRESS SYNDICATE OF THE UNIVERSITY OF CAMBRIDGE
The Pitt Building, Trumpington Street, Cambridge CB2 1RP, United Kingdom

CAMBRIDGE UNIVERSITY PRESS
The Edinburgh Building, Cambridge CB2 2RU, United Kingdom   http://www.cup.cam.ac.uk
40 West 20th Street, New York, NY 10011–4211, USA   http://www.cup.org
10 Stamford Road, Oakleigh, Melbourne 3166, Australia

First published 1999

Printed in the United Kingdom at the University Press, Cambridge

Typeset in Sabon 10/13 pt. [CE]

A catalogue record for this book is available from the British Library

Library of Congress cataloging in publication data

The Cambridge companion to modernism / edited by Michael Levenson.
p.   cm. (Cambridge companions to culture)
Includes bibliographical references and index.
1. Modernism (Literature)   2. Modernism (Art)
I. Levenson, Michael H. (Michael Harry), 1951– .   II. Series.
PN56.M54C36   1998
700'.411 – dc 21   98–13355   CIP

ISBN 0 521 49516 4 hardback
ISBN 0 521 49866 x paperback

CONTENTS

ILLUSTRATIONS

CONTRIBUTORS

MICHAEL BELL is the author of *The Sentiment of Reality: Truth of Feeling in the European Novel* (1983), *D. H. Lawrence: Language and Being* (1992), and most recently *Literature, Modernism and Myth: Belief and Responsibility in the Twentieth Century* (1997). He is Professor of English at the University of Warwick.

SARA BLAIR is Associate Professor of English and American literature at the University of Virginia and the author of *Henry James and the Writing of Race and Nation* (1996). She is currently completing a book on modernist cultures in their urban and metropolitan contexts entitled *The Places of the Literary*.

MARIANNE DEKOVEN, Professor of English at the Rutgers University, is the author of *A Different Language: Gertrude Stein's Experimental Writing* (1983), and *Rich and Strange: Gender, History, Modernism* (1991).

CHRISTOPHER INNES is Distinguished Research Professor at York University (Toronto) and a fellow of the Royal Society of Canada. The most recent of his various books on theatre are *Modern British Drama: 1890–1990* (1992) and *Avant-Garde Theatre: 1892–1992* (1993). He was an editor of the journal *Modern Drama* from 1987 to 1997.

MICHAEL LEVENSON is Professor of English at the University of Virginia. He is the author of *A Genealogy of Modernism* (1984) and *Modernism and the Fate of Individuality* (1991).

JAMES LONGENBACH is Joseph Gilmore Professor of English at the University of Rochester and the author most recently of *Modern Poetry after Modernism* (1997) and *Threshold*, a book of poems.

GLEN MACLEOD is a professor of English at the University of Connecticut at Waterbury. He is the author of *Wallace Stevens and Company* (1983) and *Wallace Stevens and Modern Art* (1993).

LAWRENCE RAINEY is the Chair in Modernist Literature at the University of York, he edits the journal *Modernism/Modernity* and has written *Ezra Pound and the Monument of Culture* (1991) and *Institutions of Modernism: Literary Elites and Public Culture* (1998).

DAVID TROTTER is Quain Professor of English at University College, London, and author of *The English Novel in History, 1895–1920* (1993) and other books and essays about nineteenth- and twentieth-century fiction and poetry.

MICHAEL WOOD is Professor of English at Princeton University and the author of *America in the Movies* (1975), *The Magician's Doubts* (1995), and the forthcoming *Children of Silence.*

1890   James George Frazer, first volumes of *The Golden Bough*
(1890–1915)
William Morris, *News from Nowhere*
Henrik Ibsen, *Hedda Gabler*
William Booth, *In Darkest England*
The dismissal of Bismarck

1891   Thomas Hardy, *Tess of the D'Urbervilles*
Oscar Wilde, *The Picture of Dorian Gray*
Arthur Conan Doyle, Sherlock Holmes stories begin in *Strand*
magazine
Franco-Russian *entente*

1893   Arthur Wing Pinero, *The Second Mrs. Tanqueray*
Formation of the Independent Labour Party
The four-wheel car of Karl Benz

1894   The quarterly journal, the *Yellow Book* launched
George Moore, *Esther Waters*
George Bernard Shaw, *Arms and the Man*
Claude Achille Debussy, *L'Après-midi d'un Faune* (music)
The conviction of Dreyfus for treason

1895   Oscar Wilde, *The Importance of Being Earnest*
Joseph Conrad, *Almayer's Folly*
Founding of the London School of Economics
The trial of Oscar Wilde
Roentgen's discovery of X-rays
Guglielmo Marconi invents telegraphy

1896   Anton Chekhov, *The Seagull*
Founding of the *Daily Mail*, London
First modern Olympiad, Athens

The last Gilbert and Sullivan opera, *The Grand Duke*
Giacomo Puccini, *La Bohème* (opera)

1898   Thomas Hardy, *Wessex Poems*
H. G. Wells, *War of the Worlds*
Oscar Wilde, *Ballad of Reading Gaol*
The Curies discover radium and plutonium

1899   William Butler Yeats, *The Wind among the Reeds*
Frédéric François Chopin, *The Awakening* (music)
Leo NikolayevichTolstoy, *Resurrection*
Beginning of the Boer War (1899–1902)
Peace Conference at The Hague

1900   Joseph Conrad, *Lord Jim*
Sigmund Freud, *The Interpretation of Dreams*
"Boxer rebellion" in China

1901   Thomas Mann, *Buddenbrooks*
Johan August Strindberg, *Dance of Death*
Rudyard Kipling, *Kim*
Death of Queen Victoria

1902   André Gide, *The Immoralist*
John Atkinson Hobson, *Imperialism*
Vladimir Ilyich Ulyanov Lenin, *What is to be Done?*
William James, *Varieties of Religious Experience*

1903   Samuel Butler, *The Way of All Flesh* (published posthumously)
Henry James, *The Ambassadors*
George Bernard Shaw, *Man and Superman*
G. E. Moore, *Principia Ethica*
The Great Train Robbery (film)
First successful flight of the Wright brothers
Emmeline Pankhurst founds the Women's Social and Political
Union

1904   John Millington Synge, *Riders to the Sea*
Anton Chekhov, *The Cherry Orchard*
Joseph Conrad, *Nostromo*
Giacomo Puccini, *Madame Butterfly* (opera)
Beginning of the Russo-Japanese War (1904–5)

1905   Richard Strauss, *Salomé*
Oscar Wilde, *De Profundis*

Edith Wharton, *The House of Mirth*
Albert Einstein proposes the theory of relativity
The founding of Sinn Fein, the Irish nationalist party

1907   Pablo Picasso, *Les Demoiselles d'Avignon* (painting)
Cubist exhibition in Paris
Joseph Conrad, *Secret Agent*
John Millington Synge, *Playboy of the Western World*

1908   Gertrude Stein, *Three Lives*
Arnold Bennett, *The Old Wives' Tale*
Jacob Epstein, *Figures* for the British Medical Association
Ford Madox Ford edits *English Review*
George Sorel, *Reflections on Violence*
Bela Bartók, first string quartet

1909   Gustav Mahler, *Symphony No. 9*
Henri Matisse, *The Dance* (painting)
Frank Lloyd Wright, Robie House
Ezra Pound, *Personae*
Arnold Schönberg, *Five Orchestral Pieces*
Lloyd George's "People's Budget"
Sergei Pavlovich Diaghilev produces the Russian Ballet in Paris
Sigmund Freud lectures on psychoanalysis in the US

1910   Post-impressionist exhibition in London
Igor Stravinsky, *The Firebird* (ballet)
E. M. Forster, *Howards End*
Bertrand Russell and A. N. Whitehead, *Principia Mathematica* (1910–1913)
Japanese annexation of Korea
Death of Edward VII, accession of George V

1912   Marcel Duchamp, *Nude Descending a Staircase* (painting)
George Bernard Shaw, *Pygmalion*
Arnold Schönberg, *Pierre Lunaire* (music)
Sarah Bernhardt in the film *Queen Elizabeth*
Sinking of the Titanic
Beginning of the Balkan Wars (1912–13)

1913   Willa Cather, *O Pioneers!*
D. H. Lawrence, *Sons and Lovers*
Thomas Mann, *Death in Venice*
Robert Frost, *A Boy's Will*

Marcel Proust, *Swann's Way*
Igor Stravinsky, *Le Sacre du Printemps* (ballet)
Edmund Husserl, *Phenomenology*
Suffragette demonstrations in London

1914 James Joyce, *Dubliners*
Joseph Conrad, *Chance*
Robert Frost, *North of Boston*
Founding of *Blast*
Outbreak of World War I

1915 Virginia Woolf, *The Voyage Out*
D. H. Lawrence, *The Rainbow*
Somerset Maugham, *Of Human Bondage*
Ezra Pound, *Cathay*
Cecil B. de Mille, *Carmen* (film)
D. W. Griffith, *Birth of a Nation* (film)

1916 James Joyce, *A Portrait of the Artist as a Young Man*
D. W. Griffith, *Intolerance* (film)
Dadaism in Zurich

1917 T. S. Eliot, *Prufrock and Other Observations*
Paul Valéry, *La Jeune parque*
Amy Lowell, *Tendencies in Modern American Poetry*
Serge Sergeyevich Prokofiev, *"Classical" Symphony*
Carl Jung, *The Unconscious*
Revolutions in Russia

1918 James Joyce, *Exiles*
Lytton Strachey, *Eminent Victorians*
Paul Klee, *Gartenplan* (painting)
Votes for women age thirty and over in Britain

1919 Pablo Picasso, *Pierrot and Harlequin* (painting)
Thomas Hardy, *Collected Poems*
Ezra Pound, *Hugh Selwyn Mauberly*
Robert Weine, *The Cabinet of Dr. Caligari* (film)
Sherwood Anderson, *Winesburg, Ohio*
John Maynard Keynes, *The Economic Consequences of the Peace*
Bauhaus founded at Weimar by Walter Gropius
Treaty of Versailles, end of World War I

1920 D. H. Lawrence, *Women in Love*
George Bernard Shaw, *Heartbreak House*

Edith Wharton, *The Age of Innocence*
Katherine Mansfield, *Bliss and Other Stories*
Sinclair Lewis, *Main Street*
Eugene O'Neill, *The Emperor Jones*
Henri Matisse, *L'Odalisque* (painting)
American women achieve the vote

1921   Luigi Pirandello, *Six Characters in Search of an Author*
John Dos Passos, *Three Soldiers*
Pablo Picasso, *Three Musicians* (painting)
Edvard Munch, *The Kiss* (painting)
Charles Chaplin, *The Kid* (film)
D. W. Griffith, *Orphans of the Storm* (film)
New Economic Policy in the USSR

1922   T. S. Eliot, *The Waste Land*
James Joyce, *Ulysses*
Virginia Woolf, *Jacob's Room*
Sinclair Lewis, *Babbit*
Bertolt Brecht, *Drums in the Night* (play)
Ludwig Wittgenstein, *Tractatus Logico-Philosophicus*
Fritz Lang, *Dr. Mabuse* (film)
Friedrich Murnau, *Nosferatu* (film)
Founding of *Criterion*
Founding of the British Broadcasting Company (BBC)

1924   E. M. Forster, *A Passage to India*
Thomas Mann, *The Magic Mountain*
Sean O'Casey, *Juno and the Paycock*
Cecil B. de Mille, *The Ten Commandments* (film)

1925   Virginia Woolf, *Mrs. Dalloway*
Gertrude Stein, *The Making of Americans*
Willa Cather, *The Professor's House*
Scott Fitzgerald, *The Great Gatsby*
Theodore Dreiser, *An American Tragedy*
Ernest Hemingway, *In Our Time*
Franz Kafka, *The Trial* (posthumous)
Sergei Eisenstein, *Battleship Potemkin* (film)
Charles Chaplin, *The Gold Rush* (film)
Pablo Picasso, *Three Dancers* (painting)
A. N. Whitehead, *Science and the Modern World*
Adolf Hitler, *Mein Kampf*

1926   Ernest Hemingway, *The Sun Also Rises*
T. E. Lawrence, *The Seven Pillars of Wisdom*
William Faulkner, *Soldier's Pay*
Fritz Lang, *Metropolis* (film)
Jean Renoir, *Nana* (film)
Henry Moore, *Draped Reclining Figure* (sculpture)
General strike throughout Britain

1927   Virginia Woolf, *To the Lighthouse*
Ernest Hemingway, *Men without Women*
Marcel Proust, *Le Temps retrouvé* (posthumous)
Jacob Epstein, *Madonna and Child* (sculpture)
Jerome Kern and Oscar Hammerstein, *Show Boat* (stage)
Martin Heidegger, *Being and Time*
Sigmund Freud, *The Future of an illusion*

1928   W. B. Yeats, *The Tower*
D. H. Lawrence, *Lady Chatterley's Lover*
Aldous Huxley, *Point Counter Point*
Sergei Eisenstein, *October* (film)

1929   Robert Bridges, *The Testament of Beauty*
Robert Graves, *Goodbye to All That*
Virginia Woolf, *A Room of One's Own*
Alfred Hitchcock, *Blackmail*
Second Surrealist manifesto
Opening of the Museum of Modern Art, New York
Collapse of the New York stock market

1930   W. H. Auden, *Poems*
Hart Crane, *The Bridge*
William Faulkner, *As I Lay Dying*
Evelyn Waugh, *Vile Bodies*
F. R. Leavis, *Mass Civilisation and Minority Culture*
Sigmund Freud, *Civilisation and its Discontents*

1931   Eugene O'Neil, *Mourning Becomes Electra*
Tristan Tzara, *L'Homme approximatif*
Henri Matisse, *The Dance* (painting)
Fritz Lang, *M* (film)
Charles Chaplin, *City Lights* (film)
Mussolini and Forzano, the 100 Days

1932   Bertolt Brecht, *The Mother*
Louis-Ferdinand Céline, *Voyage au bout de la Nuit*
W. H. Auden, *The Orators*
Aldous Huxley, *Brave New World*

1933   Gertrude Stein, *The Autobiography of Alice B. Toklas*
André Malraux, *La Condition humaine*
T. S. Eliot, *The Use of Poetry and the Use of Criticism*

1935   T. S. Eliot, *Murder in the Cathedral*
W. H. Auden and Christopher Isherwood, *The Dog Beneath the Skin*
George Gershwin, *Porgy and Bess* (stage)
Salvador Dali, *Giraffe on Fire*
Dmitri Shostakovich, *Symphony No. 1*
Clifford Odets, *Waiting for Lefty*

1936   Dylan Thomas, *Twenty-five Poems*
Stevie Smith, *Novel on Yellow Paper*
Piet Mondrian, *Composition in Red and Blue* (painting)
Charles Chaplin, *Modern Times* (film)
A. J. Ayer, *Language, Truth and Logic*
John Maynard Keynes, *General Theory of Employment, Interest and Money*

1938   Elizabeth Bowen, *The Death of the Heart*
Jean Anouilh, *Le Voyageur sans bagage*
Jean Cocteau, *Les Parents terribles* (film)
Bela Bartók, *Violin Concerto*
Lewis Mumford, *The Culture of Cities*
Pablo Picasso, *Women in Easy Chair* (painting)
Sergei Eisenstein, *Alexander Nevsky* (film)

1939   James Joyce, *Finnegans Wake*
Thomas Mann, *Lotte in Weimar*
T. S. Eliot, *The Family Reunion*
Pablo Picasso, *Night Fishing at Antibes* (painting)
Jean Renoir, *The Rules of the Game* (film)
Beginning of World War II

MICHAEL LEVENSON

Introduction

Still we call it Modernism, and this despite the anomaly of holding to such a name for an epoch fast receding into the cultural past. Not long after this volume is published, "Modernism" will be the name of a period in the beginning of a previous century, too distant even to serve as a figure for the grandparent. Uneasily but inevitably, we have reached a time when many feel the obsolescence of a movement still absurdly wearing such a brazen title. The temptation, much indulged in recent years, has been to dance beyond the reach of the aging, dying giant, to prove that one can live past the epoch marked by such names as Joyce and Woolf, Pound and Eliot, Eisenstein and Brecht, Freud and Marx. Certainly, many forces have joined to change the vectors of late twentieth-century culture. But our contemporary imperative to declare a new period and to declare ourselves citizens of a liberated postmodernism has badly distorted and sadly simplified the moment it means to surpass.

No one should be surprised by the distortions and simplifications of Modernism. Nor should anyone waste tears of sympathy on figures who themselves were more than willing to cut the shape of the past to suit present polemical purposes. And yet the task of rendering a fuller account is justified not only by the desire to provide richer, thicker narratives but also by a pressing need to clarify our own late-century, new-millennial position. A coarsely understood Modernism is at once an historical scandal and a contemporary disability.

Do we call for a return to Modernism? Certainly not, if this implies a nostalgic attempt to undo the last decades in order to share the dream of a movement that would never age and never end – but incontestably, if it means availing ourselves of the great timeliness of a revaluation. The influence of the first thirty years of the century over the next fifty was so great that the achievement of a distance from Modernism remains an event in contemporary culture. We are still learning how not to be Modernist, which is reason all the more to see what such an ambition could mean.

No clarification will be possible unless we who live at a moment of cultural skepticism are able to acknowledge the force of cultural conviction. When Gertrude Stein exploded stylistic propriety in order to release new rhythms in language, when Picasso painted primitive masks over the faces of his Demoiselles d'Avignon, when Antonin Artaud howled "No more masterpieces," when Woolf conjured a sister to Shakespeare, when Joyce trained himself to "scorch" the culture that nourished him, they all knew themselves to be engaged in forms of creative violence. For these figures the aim could never be simply to set the imagination free; it was rather first of all to challenge an unfreedom, the oppressions of journalism, of genteel audiences, of timid readers, of political and religious orthodoxy. So much of the story that these figures told themselves was a tale of tyranny and resistance. The name of the tyrant changed – the Editor, the Lady, the Public, the Banker, the Democrat – but whatever the scenario, the narrowness of the oppressor was seen amply to justify the violence of the art.

Much of this narrative was strategic, a means of rousing the will of the artist and of stimulating the useful anger of the public. We late-century historians can now see and show that the agon between revolutionary artist and benighted traditionalist was a caricature and that, as Lawrence Rainey argues below, high Modernist purpose was closely wound in the web of the commercial market. Rather than paint them as elite purists seeking a magic circle for the imagination, we can better see these artists as sharply conscious of their historical entanglements, their place within an epoch of accelerating social *modernization* that was always a challenge to a cultural Modernism.

Because its leading voices eagerly assumed not only the burden of making new artifacts, but also the responsibility for offering new justifications, the misunderstandings of Modernism began at the start, began with the ambition of writers and artists to set the terms by which they would be understood, where this often meant setting the terms by which others would not qualify for understanding. The circle of initiates was closed not only against the unwashed public, but also against rival artists who were excluded from the emerging narrative of Modernism triumphant. In the last twenty years this once dominant narrative has lost its power to control responses to the period, and we now have a dramatically enlarged perception of the range and reach of achievement. What once seemed the exclusive affair of "modern masters," the "men of 1914" (as Wyndham Lewis called them), now stands revealed as a complex of inventive gestures, daring performances, enacted also by many who were left out of account in the early histories of the epoch, histories offered first by the actors themselves and later produced within an academic discourse, willingly guided by the precedents of the eminent artists. As Marianne DeKoven shows in her chapter, it is now deeply startling to realize how Stein's literary radicalism was omitted by the canonical narratives. And as Sara Blair securely demonstrates, the challenge of the Harlem Renaissance must belong to any account of Modernism with even modest aspirations to historical density.

No one should expect that our recession from these early century decades will allow the many varied performances to assume at last the crisp shape of unity. Nor should we regret the loss. Within the emerging historical revision there can still be found certain common devices and general preoccupations: the recurrent act of fragmenting unities (unities of character or plot or pictorial space or lyric form), the use of mythic paradigms, the refusal of norms of beauty, the willingness to make radical linguistic experiment, all often inspired by the resolve (in Eliot's phrase) to startle and disturb the public. Increasingly, though, attention has fallen upon a range of irreducibly local ambitions, highly particular projects not broadly shared but peculiar to a band of eager practitioners working in a sharply delimited field. The course of modern drama narrated here by Christopher Innes needs to be preserved in the specificity of its medium, as do the provocations of painting and cinema, described by Michael Wood and Glen MacLeod. As we acknowledge the full compass of the work, it will prove better to be minimalist in our definitions of that conveniently flaccid term *Modernist* and maximalist in our accounts of the diverse *modernizing* works and movements, which are sometimes deeply congruent with one another, and just as often opposed or even contradictory.

So much of the artistic passion of the period was stirred by questions of technique, where "technique" should not suggest attention to "form" as opposed to "content," but should imply rather the recognition that every element of the work is an instrument of its effect and therefore open to technical revision. Nothing was beyond the reach of technical concern: not the frame of a picture, not the shape of a stage, not the choice of a subject, not the status of a rhyme. If a new medium such as film was extravagantly bound up with problems of technique, so too was an ancient genre such as lyric poetry. And as David Trotter's chapter shows in great detail, novels of the period continually enacted strenuous negotiations between new formal strategies and the unprecedented social matter that they sought to absorb.

One of the notable effects of the regime of technique was precisely to bring attention to the close particularities of a specific genre. How long should a poem be? Could a still life rise off the surface of a painting? The general disposition – to radicalize the techniques of art – resolved into a rich multiplicity of different strategies, strongly localized experiments.

Despite a variety of efforts to bind the arts into a common cultural front, as in Pound's eagerness in 1914–15 to write poems somehow congruent with the experimental painting of Wyndham Lewis, the artistic results were most often short-lived and unpersuasive. The result is that the period 1890–1930 saw the sharply uneven development of the separate enterprises. Within prevailing narratives of English Modernism, the achievements in poetry and the novel between, say, 1914 and 1922 have been taken as the paradigm of modernist achievement. Useful as this view may be in comprehending the "men of 1914" – Pound, Eliot, Lewis, chief among them – it has become demonstrably inadequate to the enlarged domain. As Christopher Innes pointedly observes, such a paradigm has never been able to account for the development of twentieth-century drama. James Longenbach implicitly demonstrates that such a reading makes no better sense of the careers of Frost, Moore, or Stevens. Nor can it comprehend major episodes in painting and in film.

Crisis is inevitably the central term of art in discussions of this turbulent cultural moment. Overused as it has been, it still glows with justification. War! Strike! Women! The Irish! Or (within the popular press), Nihilism! Relativism! Fakery! This century had scarcely grown used to its own name, before it learned the twentieth would be the epoch of crisis, real and manufactured, physical and metaphysical, material and symbolic. The catastrophe of the First World War, and before that, the labor struggles, the emergence of feminism, the race for empire, these inescapable forces of turbulent social modernization were not simply looming on the outside as the destabilizing context of cultural Modernism; they penetrated the interior of artistic invention. They gave subjects to writers and painters, and they also gave forms, forms suggested by industrial machinery, or by the chuffing of cars, or even, most horribly, the bodies broken in the war.

If the social cataclysms left traces on modernist art, so did that art inform and to an extent *form* the conception of social life within historical crisis. Along with the massive intellectual challenge offered by Marx and Nietzsche, Freud and Frazer, Heidegger and Wittgenstein, chronicled in Michael Bell's chapter, the new art of film changed habits of perception, and the experiments enacted within the older arts of painting, poetry, drama, and novel incited the consciousness of breakdown.

Yet if the milieu of crisis incontestably affected the spirits of artists, who like others in their generation sometimes succumbed to great personal demoralization, it would be a mistake to paint these decades in unending shades of gray. Was modern civilization all a "Heart of Darkness?" Was it an arid "Waste Land?" True enough, figures of nihilism, of degeneration and despair, circulate quickly both in the work and in the responses to the work. The loss of faith, the groundlessness of value, the violence of war, and a nameless, faceless anxiety – no one is likely be surprised by such a list of disturbances, at once individual and social. But here we come to a further complex effect of the passion for technique. Not only did it solicit attention to the close particulars of a genre at a given historical moment; it also opened a field of action, a theatre of conviction, within the wider social failure.

It is fair, and indeed important, to preserve memory of an alienation, an uncanny sense of moral bottomlessness, a political anxiety. There was so much to doubt: the foundations of religion and ethics, the integrity of governments and selves, the survival of a redemptive culture. But if the fate of the West seemed uncertain and shadowy, the struggles with the metrical scheme of lyric poetry or the pictorial space of a cubist painting could seem bracingly crisp. Shining luminously from so much of the work is the happiness of concentrated purpose and the pride of the cultural laborer, believing fully in the artistic task at hand.

Only a decade or two after Oscar Wilde's witty campaign against earnestness, these early century Modernists are distinguished precisely by the earnestness of their resolve. A deep, sometimes even dour, seriousness allowed many fragile personalities to carry on through private hardship. And if there is one temperamental difference sharply separating our late-century selves and our early century progenitors, it may be our own instinctive distance from the belief that the publication of a poem or the exhibition of a painting can so triumphantly confirm the creator and so decisively serve the culture. Among these Modernists were many connois-seurs of irony, but the irony was characteristically in the service of high-minded conviction that became still more explicit – more politically strenuous, more religiously ambitious – as the movement wore on.

What is so distinctive about such occasions of high conviction is how rarely they belonged either to solitary figures capable of pleasing themselves or to those who enjoyed comfortable relations with the wider public. The will to live out the risks of technical experiment – and the celebrity achieved later in the century should not obscure the extent of the risk – was characteristically nourished within small groups of mutually confirming artists, able to defend one another against neglect, incomprehension or often biting critique. The circles forming around Stein, Woolf, Pound, and DuBois, the collaborations of Picasso and Braque or Ford and Conrad, the trooping together of Dadaists and Surrealists were as much the condition of what we call Modernism as any set of formal gestures. In January 1923 Woolf filled pages of her diary with an account of a Bloomsbury party the evening before, which in her heightened presentation comes to seem an emblem of her cultural position, even an allegory of her modernity.

> Suppose one's normal pulse to be 70: in five minutes it was 120: & the blood, not the sticky whitish fluid of daytime, but brilliant & prickling like champagne. This was my state, & most peoples. We collided, when we met: went pop, used Christian names, flattered, praised, & thought (or I did) of Shakespeare . . . We were all easy & gifted & friendly & like good children rewarded by having the capacity for enjoying ourselves thus. Could our fathers? . . . There is something indescribably congenial to me in this easy artists talk; the values the same as my own & therefore right; no impediments; life charming, good & interesting; no effort; art brooding calmly over it all.[1]

Woolf would write in other tones about many other evenings, but this passage speaks eloquently to the positive conditions of a Modernism of small social cells, nourished on the pleasures and powers of comradeship. In light of this description, and countless other such passages, we can speak of the micro-sociology of modernist innovation, within which small groups of artists were able to sustain their resolve – or more than sustain, able to create small flourishing communities based on the powers of reciprocal acknowledgment. Whether the opponent took on the aspect of the outraged traditionalist or the bored and inattentive distraction-seeker, the regular presence of the collaborator, or the group, was often enough to keep the will to cultural insurrection alive. Within this context the idea of a "party" takes on an important double signification: as a festivity and also as a cadre of insurrectionists. At such happy moments as this evening of 1923, the two senses combine, and it was possible to experience keen enjoyment while feeling that an advance was being made against the empire of those "fathers," who never could enjoy themselves and whose moralism blocked the flow of artists' talk.

Through the early decades of modernist experiment, the mix of skepticism and ardor – skepticism about the destiny of the species, ardor for the latest innovation in a brush stroke or a rhyme scheme – might well have led to the state of affairs familiar in recent caricatures of Modernism: the proud political abstention of those who sought perfection of the work at the expense of social engagement, who curled inside the "autonomy" of art, safe from the historical instability towards which they remained cool, indifferent, fastidious. We need not doubt the lure of abstention or the siren call of autonomy, but the more complete our historical recovery and the less constrained by polemical need, the clearer it is that the late, sometimes infamous, political turns were prepared during times of apparent social indifference. Pound's *Jefferson and/or Mussolini* and Picasso's *Guernica* are radically different works, but both strong political statements grew out of earlier aggressions performed within the politics of culture. The efforts to slay the authority of George Eliot or poetic rhetoric or the conventions of pictorial realism were a preparation for the often bombastic social politics of late Modernism.

Pound's bellowing cry, "I want a new civilization," was more peremptory than others and more unfortunate in its effects, but it was hardly a lone demand for the extension of formal concentration into the broadest realms of politics. The challenge from the Left, from workers' parties within European democracies and from the example of the Russian revolution, and the challenge from the Right, from Action Française to the rise of fascism, squeezed liberal moderation and the moderate forms of art that nourished it.

The generation of artists who had created so much turbulence in their own and the century's youth reached late middle age when the whole world began to shudder. By the late twenties and the thirties, a host of new reputations had been secured. And whether or not it was due to the triumph of cultural vindication, those who had stood in artistic alliance had nearly all separated. From the position of proud isolation, they encountered the miserable years of the century.

How could the many Modernisms ever have aged gracefully? It is not simply that the young had to grow older and that revolutionary fervor was likely to fade, but also that special historical torsions placed so much strain on ambitious careers. Did Picasso play the art market with integrity-weakening cynicism? Was Pound right in saying that his cantos were "a botch," and was fascism the botching agent? Was Woolf's feminism ensnared within a deep class snobbery? Did Eliot's anti-Semitism reach down to the roots of his poetry? A movement committed to the rejuvenation of art exposed its own weaknesses as it grew older. Partly this was due to uglinesses of character that are not to be thought away, and partly it was due to the pressures of an ugly age.

As the grand artistic achievements have grown encrusted with cliché, the inescapable failings of an aging and increasingly divided Modernism – sometimes moral failings, sometimes aesthetic – have understandably encouraged the desire to consign those decades to a closed past. Certainly, whether we desire it or not, a new age is where we must live. But the long span of Modernism, longer now than ever, is a serious test of our own historical character. It is so tempting to make the many Modernisms into one thing, and then to place that one thing into a single chapter within a tidy narrative.

A *Companion* cannot be a friend to everyone. It cannot invite all achievement to the table; and ambitious though this volume is, it must perform resolute acts of exclusion in order to begin speaking at all. The strong central emphasis falls upon Anglo-American Modernism from the last decade of the nineteenth century up to the beginning of the Second World War. But this act of attention aims to be a focus not a prison. My own keen hope is that the following chapters will encourage an eye for new distinctions that will free the reader from the sight of any dull monolith in these originary decades and will make it possible for those of widely different tastes and temperaments to recognize the profusion within which there is ample room for reverence and resistance.

NOTES

1 *The Diary of Virginia Woolf*, vol. II, 1920–4, ed. Anne Olivier Bell (Harmondsworth: Penguin, 1978), pp. 223–4.

I

MICHAEL BELL

The metaphysics of Modernism

I Approaching Modernism

Although the difficulties of defining Modernism are properly aired else-where in this volume, its broad outlines are now only too familiar: its peak period in the Anglo-American context lay between 1910 and 1925, while its intellectual formation encompassed a coming to terms with the lines of thought associated with Marx, Freud, and Nietzsche. Yet despite its apparent familiarity, interpretation of the literature of the period has become less rather than more clear by the end of the century. In particular, as Modernism becomes the assumed background against which to define postmodernism, it is in danger of being both banalized and misappreciated at the same time. Since the change from Modernism to postmodernism is not a difference in metaphysic so much as a different stage in the digestion of the same metaphysic, this chapter focuses on how new thought was assimilated at the time. And similarly, rather than giving an encyclopedic synopsis of intellectual developments within and preceding the period, it concentrates on the interpretative cruxes of Modernism, which are in many ways precisely a testing of this body of thought.

Indeed, one of the reasons it is hard to avoid approaching Modernism on the purely intellectual plane is that the question of interpretation lies at its heart. Each of the great triumvirate turned human life into a fundamentally hermeneutic activity. Marx had analyzed the external realm of social and economic process and laid bare the "false consciousness" by which the advantaged classes unwittingly rationalized their own condition.[1] Freud investigated the inner realm of the psyche and showed how, through the processes of "sublimation," consciousness may itself act as a sophisticated barrier to recognizing the true nature of instinctual desire. And this is not just a personal problem to be diagnosed, it is the necessary basis of civilization.[2] Meanwhile, Nietzsche diagnosed the whole tradition of Western metaphysics from Socrates onwards as a subtle form of falsehood

9

reflecting an inner suppression and outer domination. Christianity in particular was a gigantic fraud perpetrated by the psyche on itself.[3] In all three cases it is not just that external appearances, and the commonsensical or rational means of understanding them, are limited and fallible. It is that such appearances and reasoning may be actively disguising contrary truths to which, by definition, there is no other access. The very principle of reason collapses unnervingly into possible rationalization while reason remains the only means of negotiating this recognition. On this reading, the attempt of the European Enlightenment to bring about a rational and humane order not only suffered the dangers of rationalistic and utilitarian narrowness, to which romanticism was partly a reaction, but was tainted in itself. On the darkest interpretation, neither Enlightenment nor its alternatives are viable.

The specific theories, judgments, and premises of these three cultural diagnosticians have themselves been increasingly subjected to radical critique as their own cultural and period formations have become more evident, but their underlying legacy of hermeneutic suspicion remains. Indeed, they have been most effectively fought by those who could best use their own weapons against them and that effectively epitomizes the relation of the modern to the postmodern. A new cultural moment, and new forms of artistic expression, have undoubtedly come into being, yet they are inevitably still working out the inner possibilities of the earlier period. The shift is in the cultural and political interpretation of the same metaphysic. But when an idea is differently lived, or is lived in a different historical world, it is in some sense a different idea and hence the need to clarify the underlying metaphysics of Modernism as understood in its day. Indeed, the question of living is crucial here since modernist literature is often concerned with the question of how to live within a new context of thought, or a new worldview. This is why, although much literature of the period is notoriously self-conscious about its own form, this frequently goes with a remarkable implicitness as to its meaning. As Pound said, "An "idea" has little value apart from the modality of the mind which receives it."[4] This caveat, and the very bracketing of the word "idea," catches a common modernist resistance to concepts as such and suggests the importance of the implicit dimension, of what Wittgenstein called the "form of life," as the level at which literary form becomes meaningful.[5] Indeed, translating modernist literature into ideas may be the way to miss the most fundamental point. To appreciate the force of this it is helpful to start with the most objective and prestigious mode of knowledge to be challenged by the living metaphysic of several modernist writers: namely, natural science.

II Science

The modernist generation, both critically and creatively, was centrally concerned with the relations between literary form and modes of knowledge or understanding. Throughout much of the nineteenth century natural science had been the paradigmatic form of truth statement; as was evident in the way the fiction of the period constantly modeled itself, whether literally or metaphorically, on science. Zola's naturalism, theorized in *The Experimental Novel* (1880), was the culminating example. But well before the turn of the century science itself was losing some of its epistemological self-evidence and privileged status. Einstein's relativity theory was to catch the headlines and, like Heisenberg's "indeterminacy," it seemed to have an analogical application to other, nonscientific spheres.[6] But the true impact of the shift in scientific thinking arose from the last two decades of the nineteenth century; the same decades that saw the most intense unease about realist form. For fiction was also involved in the radical modern departure, across all of the arts, from representational verisimilitude. However problematic they are, the terms "realism" and "verisimilitude" inevitably suggest some truth value in their mode of imitation and the general shift is part of an epochal epistemological change for which science provides the clearest focus.

Two books intended for educated lay readers conveniently bracket the period: Karl Pearson's *The Grammar of Science* (1892) and Arthur Eddington's *The Nature of the Physical World* (1928). In the middle of the nineteenth century physical science still seemed an irrefragably inductive structure built on the testable foundation of empirical observation. And in the layman's conception this remained the case. But as scientific inquiry addressed itself to astronomical and subatomic scales, the underlying notion of observation was increasingly problematic. It became evident that the universe at these levels behaved in a different way from the commonsense world of everyday experience while the necessary questions could only be asked through highly speculative theory. The last decade of the century saw a running controversy as to whether the basic material of the universe behaved like waves or particles; a controversy for which there was no direct observation.[7] Pearson expressed this for a general public by saying that science does not "explain" the workings of the universe, it merely describes what happens in given conditions. Quite evidently, this recognition of epistemological limitation did not impede the progress of science, indeed it reinforced the creative need to think outside commonsense or inherited terms, but it brought home the recognition that science is a construction of the human mind before it is a reflection of the world. And where there were serious doubts about the hegemony of scientific thinking in the culture at large, this provided a philosophical argument for relativizing its value. As Nietzsche put it in 1872, "great men . . . have contrived, with an incredible amount of thought, to make use of the paraphernalia of science itself, to point out the limits and relativity of knowledge generally, and thus to deny decisively the claim of science to universal validity and universal aims."[8] This was crucial to several modern writers who deliberately used science as just one of the possible orders of understanding rather than as the ultimate form of truth statement. The "Ithaca" episode of *Ulysses*, the first part of *The Magic Mountain*, Lawrence's essays on psychoanalysis, and Proust's use of scientific analysis and metaphor all carry this implication.

But there is a more complex and positive point here than the epistemological limitations of natural science. Eddington, looking back on the period, opens with a homely but telling image. The modern physicist, he says, lives in two worlds at once. He uses the same solid plane surface of the writing table as anyone else, but he also knows that the table is "really" a mass of moving particles through which, given the appropriate technique, it would be possible to penetrate without disturbance.[9] Roentgen had invented the X ray in 1895, and it was pregnantly used in Thomas Mann's *The Magic Mountain* (1924).[10] That was Mann's most synoptically modernist work and the X ray remains a suggestive image of Modernism. For Eddington implies a living synthesis of different world conceptions. The modern physicist continues to live in the Newtonian world of the layman while knowing its limited, almost illusory, character. Or in other words, the commonsense table continues to exist but only within a human scale of reference. Several of the greatest works of modern literature are characterized by such a double awareness. They use realist representation, indeed they often use it consummately, yet with an X ray awareness of its constructed, or purely human, character. The modernist decades were a time of epochal shift, like that of Shakespeare and Cervantes, and the most summative works of the period were frequently those which, like them, owned a dual loyalty. Different world conceptions are held together in a mutually defining, mutually testing, relation. The past is criticized, yet it is also preserved on a new basis and one consequence is that it becomes necessary to speak not of *the* world so much as of the human "world."

III   The human "world"

The force of this can be seen in Martin Heidegger's retrospective definition of modernity as the "Age of the World Picture":

The expressions "world picture of the modern age" and "modern world picture" . . . assume something that never could have been before, namely, a medieval world picture and an ancient world picture. The world picture does not change from an earlier medieval one into a modern one, but rather the fact that the world becomes picture at all is what distinguishes the essence of the modern age.[11]

Heidegger sees this relativistic consciousness as a defining characteristic of modernity, and he goes on to cite both modern humanism and the rise of anthropology as aspects of this. For the awareness of living simultaneously on a human and a nonhuman plane inevitably problematizes the human itself as a worldview, or a congeries of overlapping worldviews. In the later twentieth century it has become common to speak disparagingly of humanism as an unacknowledged ideology naturalizing the given social order, and then to see Modernism in turn as tainted with this.[12] But the opposite is closer to the truth: the relative status of the human was a central recognition of Modernism itself. Lawrence, for example, writing in 1914 about the work which was to become *The Rainbow* (1915) and *Women in Love* (1920), rejected the "old stable ego" of humanist ethical characterization because he only cared "about what the woman *is* – what she *IS* – inhumanly, physiologically, materially – . . . what she *is* as a phenomenon (or as representing some greater, inhuman will), instead of what she feels according to the human conception."[13] Yet of course he was equally interested in what his characters felt as individuals, and the category of the individual retained a crucial importance for him. In the same letter, therefore, he criticizes the Italian Futurist Marinetti for seeking a purely scientific or technological vision when a human being was in question.[14] This precisely epitomizes the modernist synthesis as outlined above. Marinetti's Futurism, with its celebration of the machine, represented a debunking of humanism whereas Lawrence was incorporating something of Marinetti's spirit into an enlarged conception. In this he was one with Joyce and Thomas Mann.

Many writers thus "saved the appearances" of humanism, holding that in these areas appearances may be all that can matter to human beings.[15] The fact that the world itself does not privilege the human, which was a matter of shock to Thomas Hardy and other Victorian agnostics, was incorporated into a more self-standing humanist conception. Victorian attempts to base humanistic values, such as ethics and criticism, on science persisted well into the twentieth century, but the modernist decades started to reverse this relation.[16] Virginia Woolf's Mr. Ramsay, as a portrait of Woolf's father, the Victorian critic Leslie Stephen, catches the note of absurdity that begins to surround the figure of the earnestly scientistic agnostic. The modernist writers were immensely serious, although it was no longer important to be earnest, and to read them either humanistically or antihumanistically, therefore, is to miss the point since humanism, the necessary human standpoint, is acknowledged in its ultimate groundlessness.[17] *Ulysses* is the classic instance. With its burlesque jostling of cultural structures, myths, discourses, and intellectual disciplines, it reenacts in contemporary terms an ancient tale of homecoming and thereby expresses a modern sense of what the human home is: a construction within a void.[18] This recognition of the self-grounding character of the human world is the truest meaning of the modernist use of myth. Myth could be many things, including nostalgia for a lost unity, a fascistic regression, or a literary structure, but its most important meaning was as an emblem of the human world as self-created. Of course, Joyce's comedic inflection of this was not the only possibility. Kafka was the obverse. Whereas Joyce's apparent verbal density is ultimately transparent, allowing the reader to possess its world and know there are no other transcendental meanings, Kafka's enigmatic simplicity incites interpretation, a need for meaning, only to frustrate it. The anguish of Kafka's fiction, whatever its other causes or implications, comes from a desire still to find, rather than create, a meaning.

If the prestige of science as objective truth was dislodged, this suggests another aspect of the departure from traditional realism. For realism in fiction had been embodied in a narrative model of history which had itself been given a strongly scientific inflection, yet by the end of the century a number of thinkers were reacting against the dominance of the historicist mode of understanding which had developed since the late eighteenth century.[19] The prestige of historicism was undermined by the questioning of the scientific model, for the word *history* refers both to the unimaginably vast process of events making up collective human life and to the interpretative discipline through which it is understood. Meanwhile the factual concern of the discipline can give it a misleading impression of objectivity. But F. H. Bradley, Dilthey, and Benedetto Croce all emphasized, in turn, that history is written from the standpoint of the present and expresses values which cannot themselves be based in science or research.[20] Nietzsche's early essay on "The Uses and Disadvantages of History for Life" (1874) brought several of these concerns together and proved to be effectively a manifesto for this aspect of Modernism whereby history is understood under the sign of myth.

IV History, myth and tradition

Modernist writers were almost obsessively concerned with history in a double sense: they were concerned both about what was happening in their world and with the nature of historical understanding as such. The mythopoeic basis of history has several very different aspects, but it importantly includes an underlying recognition of the projective nature of all historical meaning. Insofar as myth is an affirmation of values, it may be a form of historical motivation; as it proves to be, through the retrospective understanding of the poet, for the patriots of Yeats's "Easter 1916."[21] Yet insofar as myth is concerned with values which are in some measure transhistorical, myth can also reflect a version of what Nietzsche called the "superhistorical" spirit.[22] When a great range of historical knowledge spanning different cultures and times has been assimilated, its effect, Nietzsche argues, may be to reveal the partiality and limitation of all those issues which seem supremely important to one's contemporaries. The superhistorical spirit transcends historical time and may focus this in a mythic timelessness such as Joyce finds in the Homeric parallel of *Ulysses*, or Yeats attributes to the sage "chinamen" of "Lapis Lazuli" (*Collected Poems*, pp. 336–9). Myth is highly ambivalent, therefore, in its relation to history: it may be a way of acting purposefully *within* history or a way of transcending, which is to say withdrawing *from*, it. Meanwhile the capacity for transcendence is not necessarily negative: it may rather be a condition of properly living within history: a secular equivalent of T. S. Eliot's more religious thought, "teach us to care and not to care."[23]

The mythic structures of Yeats, Joyce, Lawrence, and Mann are all concerned with this problematic awareness, and the formal index of this is their development of spatialized rather than chronological structures.[24] The action takes place in time, but the meaning is created spatially; or, as Thomas Mann said, "musically."[25] On a larger scale, the cyclic conceptions of history in Oswald Spengler and Arnold Toynbee have a related implication.[26] The causal process enacted within historical and personal time is set against, not so much the timeless, as the intrinsic, values represented emblematically in myth. For this is the important emphasis: not a withdrawal into some realm of the timeless but a recognition of the intrinsic and foundational import of these values for the given community or "world."

Of course, not every use of myth embodies this metaphysical implication. T. S. Eliot's grail legend in *The Waste Land* affirms a fertility which is largely belied by the sexual disgust in the poem itself, and Eliot's use of myth proved to be rather a placeholder for the religious faith which he was subsequently to adopt. Where Eliot came closest to the spirit of myth as defined through these other writers is in his sense of tradition.[27] Tradition, for Eliot, was not what he called an "orthodoxy," a rule to be followed, but a largely unconscious inheritance being continually modified within the self. Like Pound and other Modernists, Eliot thought closely about the paradoxes of tradition in relation to creativity; the most original talent is not only bound within a tradition but is most likely to reaffirm it; in this connection, "renewing" is a bottomlessly ambiguous term. And it was within this sense of the greater, transindividual "mind of Europe" that he was able to project his truly mythopoeic imagination. The "dissociation of sensibility" occurring during the seventeenth century was one of Eliot's powerful interpretations which, although offered as a literary historical argument rather than as a myth, continued to grip the contemporary imagination with a mythic power even after he had distanced himself from it.[28] Its essentially mythopoeic status is reflected in the fact that his evidence for dissociation was not an historical argument so much as a close reading of language understood as itself the embodiment of a quality of life. But that leads to another major theme for the modernist generation.

V The linguistic turn

The pervasive concern with the construction of meaning helps explain the emphasis in all the modernist arts on the nature of their own medium; and in the case of literature this means, as well as literary genres and forms, language itself. Furthermore, by the early teens of the century there had occurred what has come to be known as the linguistic "turn": rather than describing or reflecting the world, language was now seen to form it. And whereas nineteenth-century study of language was predominantly historical, concerned with origins and development, Ferdinand de Saussure's *Course in General Linguistics*, published in 1916 after his death, emphasized the synchronic and structural dimension.[29] He showed how the linguistic sign stands in an arbitrary relation to its external referent while meaning is created relationally within the system of language itself. It is a precise reversal of the Adamic model of meaning as giving names to preexisting things, it sees that we only come to have things by creating names for them. Wittgenstein in the *Tractatus Logico-Philosophicus* (1921) was to develop a related point: "The limits of my language mean the limits of my world."[30] The modernist generation were conscious contemporaries of this linguistic turn but they also represent an important watershed in its interpretation.

Ulysses started to appear at this time and its linguistic self-consciousness reflects an epochal ambiguity. The episode specifically devoted to language, "Oxen of the Sun," creates a running parallel between the growth of the English language through a succession of literary prose styles and the development of a fetus. Nineteenth-century historical thinking about language had been strongly influenced by organicist conceptions and saw language as the manifestation of a particular national character. Such a legacy was of special interest to Joyce as an Irishman whose "mother" tongue was English. On the face of it this episode seems to celebrate the language on this most organic of analogies, yet the parallel with fetal development occurs in a spirit of burlesque which might alert the reader against any too simple an interpretation. Joyce is treading a watershed between different views of language. On the one hand, the organic evolution of language is perhaps only a parodic, rather than a real, parallel of fetal development since the episode is after all demonstrating that these historical and personal styles are themselves subsystems, or codes, within the language which can be individually cracked and reproduced. Even Dickens' self-bestowed title of the "Inimitable" is put in question. Yet the episode plays with, and within, language as if in a sea of possibility, so that behind the particular style language itself is enjoyed as a protean second nature. Hence, while the parodic tone hints at the literal absurdity of the analogy, it also highlights its metaphorical appropriateness. As usual, Joyce admits of opposite readings with equal plausibility, as if he had deliberately built into his work the revelatory doubleness of meaning which Hans Blumenberg calls "epochal ambivalence."[31]

Over the same years as the instalments of *Ulysses* were being published, Eliot, Pound, Lawrence, and Proust were thinking critically about language as the medium of cultural tradition. Their thinking was not sentimentally organicist either, but they all recognized, in their different ways, the complexity of language as the fundamental medium of culture in its historical, creative, and unconscious dimensions. In fact, there emerged from this period two rival, apparently incommensurable interpretations of the linguistic turn. One view, which has its most philosophically magisterial expression in Martin Heidegger, sees the human involvement in language as resistant to technical or external analysis. Linguistic analysis has its uses but it cannot encompass the human use of language.[32] Lawrence and Rilke are among the most telling literary embodiments of this understanding.[33] The other view seeks to build on Saussure's perceptions to provide a radical analysis of culture, and an exposure of its ideology, through language. This has had a more French provenance with a very explicit variant, for example, in Roland Barthes.[34] On this view, if language is the index, and perhaps even the creating structure, of the human world, then it gives a complete critical insight into that world. This is the basis of what Paul Ricoeur has called "the hermeneutics of suspicion" and it is worth noting that Saussure became an important influence outside linguistics only in the latter part of the century, when his analysis of linguistic structure began to be accorded a quasi-metaphysical significance, as if he were saying that meaning itself is arbitrary.[35] Eliot and Pound were somewhere between these positions. On the one hand they saw that civilization depends on words and it is the function of the poet and the critic to keep words accurate. On the other hand, as with the sense of tradition, they recognized a properly unconscious and implicit dimension in this. It would be neither possible nor desirable to bring the whole form of life implicit in language into consciousness. In this aspect they were closer to Heidegger. They were forerunners of ideology critique but they also saw language as being, like the moon in Joyce's "Ithaca" episode and Lawrence's "Moony" chapter of *Women in Love*, an inscrutable surface sustained by an invisible body whose dark side cannot be known.

The difficulty of getting an analytic grip on language is compounded by another epochal phenomenon. Cultural periods are often characterized by dominant metaphors such as the medieval and Renaissance great chain of being, the eighteenth-century clock or machine, or the nineteenth-century organism. In the twentieth century, language itself became the pervasive metaphor. By the mid-century, even the act of conception had become a matter of a genetic "code." This has led, in the latter part of the century, to a solipsistic hyper-consciousness of language whereby the recognition that language forms reality has acquired a newly literalistic meaning; as if the analysis of ideology in language can completely encapsulate the life world of its user. This hyper-conscious reification of language has its partial origin in the modernist period, but there it was generally balanced by a sense of the unconscious or tacit dimension. In this respect, the gradual shift to the computer as a common model of the mind suggests that the metaphor of language is now giving way to an even more two-dimensional one. But the larger point here is that a view of language entails a view of the world, a usually implicit philosophy, and the divided responses to the linguistic turn have themselves to be understood in a broader philosophical context.

VI The collapse of idealism

If it was Heidegger who most fully developed the rival conception of language to the Saussurean tradition, this was because of his part in a larger shift in philosophical outlook in the early part of the century: the effective demise of the idealist tradition which had lasted, in various transformations, almost since the time of Immanuel Kant. Kant's *Critique of Pure Reason* (1781) was a foundational text of modern thought. It answered the skepticism of David Hume, and radically changed the dualism of Descartes, by indicating how the world can be known only through the necessary categories of thought; the structure of thought is the structure of the world. He used the word "transcendental," therefore, not to refer to some realm *beyond* the phenomenal world, but to indicate the conditions of possibility for *experiencing* it. The philosopher J. W. Fichte, however, whose lectures at the University of Jena in the 1790s influenced a generation of German romantics, gave this philosophy a subjective inflection. He interpreted Kant as saying that the world is an aspect of the mind. F. W. Schelling reacted in turn by claiming that the mind is an aspect of the world. Despite its being subjected to radical critiques, the metaphysical preoccupation with the transcendental conditions of experience remained dominant throughout the nineteenth century, and it was only in the new century that some form of idealism ceased to be the central premise of philosophical activity. T. S. Eliot wrote a Ph.D. thesis on the "objective" idealist F. H. Bradley and yet claimed later in life that he no longer understood it.[36] However literally we take Eliot's remark, it has a representative value for the relation of Modernism to this earlier tradition for, at one level, the modernist period, in Nietzsche, Heidegger, and Wittgenstein, was a turn not just against idealism, but against metaphysics as such. The later world no longer believed in the questions, let alone agreed with the answers, of the earlier one. And yet, as several critics have noted, Eliot's poetry is full of the concerns, and formation, of Bradley's thought and this transformed continuity is equally representative of the period at large for the important thinking of the modern age was where it attempted to meet, rather than ignore, the earlier tradition.[37] In the Anglo-American context the demise of idealism can be seen in William James's pragmatism, Bertrand Russell's mathematical logic, and Wittgenstein's restriction of the philosophical enterprise to an analysis of language use. Wittgenstein provides a revealing fault line here. In the later Anglophone world he was associated with the metaphysical philistinism of A. J. Ayer rather than recognized as an antimetaphysical thinker.[38] Even Russell seemed not fully to comprehend this aspect of Wittgenstein. Wittgenstein was like Joyce in being profoundly superficial, in understanding the limits of what could be said, whereas Ayer was merely superficial in thinking there was nothing of interest outside what he could say. But the most serious onslaught on the metaphysical tradition had come from Nietzsche before the turn of the century, while Heidegger was in turn his most productively critical reader; and the shift from Nietzsche to Heidegger helps to clarify much that was going on even in the Anglo-Saxon literary context in which Heidegger himself was unknown.

Heidegger endorsed Nietzsche's exposure of the whole tradition of metaphysics from Plato onwards as an enormous falsehood and psychological deceit; a quite different kind of "great lie" from what Plato had in mind in *The Republic*. In particular, the centrality of epistemology, the problem of knowledge, had grown, as they both thought, from an unwitting reification of consciousness and world into separate entities, the subjective and objective. Nietzsche proposed instead that the question of value was more primary than that of knowledge: we know, or question, what is of interest to us as living beings and the ideal of academic disinterestedness is only a misleading exception to this general truth. Heidegger approved all this but went on to argue that Nietzsche was not the end of metaphysics, as he had claimed, because the question of Being was more primary again than that of value.[39] Heidegger capitalized Being to indicate that his concern was not with individual beings but with the sheer mystery of Being at all. Our everyday instrumental dealing with individual beings, whether human or not, deadens us to Being; and philosophical activity, as traditionally practiced, only reinforces this. For Heidegger this loss, or forgetting, of Being had set in since pre-Socratic times. Quite independently, Lawrence and Pound had the same conviction and invoked the supposedly predualistic sensibility of that time to define its mythopoeic relation to the world. This leads to a central paradox of Modernism: the most sophisticated achievement of the present is a return to, or a new appreciation of, the archaic. As Thomas Mann put it in his lecture on Freud, "In the life of humanity the mythic is indeed an early and primitive stage but in the life of the individual it is a late and mature one."[40] To appreciate this it is necessary to trace the development of another important area of inquiry, anthropology, which provided the contemporary models of the primitive and the archaic.

VII Anthropology and the "primitive"

Primitivism is almost as old, it may be supposed, as civilization; both terms, of course, being relational.[41] As a literary convention primitivism allows the civilized to inspect, or to indulge, itself through an imaginary opposite. It is often a self-critical motif within the culture, like Montaigne's essay on cannibals.[42] But in the modernist period a radical questioning of the present civilization along with the close study of tribal peoples gave a new edge to the primitivist impulse.

In the past "primitive" peoples had been seen, whether nostalgically or condescendingly, as a simpler version of the "civilized." Only their circumstances and social organization made them different. This had been the case with Rousseau and was still so for James Frazer's *The Golden Bough*.[43] By thinking of their circumstances, one could imagine their frame of mind. But in the first decades of the twentieth century a new conception of the primitive was developed. For the generation of anthropologists typified by Lucien Levy-Bruhl's *How Natives Think* (1922), primitive man was believed to have a different way of thinking and of relating to the universe. This conception was developed through scholarly study and often fieldwork, although the fieldwork was still frequently at secondhand and the meaning of such primitive sensibility is best understood through its contemporaneity with the theme of forgetfulness of Being. For it is still partly a projected *alter ego* of the European observer. In this conception, clearly owing much to romantic thought, primitive man was believed to have had, like the pre-Socratic Greeks, a psychological continuity with his world; the practice of sympathetic magic, for example, suggesting this predualistic relation. His sense of space and time were radically different from "ours." Rather than being objectively measurable, they followed the contours of the psyche and of the sacred. This was not just prescientific, but a wholly opposed worldview and the Kantian philosopher, Ernst Cassirer, was to articulate at length the philosophical character of this archaic worldview as seen by early twentieth-century anthropology.[44] By the latter half of the century it was becoming clear that this whole conception was itself quite unscientific and not least in its reification of a generalized "primitive mind" and its assumption that modern "primitives" represent an early stage of a universal development including that of modern Europeans. But if it was not scientifically true it is only the more telling as an epochal reflection and its value as a literary or philosophical vision is not necessarily to be discounted; indeed, it may be increased.

The crucial point here is that the primitive should have been accorded not just an alternative state, but an alternative worldview. As Heidegger said, anthropology underwrites the experience of modernity as "the age of the world picture." In many ways the universalism, and the valorizing, of the "primitive mind" in these decades had a progressive, critical force against the home culture and the relativity of worldviews was an enabling condition for this. It made it possible for the primitive to acquire such a value of radical difference. In this way, the scientific study of myth throughout the nineteenth century eventually produced a reflector in which the scientific observer could see the scientific viewpoint itself as only one form of life, a lived worldview, a myth. Yet this was not a position of vulgar or open relativism. Any given life form is lived as life not as a relative world picture; and likewise archaic myth, which seemed to be inhabited without the category of disbelief, exemplified the holism and faith with which any life form must be lived. This is why many of the modern writers, even while exhibiting formal self-consciousness, allowed the underlying metaphysic of a conscious worldview to remain implicit. They were concerned to absorb and live with this "tacit dimension" rather than make it the overt point of the work.[45] As Serenus Zeitblom, the "humanist" narrator of Thomas Mann's *Doctor Faustus* put it, "Belief in absolute values, illusory as it always is, seems to me a condition of life."[46] It was a central characteristic of the period to hold these contradictory aspects in conjunction.

This gives rise to complex truths and evident dangers. Myth, in the modern sense of a lived worldview, is highly ambivalent. The vulgar cooption of myth by fascism has shorn this central modernist term of its allure despite the efforts of Karl Kerenyi, the anthropologist, and Thomas Mann to save the humanistic value of its bracketing of belief.[47] Mann's own humanism lay not just at the level of narrative values but in the tolerant skepticism with which the narrative is constructed. "Man is the lord of counterpositions" and it is by inhabiting beliefs in this spirit of modernist mythopoeia that one is most truly free from the seductions of modern barbarism (*Magic Mountain*, p. 496). It is ironic, but perhaps deeply fitting, that the same term "myth" should hold in counterpoint two opposite tendencies of the period: political regression and humane relativity. On the European political stage, a word that may be used advisedly here, virulent nationalisms were supported by a hand-me-down nineteenth-century mythic essentialism while the finer minds of the period had been dissolving nationhood itself into a mythic self-consciousness.

Modernist mythopoeia was universalistic and seemed to be endorsed in this by Frazer's fertility rituals, Freud's psychic structures and Levy-Bruhl's primitive mind. The unwitting Eurocentrism of this supposed universalism has since become apparent, but in its time it had a mainly progressive value in the tradition of the Enlightenment. It criticized the Enlightenment from within while the historic catastrophe of the Great War exposed the evils of nationalism in an urgent and practical way. At the same time, while in *The Rainbow* and *Ulysses* the mythopoeic invocations of the Bible and Homer raised humble provincial characters to a primary level of seriousness, both books are densely of their localities. Their national and local dimensions are present but are understood as formations rather than essences. That is why the reflexive self-consciousness of worldviews, the conscious relativity of forms of life, is a key to understanding the inner process, however gradual and groping it was, by which the evils of colonialism came to be recognized.

VIII   The colonial "other"

Anthropology grew up in the era of colonial expansion and had given "scientific" endorsement to the colonial "mission." But by the early twentieth century the tradition of European Enlightenment, and indeed the whole post-Socratic conception of civilized culture, was being thrown into question and the primitive *alter ego* was coming to be seen more honorifically. A changing attitude to the colonial "other" reflects a changing self-perception in the European. Freud was fascinated by primitive life and artifacts, and the relationship of consciousness to the unconscious in his metaphorical discourse reflects the structure of colonialism with the unconscious as the region to be colonized and controlled by the ego. *Civilization and its Discontents* (1930) summed up his view that civilization was necessarily, and tragically, built on the suppression and sublimation of instinct. This was the white man's burden externally and internally. C. G. Jung or Lawrence, on the other hand, would argue that the instinctual realm became destructive only because it was repressed rather than respected.[48] The homology between the two realms, of psyche and of empire, gives each a double meaning whereby internal and external liberation are linked. Three literary moments show the stages of this.

Joseph Conrad's *Heart of Darkness* (1899) recognized that the darkness lies not in Africa but in the human, and specifically European, heart. It took the crucial step of internalizing the problem even while retaining the "Freudian" model of tragic legitimacy. For Conrad is still committed to the colonial idea and, as a man of his time, he accepts the current views of Africa and its inhabitants. Indeed, as a naturalized Briton, and on the principle that a convert is more Catholic than the Pope, he deflects the major evil on to Belgium while Kurtz, with his German name, raises colonial brutality to a level of philosophical self-consciousness. The power of the book lies in its not quite suppressing its own deepest insight, and it is hard to say whether Conrad's creative struggle was the more invested in suppression or recognition. The tortured mystifications of the book reflect its significance as a cultural document. The heroizing of Kurtz as one able to face this dark knowledge of the self is a displaced reflection of what the book itself almost faces about the colonial relation at large and in his day Conrad himself showed courage in peering into this abyss whose meaning has since become banal.

Lawrence's *The Rainbow* (1915) is a generation later and from a native Englishman who had no illusions about the British governing classes. His character, Anton Skrebensky, another half-Polish émigré of genteel background, returns from colonial service in Africa to tell Ursula Brangwen of the strange exotic thrill, the repellent fascination, of the "African darkness."

> One breathes it, like a smell of blood. The blacks know it. They worship it, really, the darkness. One almost likes it – the fear – something sensual.
> She thrilled again to him. He was to her a voice out of the darkness. He talked to her all the while, in low tones, about Africa, conveying something strange and sensual to her: the negro, with his soft loose passion that could envelope one like a bath.[49]

Skrebensky has long been detected by Ursula as a hollow man, but she is momentarily affected by him here because through his "African" experience he has made some contact, however repressive and unacknowledged, with his inner self. His Africa is manifestly an Africa within and only through the projection on to a primitive "other" can he make contact with a lost aspect of himself. It is evident why Lawrence was at once the most important modern primitivist and the most serious critic of primitivism as a decadent symptom. What Skrebensky is "conveying" for the reader is a remarkable understanding of the inner structure of the colonial relation, but the aspect to be noted for present purposes is that the book is not mainly about colonialism or the primitive. The clarity of insight in the episode arises from Lawrence's more general modernist awareness throughout the book of how characters and cultural communities inhabit their own "worlds." Skrebensky lives in a different "world" from Ursula, and his Africa is created as the effect of a voice in an English darkness. If modernity is the "age of the world picture," the second decade of the century is where this recognition becomes critically self-conscious and the present episode suggests the seismic implications. Of course, none of this is evident to Skrebensky himself and after his rejection by Ursula he goes off to colonial service in India; and indeed E. M. Forster's *A Passage to India* (1924) exemplifies the next stage in the process of internal liberation.

Lawrence was not concerned with the colonial question as such, which may be why he had this insight into it. His setting in what George Eliot called the heart of England indicates where the true heart of the problem lay, and his representation of his characters' world projections is so naturalized that it hardly emerges as a conscious "theme." E. M. Forster was more directly concerned with colonial relations, yet still as part of an, even more overt, thematizing of conflicting worldviews. For in *A Passage to India* different world projections are not a matter of internal psychological conflict so much as the institutionalized traditions of different world religions: Christianity, Islam, and Hindu. Of course, despite its liberalism, the standpoint of the book is still one of European self-inspection, and the book is not much more about India than Conrad's was about Africa, but the positive meaning of this fact has to be understood. External liberation, in this instance, is partly a consequence of internal liberation and these three novels show a progressive process of inner recognition from which the present-day reader benefits as orthodoxy. These writers, however inadequate they may now seem in their racial perceptions, resisted the orthodoxies of their own day to start the liberation of European consciousness from one of its most pernicious and deep-lying formations. The conscious world creation of Modernism was a significant means to this. It is revealing, however, that in all three of these books the repressive relation to the colonial "other" is linked to sexual repression, and that leads to a parallel modernist theme of liberation inviting a different commentary.

IX Sexuality and liberation?

Sexual liberation, and liberation through sexuality, were conscious and central projects of the time. Sex came out of the closet in Freud, Havelock-Ellis, and others, and the sheer openness of treatment was a significant point in, for example, Franz Wedekind's *Spring Awakening* (1891), in which young men masturbate on stage.[50] But sexuality was seen through highly ideological lenses, as in the extreme instance of Otto Weininger's misogynistic *Sex and Character* (1903), and it has taken much longer for the gendered construction of sexuality itself to be recognized. Whereas for many male writers and thinkers sexuality might be a mode of liberation, for women it was just as likely to be another mode of suppression, and women writers were therefore more aware of underlying contradictions which possibly made it more difficult to achieve, or to desire, the grand syntheses of some male Modernists. The immediate explosion of sexuality in the period largely hid the time bomb of gender which was to explode later, and is dealt with in Marianne DeKoven's chapter in this volume.

Different levels of liberation can be seen in Joyce's treatment of Leopold Bloom. Through Bloom, Joyce's own voyeuristic tendencies and his masochistic fantasies about his wife's unfaithfulness, the theme explored in *Exiles* (1918), are acknowledged in a spirit of acceptance. The exemplary acceptance is bold and admirable in itself, yet is still based on naturalizing the effects of a repressive culture or condition. Internal liberation, perhaps, does not come at a stroke or in one generation. But a more vital aspect of Bloom is his female identification. He is first seen cooking the breakfast and his womanliness is continually highlighted against the absurd virility of other characters. Lawrence's female side was so developed he was always fighting it and having to assert his maleness while some of his earliest reviews assumed him to be female.[51] Lisa Appignanesi has identified in Modernism at large a connection between femininity and creativity even where the feminine, as in Proust, may not be biologically female.[52] Edward Carpenter proselytized strongly for a view of homosexuality as a creative and liberated condition.[53] Although Stephen Dedalus's explicit theorizing about artistic creation privileges intellectual fatherhood as against mere biological motherhood, it is the "womanly" Bloom who is associated with Shakespeare.

Hence, in the early modern period, "woman" was often valued for qualities related to the philosophical concerns already indicated. Dorothy Richardson spoke of woman's "awareness of being, as distinct from man's awareness of becoming" and Yeats and Lawrence had a strong investment in such a view.[54] When Yeats, in "Easter 1916," said of Constance Markiewicz, who was to be the first woman MP in Britain, "that woman's days were spent in ignorant good will, her nights in argument," he clearly preferred the pre-political days when "young and beautiful she rode to harriers." Yet his critique bears not against a woman in politics so much as against politics as such. Because "woman" is more whole, she suffers the greater damage, or constitutes the greater waste, when drawn into the shrillness of politics or the shallowness of opinion. In this respect the understanding of "woman" in this period reflects, among other things, its central problematic of Being.

X   Aesthetics and Being

A central ambiguity about Modernism lies in the understanding of the "aesthetic," the meaning of the artistic realm as such. For Modernism is importantly not aestheticist, it is rather a turn against an earlier generation's aestheticism, but it uses highly self-conscious aesthetic means to do so and Edmund Wilson had good reason to see the period, in *Axel's Castle* (1931), as a continuation of aestheticism. Wilson's interpretation implies a measure of withdrawal from historical commitment and a comparable charge was made by the Modernist writer and artist Percy Wyndham Lewis in *Time and Western Man* (1927). Lewis attacked the pervasive preoccupation with time in this period extending from Bergson, Einstein and A. N. Whitehead in philosophy and science through to Joyce and Proust in literature. He saw time as a less real dimension than space since, apart from the fleeting present, experience in time is only known in the imaginative mode of memory and anticipation. Hence this whole preoccupation with time was an indulgent withdrawal in keeping with Wilson's interpretation; and indeed with the Marxist view of Modernism, expressed by Georg

Lukacs, as an indulgent turning inwards of the Western bourgeois self.[55] But the category of the "aesthetic," like Nietzsche's "superhistorical" spirit, is deeply ambivalent and it went through a crucial transformation in the period which can be understood through Nietzsche's parallel transformation of Schopenhauer's thought on this subject since Schopenhauer stands to the nineteenth-century symbolist and aesthetic movements as Nietzsche stands to Modernism.

Schopenhauer's pessimistic philosophy in *The World as Will and Idea* (1818) saw human consciousness as evolved by nature to achieve its own blind "purpose" in the same way that wings or claws have done. But the irony of consciousness is that it works by imagining itself to be independently purposive rather than merely reflecting the great process, or Will, of nature. For him, all human purposes are an illusion. Given this understanding of things, the only dignified posture for the individual intelligence is mental withdrawal from the whole process and, adapting Kant's definition of the artistic realm, in the *Critique of Judgement* (1790), as "purposiveness without purpose," Schopenhauer saw artistic experience as the principal means to this end. Art gives intensity with detachment. Nietzsche was strongly influenced by Schopenhauer, and always accepted his philosophical nihilism, but he gradually turned the structure of Schopenhauer's thought on its head to serve a vitalistic affirmation. This inversion can be seen in the early *Birth of Tragedy out of the Spirit of Music* (1872) and in the late *Twilight of the Idols* (1888). In the first, he adapts Schopenhauer's metaphysic of illusion to affirm the dream itself: "It is a dream. I will dream on." Only as a conscious dream, or as an "*aesthetic phenomenon*" are "human existence and the world eternally *justified*" (Nietzsche's emphases).[56] In the later work, however, he turns more critically against Schopenhauer for the sake of what seems to be a simpler vitalism. Artistic beauty, instead of standing in opposition to natural impulse, is now merged with the attraction of sexuality as part of a procreative affirmation. But Nietzsche was not abandoning the category of the aesthetic, rather he was making it the model of all experience and therefore eliding it by assimilating it. Life, like art, is a "purposiveness without purpose"; it is lived for its intrinsic value rather than for some transcendental end. Whereas aestheticism saw life in opposition to art, Nietzsche now saw art as the most telling image for the "joyful and trusting fatalism" with which life should be accepted.[57] This is a complex and subtle point to be understood through close reading of at least Nietzsche, Yeats, Joyce, and Lawrence, but the principal upshot is an elision of the category of the aesthetic into a life term.[58] It is like Wittgenstein's "ladder" at the end of the *Tractatus*, an argument you realize you must throw away when you have climbed up it.

So too, the category of the aesthetic is necessary to see the point but the point is also the dissolution of the category.

Where Nietzsche was concerned with the aesthetic as a "justification" of human existence, as a constation of values in life, his elision of the categories opened the way to a different inflection which was most clearly expressed in Heidegger, namely art as an intuition of Being. For just as Heidegger saw the question of Being as more primordial than that of value, so he saw the function of art as preeminently the expression of Being. "Purposiveness without purpose" now suggested freedom from the instrumental relation to individual beings which commonly occludes Being. A favorite quotation of his was Hölderlin's "poetically man dwells upon the earth."[59] Art lets us know what it is to "be," and this Heideggerean dimension is evident in Lawrence and Rilke; and perhaps in an inverted way in Kafka and Beckett. The "aesthetic," of course, continued to mean many different things within the period, and even the line of thought sketched here is controversial and often misunderstood.[60] But it would be more generally agreed that the aesthetic assumes some greater burden in the period even if the nature of the burden itself is disputed, and that leads to a further question: the rise, and the changing status, of literary criticism within the modernist decades.

XI Literature and criticism

T. S. Eliot's obituary compliment to Henry James, that he "had a mind so fine that no idea could violate it" strikes an important modernist note in its skepticism about ideas as such.[61] As part of the larger turn against metaphysical concerns, Eliot implies that truth is to be found not in philosophical ideas or systems but by collapsing philosophical concerns into a close scrutiny of experience, and more particularly of language. Such a spirit is echoed in William James, the brother of the novelist, and in Wittgenstein. Where Eliot became a poet, Wittgenstein several times gave up philosophy and advised bright students to find an honest manual trade. The effect of this, for Eliot, Pound, and Lawrence, was to place an especially primordial philosophical burden upon imaginative literature, and through that on literary criticism, although Eliot's own turn to religious faith ultimately prevented him from allowing literature this full weight. The modernist writers were remarkable and original critics, and would perhaps not be so comprehensible without their criticism. And the period of Eliot's influence especially saw the rise of literary criticism as an academic discipline partly sustained by a belief in literature as a primordial constation of values not to be reached or grounded by other means. The Arnoldian sense of literature as the modern substitute for religion was increasingly realized not, as the classicist Arnold had thought, as a source of transmitted wisdom, "the best that is known and thought in the world," but rather as the active means of questioning and discovering fundamental values, truths, and understandings for which there was no alternative grounding.[62] The critic who took this most fully and openly to heart was F. R. Leavis, and the history of his reception, including the common misreading of him as a naïve moralist, is an index of the history of this understanding since he made overt what is otherwise the largely unacknowledged basis of criticism in the twentieth century.[63] Leavis, who had always an embattled relation to the institutionalized practice of criticism, provided a lightning conductor for this widespread refusal of acknowledgment. A central philosophical feature of Modernism, reworking a strain of romantic thought, is its claim for literature itself as a supreme and irreplaceable form of understanding.

NOTES

1 Apart from the economic theory in *Das kapital*, 3rd edn (1889), Marx, with Engels, analyzed the cultural manifestations of capitalism.

2 See especially *The Interpretation of Dreams* (1900), *Five Lectures on Psychoanalysis* (1910), *Totem and Taboo* (1930), *Civilization and its Discontents* (1930).

3 See especially *The Birth of Tragedy out of the Spirit of Music* (1872), *The Uses and Disadvantages of History for Life* (1874), *The Genealogy of Morals* (1887), *Twilight of the Idols* (1888).

4 Ezra Pound, *The Literary Essays of Ezra Pound*, ed. T. S. Eliot (London: Faber, 1954), p. 341.

5 See, for example, Ludwig Wittgenstein, *Philosophical Investigations*, trans. G. E. M. Anscombe, 2nd edn (Oxford: Blackwell, 1958), p. 88.

6 Albert Einstein's "Special Theory of Relativity" was published in 1905; Werner Heisenberg's "uncertainty principle" in 1927.

7 William Crookes discovered in 1879 that cathode rays were bent by a magnetic field. The resulting controversy over waves or particles was settled by Heinrich Herz's experiment of 1892 and J. J. Thomson's discovery of the electron in 1897. See *Encyclopaedia Britannica*, Macropaedia, 15th edn (Chicago: Chicago University Press, 1992), vol. XIV, pp. 345–6.

8 Friedrich Nietzsche, *The Birth of Tragedy out of the Spirit of Music*, trans. Walter Kaufmann (New York: Random House, 1967), p. 112.

9 See Arthur Eddington, Introduction to *The Nature of the Physical World* (Cambridge: Cambridge University Press, 1928), pp. xi–xix.

10 Thomas Mann, *The Magic Mountain*, trans. H. T. Lowe-Porter (New York: Knopf, 1955), p. 218.

11 Martin Heidegger, "The Age of the World Picture" in *The Question of Technology and Other Essays*, ed. and trans. William Lovitt (New York: Harper and Row, 1977), p. 130.

12 A much quoted expression of this view is Fredric Jameson, "Postmodernism and

Consumer Society" in Hal Foster, ed., *The Anti-Aesthetic: Postmodern Culture* (London: Pluto, 1985), pp. 111–25.

13 D. H. Lawrence, *The Letters of D. H. Lawrence*, vol. II, ed. James T. Boulton and George J. Zytaruk (Cambridge: Cambridge University Press, 1981), p. 182.

14 Filippo Tommaso Marinetti (1876–1944). For a good discussion of Futurism in a broad context of European artistic movements, see Peter Nicholls, *Modernisms* (London: Macmillan, 1995), esp. pp. 84–111.

15 For the significance of the phrase "saved the appearances" in relation to modernity, see Owen Barfield, *Saving the Appearances: A Study in Idolatry* (New York: Harcourt Brace Jovanovich, 1965).

16 For a full discussion of this topic, see Peter Alan Dale, *In Pursuit of a Scientific Culture* (Madison: University of Wisconsin Press, 1989).

17 The allusion to Wilde here is relevant to changing conceptions of art and truth in the period as in his "The Decay of Lying" (1889).

18 ". . . because founded, like the world, macro and microcosm, upon the void." James Joyce, *Ulysses*, ed. Walter Gabler (Harmondsworth: Penguin, 1986), p. 171.

19 On this general topic, see James Longenbach, *Modernist Poetics of History* (Princeton: Princeton University Press, 1987).

20 See F. H. Bradley, *The Presuppositions of Critical History* (1874), Benedetto Croce, *History: Its Theory and Practice* (1917), *Meaning in History: Dilthey's Thoughts on History and Society*, ed. H. P. Rickman (London: Allen and Unwin, 1961).

21 W. B. Yeats, *Collected Poems of W. B. Yeats*, 2nd edn (London: Macmillan, 1950), pp. 202–5.

22 See Friedrich Nietzsche, *Untimely Meditations*, trans. R. J. Hollingdale (Cambridge: Cambridge University Press, 1983), pp. 64–6.

23 "Ash Wednesday." See T. S. Eliot, *The Complete Poems and Plays* (New York: Harcourt Brace and World, 1971), p. 67.

24 The classic first treatment of this theme was Joseph Frank, "Spatial Form in Modern Literature," *The Widening Gyre: Crisis and Mastery in Modern Literature* (New Brunswick, NJ: Rutgers University Press, 1963), pp. 3–62.

25 Thomas Mann, "The Making of *The Magic Mountain*" *Atlantic Monthly* (January 1953); reprinted in Lowe-Porter, trans., *The Magic Mountain*, p. 723.

26 Oswald Spengler, *The Decline of the West* (1919), Arnold Toynbee, *A Study of History* (1934–61).

27 See T. S. Eliot, "Tradition and the Individual Talent" in T. S. Eliot, *Selected Essays*, 3rd edn (London: Faber and Faber, 1951), pp. 13–22.

28 See "The Metaphysical Poets" in ibid., esp. pp. 286–8.

29 Ferdinand de Saussure, *Cours de Linguistique Générale* (Lausanne: Payot, 1916).

30 Ludwig Wittgenstein, *Tractatus Logico-Philosophicus*, trans. D. F. Pears and B. F. McGuinness (London: Routledge, 1933), p. 115.

31 This is a central motif of Blumenberg's *The Legitimacy of the Modern Age*, trans. Robert M. Wallace (London: MIT Press, 1983).

32 See for example Martin Heidegger, "The Nature of Language" in *On the Way to Language*, trans. Peter D. Herz (New York: Harper and Row, 1971), esp. p. 98.

33 Heidegger cites Rilke but for the perhaps less evident relevance of Heidegger to

Lawrence see Michael Bell, *D. H. Lawrence: Language and Being* (Cambridge: Cambridge University Press, 1992).

34 Barthes makes the Saussurean connection explicit in *Mythologies*, trans. Annette Lavers (London: Harper Collins, 1973).

35 Ricoeur uses the phrase in *The Rule of Metaphor*, trans. Robert Czerny *et al.* (London: Routledge, 1978), p. 285.

36 T. S. Eliot, *Knowledge and Experience in the Philosophy of F. H. Bradley* (London: Faber and Faber, 1964).

37 A first important discussion was Hugh Kenner's chapter "Bradley" in *The Invisible Poet* (London: Allen and Unwin, 1960), pp. 35–59.

38 See Ludwig Wittgenstein, *Language, Truth and Logic* (London: Gollancz, 1936).

39 See, for example, Martin Heigegger, "The Word of Nietzsche: 'God is Dead'" in *The Question of Technology*, esp. p. 103.

40 Thomas Mann, "Freud and the Future" in *Essays of Three Decades*, trans. H. T. Lowe-Porter (London: Secker and Warburg, 1947), p. 422.

41 I discuss this question in *Primitivism* (London: Methuen, 1972).

42 "On the Cannibals" in *Michel de Montaigne: the Complete Essays*, trans. M. A. Screech (Harmondsworth: Penguin, 1991), pp. 228–41.

43 James Fraser, *The Golden Bough*s 1st edn, 2 vols. (1890), 2nd edn, 3 vols. (1900), 3rd edn, 12 vols. (1915), abridged edn (1922).

44 Cassirer reflected the period in developing contemporary anthropological views of archaic sensibility into a sophisticated progressive theory of symbolic forms. See *The Philosophy of Symbolic Forms*, 3 vols., trans. Ralph Mannheim (New Haven: Yale University Press, 1953–5).

45 Michael Polanyi, *The Tacit Dimension* (London: Routledge, 1967).

46 Thomas Mann, *Doctor Faustus* trans. H. T. Lowe-Porter (Harmondsworth: Penguin, 1968), p. 47.

47 See *Mythology and Humanism: the Correspondence of Thomas Mann and Karl Kerenyi*, trans. Alexander Gelley (Ithaca, NY: Cornell University Press, 1975).

48 Carl Jung (1875–1961). One-time disciple who broke with Freud and emphasized the beneficial aspects of the collective unconscious and the archetypal.

49 D. H. Lawrence, *The Rainbow*, ed. Mark Kinkead-Weekes (Cambridge: Cambridge University Press, 1989), p. 413.

50 Early publications of Havelock-Ellis include *Man and Woman* (London: Walter Scott, 1894). His multivolume *Studies in the Psychology of Sex* appeared Philadelphia, 1905–10. For a convenient summary see his *Psychology of Sex* (London: Heinemann, 1937).

51 *D. H. Lawrence: The Critical Heritage*, ed. R. P. Draper (London: Routledge, 1970), p. 3.

52 Lisa Appignanesi, *Femininity and the Creative Imagination: A Study of Henry James, Robert Musil and Marcel Proust* (London: Vision, 1973).

53 See Edward Carpenter, *Love's Coming-of-Age* (1896), *The Intermediate Sex* (1908). Both are included in *Selected Writings of Edward Carpenter*, vol. I, *Sex* (London: GMP, 1984).

54 Dorothy Richardson, "Continuous Performance: The Film gone Male", reprinted in *The Gender of Modernism*, ed. Bonnie Kime Scott (Bloomington: Indiana University Press, 1990), p. 424.

55 See Georg Lukacs, *The Meaning of Contemporary Realism*, trans. John and Neike Mander (London: Merlin Press, 1963).

56 Nietzsche, *Birth of Tragedy*, p. 44. The latter formulation occurs twice, initially p. 52, finally p. 141.

57 Friedrich Nietzsche, *Twilight of the Idols*, trans. R. J. Hollingdale (Harmondsworth: Penguin, 1968), p. 103.

58 I offer such a reading in *Literature, Modernism and Myth: Belief and Responsibility in Twentieth-Century Literature* (Cambridge: Cambridge University Press, 1997).

59 See particularly Martin Heidegger, ". . . Poetically Man Dwells . . ." in *Poetry, Language, Thought*, trans. Alfred Hofstadter (New York: Harper and Row, 1971), pp. 213–29.

60 For a counter-view of the aesthetic in post-Nietzschean modernity, see Alan Megill, *Prophets of Extremity: Nietzsche, Heidegger, Foucault, Derrida* (Berkeley and London: University of California Press, 1985).

61 T. S. Eliot, "In Memory of Henry James," *Egoist* (January 1918): 2.

62 In Matthew Arnold, "The Function of Criticism at the Present Time," *National Review* (November 1864).

63 Leavis developed his explicit thought about the primordial creativity of language in imaginative literature in his late writings especially *The Living Principle: "English" as a Discipline of Thought* (London: Chatto and Windus, 1975), which includes a close reading of T. S. Eliot's *Four Quartets*, and in *Thought, Words and Creativity: Art and Thought in Lawrence* (London: Chatto and Windus, 1976).

2

LAWRENCE RAINEY

The cultural economy of Modernism

Charles Dickens, rising to his feet, stood at the table and surveyed the vast hall in which the leading citizens of Birmingham had gathered in early 1853 to pay him homage at a banquet. It was his duty to thank them now, and he proceeded to offer his tribute.

> To the great compact phalanx of the people, by whose industry, perseverance, and intelligence, and their result in money-wealth such places as Birmingham, and many others like it, have arisen – to that great centre of support, that comprehensive experience, and that beating heart, – Literature has turned happily from individual patrons, sometimes munificent, often sordid, always few, and has found there at once its highest purpose, its natural range of action and its best reward.

"The people," Dickens concluded triumphantly, "have set Literature free." And in return for that gift of liberty, he opined, "Literature cannot be too faithful to the people."[1]

Within thirty years of Dickens's death in 1870, authors were far less confident about the beneficent effects of literature's dependency on "the people," or the prospects for a collective literary culture. In the intervening period, as many critics have noted, British popular fiction undergoes an unmistakable transformation, one in which the novel gradually acquires a class structure analogous to that of the social world surrounding it. By the decade 1900–1910, the years when Conrad is writing his best work to little acclaim, the polarization between "high" and "low" literature is firmly in place, and the modernist project issues its claim to aesthetic dignity by repudiating that Victorian literature, above all fiction, which had sold itself to a mass reading public. When Leopold Bloom, the protagonist of *Ulysses*, concludes his first appearance in the novel by cleansing himself of feces with pages torn from the popular weekly *Tit-Bits*, his gesture epitomizes the modernist contempt for popular culture.

For some scholars, that contempt is Modernism's salient characteristic.

"Mass culture has always been the hidden subtext of the modernist project," one critic urges, a project in which popular culture is construed as a threat of encroaching formlessness, gendered as female, and held at bay by reaffirming and refortifying the boundaries between art and inauthentic mass culture. More important, mass culture also marks the dividing line between Modernism and the avant-garde. In contrast to Modernism, "the avant-garde attempts to subvert art's autonomy, its artificial separation from life, and its institutionalization as 'high art,'" and this impulse accounts for its "urge to validate other, formerly neglected or ostracized forms of cultural expression," chief among them popular culture. Modernism, in this account, becomes little more than a reactionary, even paranoid, fear of popular culture. Postmodernism, instead, seeks "to negotiate forms of high art with certain forms and genres of mass culture and the culture of everyday life" and is therefore the legitimate heir of the historical avant-garde.[2]

Such formulations have brought welcome attention to the ongoing dialogue between Modernism and popular culture, but their tendency to postulate a rigorous opposition between "high" and "low" culture may be inadequate to account for the complexity of cultural exchange and circulation in modern civil society. Further, they generally draw on arguments derived solely from the reading of literary texts, a procedure that evinces excessive faith in our capacity to specify the essence and social significance of isolated formal devices and to collate them with complex ideological and social formations, slighting the institutions that mediate between works and readerships, or between readerships and particular social structures. To focus on those institutions, instead, is to view Modernism as more than a series of texts or a set of ideas that found expression in them. It becomes a social reality, a configuration of agents and practices that converge in the production, marketing, and publicization of an idiom, a shareable language within the family of twentieth-century tongues. The institutional profile of Modernism can be traced in the social spaces and staging venues where it operated, and to trace it can teach us a great deal about the relations between Modernism and popular culture as well as Modernism's shifting status in more recent debate.

Anglo-American literary Modernism was unusual in the degree to which its principal protagonists interacted with one another through shared institutional structures during a brief but important period that runs from 1912 to 1922, from roughly the formation of Imagism to the publication of *Ulysses* and *The Waste Land*. Such historical boundaries are inevitably arbitrary, slighting the extent to which Anglo-American Modernism drew on cultural traditions that extend much further back in time, minimizing developments that occurred in the decades that followed. Still, they do acknowledge the density of the particular social space that bound together the authors whose works have been deemed central to discussion of the modernist moment. To map the contours of that space, one might consider three events that best exemplify its working dynamics, the changing relations among authors and audiences that have been the subject of so much comment: a lecture on poetry that Ezra Pound gave in March 1912; the publication of *Ulysses* in February 1922; and the publication of *The Waste Land* a few months later in October.

When Ezra Pound arrived in London in September 1908, he welded his claims for literary authority to the culture of Provence. The first poem that he published in England was a *sestina*, a Provençal verse form; his first books of poetry presented a succession of albas, planhs, sestinas, ballatas, madrigales, and tenzoni; and his first work of critical prose treated the same subject, Provençal poetry. Pound had rapidly become, as one reviewer approvingly put it, "the modern troubadour," his literary identity insepar-able from the courtly lifestyle that had once nourished the poetic culture of Provence. Indeed, by a curious stroke of good fortune his very life had also become linked with analogous forms of aristocratic patronage. In March 1910 he had been introduced to Margaret Cravens, a thirty-year-old American expatriate who studied music in Paris and was a member of well-to-do Bohemia – an aristocracy of sensibility, in other words. Cravens promptly offered to become Pound's patron, and soon he was receiving about $1,000 or £200 per annum, a sum that was neither mean nor princely. On the eve of World War I in England, the average wage for the adult male industrial worker was £75 per annum, while the average annual income of the salaried class was £340. The gap between these figures represented the divide between the working class and the whole of the rest of society, a great and accepted gulf that has been termed "the major social fact of the day."[3] Patronage meant that Pound lived just beyond that divide, though never far from the abyss that yawned behind him. Pound, in fact, was acutely aware of these economic and social distinctions. Throughout the same period he was also courting Dorothy Shakespear, the daughter of an established barrister, whose parents insisted that Pound possess an income of £500 per annum before they would consent to their marriage. In early 1912, Pound was pressing his case to show that he would be a worthy son-in-law. To Dorothy's father he wrote a letter describing his income in detail: his writings were earning nearly £100 per year; he had just signed a contract with a publisher that would guarantee an additional £100 per year; and together with his £200 from Cravens, his income amounted to "about £400 per year, with reasonable chance of increase." Though "this would not go very far in England," it was a respectable, promising figure.[4]

Such considerations form the background, at once economic, personal, and ideological, to a series of three lectures that Pound gave in March 1912, designed to supplement his income and enhance his reputation among a small corpus of people with influence. The price for the three lectures was a steep one, £1 1s, slightly less than the weekly wage of the average male industrial worker. The audience was "limited to fifty," as a contemporary program announced, and the site was to be the "private gallery" of Lord and Lady Glenconner, located at 34 Queen Anne's Gate. With no expenses to cover (the event was offered "by the kind permission" of the Glenconners), Pound might earn between £50 and £60. Equally vital, however, was the effort to endow the lectures with an aura of aristocratic glitter, to distinguish them from mere offerings of the contemporary economy. Programs were not posted in public places, but privately distributed; tickets were not commodities to be purchased, but favors to be courteously requested ("TICKETS may be had on application to Lady Low," the program stated; Lady Low lived just off Kensington Gardens and hosted "evenings at home" for a circle of upper middle-class intellectuals including G. W. Prothero, editor of the *Quarterly Review*).[5] Above all, however, these ambitions found expression in the site of the lectures.

Edward and Pamela Tennant Glenconner, the owners of 34 Queen Anne's Gate, were both from remarkable families. Edward (1859–1920) was the eldest son of Sir Charles Tennant (1823–1906), the third in a succession of enterprising Scotch industrialists who had established their wealth in chemical manufacturing in Glasgow, a heritage that Sir Charles had transformed into an empire of international mining, finance and steel. (At his death he was the chairman of fourteen different companies and director of nine others.) In 1894 his daughter Margot married Sir H. H. Asquith, already a rising star in the Liberal Party. In 1895 his son Edward married Pamela Wyndham, the youngest daughter of a family with aristocratic background and artistic tastes – a house designed by Philip Webb, paintings by Rossetti and Edward Burne-Jones, carpets and curtains designed by Morris himself. After constructing their country house from 1904 to 1906, Edward and Pamela turned to their residence in town; in 1908 they purchased 34 Queen Anne's Gate and commissioned Detmar Blow to redesign it entirely. They occupied it in 1910, and in 1911 Edward was named the first Baron Glenconner by his brother-in-law Asquith, now the Prime Minister, a reward for Edward's many years of support for Asquith's costly electoral campaigns. The first storey (in American usage, second floor) contained the "private gallery" that housed Edward and

Pamela's collection of thirty-seven masterpieces by Reynolds, Hogarth, Romney, Hoppner, Gainsborough, Ramsay, Turner, Fragonard, and others. Pamela, who had published a book of poetry in 1905 and prose fiction in 1907, possessed discerning taste and genuine talents, and it was no doubt her decision that led to Pound's lectures in the "private gallery."[6] No space better epitomized the realm of elite bourgeois culture in which Pound's career had been fashioned to this point: a world withdrawn from public life and insulated from the grim imperatives of a commodity economy, a sphere in which literary culture was a privatized medium of symbolic exchange for an exiguous aristocracy of sensibility, a court of intellect now patronizing Ezra Pound.

Pound's first lecture (14 March) had concerned Guido Cavalcanti. His second (19 March) treated Arnaut Daniel, the master of "trobar clus" or "closed verse," the most hermetic vein of Provençal poetry. The gist of his lecture survives in an essay published two months later, in which Pound urged that Daniel's poems "are good art as the high mass is good art," a body of works that must be "approached as ritual" because they sought "to make their revelations to those who are already expert."[7] Pound, plainly enough, was describing his own poetry as well, and his lecture on Daniel, Daniel's poems, and their audience, was a self-referential discourse.

Pound's lecture acquires special relief when set against another lecture that took place on the same day, this one given by F. T. Marinetti, the leader of the Futurists, who had published the famous "Foundation and Manifesto of Futurism" on the front page of the Parisian newspaper Le Figaro in 1909. Two weeks earlier the first exhibition of Futurist painting had opened at the Sackville Gallery, prompting an avalanche of reviews and widespread public debate, and it was in the wake of these events that Marinetti gave a much-anticipated lecture, one that differed in almost every respect from Pound's. It was held not in a "private gallery," but in Bechstein Hall (now Wigmore Hall), a public concert room that seated 550 people. Whereas a ticket for a single lecture by Pound had cost 10s 6d, only the most expensive tickets to Marinetti's lecture had cost that much, and the lowest-priced ones had cost only 1s.[8] But perhaps the most significant difference was style: far from gratifying his audience, Marinetti berated it, castigating the English as "a nation of sycophants and snobs, enslaved by old worm-eaten traditions, social conventions, and romanticism." The spectators, one newspaper reported, "rewarded him with their laughter and applause," or as another contemporary recalled, "wildly applauded his outspoken derision of all their cherished national characteristics." And for an avid reader of newspapers such as Pound, the next day must have been unforgettable. Not one took note of his lecture on Arnaut Daniel, while

Marinetti's performance was fully reported in the morning edition of the *Daily Chronicle*, with a headline reading "'Futurist' Leader in London," and a subtitle announcing, "Makes an Attack on the English Nation." The next day a second article on Marinetti appeared in the *Morning Leader*, while the venerable *Times* devoted its editorial column to a careful analysis of Marinetti's remarks.[9] Marinetti's audience had become not just those who had attended his performance, but the millions who read about it in the *Daily Chronicle*, the *Morning Leader*, and *The Times*. Nothing could have made plainer the value of a concerted polemical onslaught, the formation of a collective identity buttressed by theatricality and publicity. Nor is it possible that Pound was unaware of these doings: the day of his lecture he had received a note from his fiancée, who had advised him that she would be attending a lecture that evening – not his, however. She was going "to hear Marinetti lecture . . . about les Futuristes."[10]

A few weeks later Pound sent off the manuscript for his next book of poetry, *Ripostes*, at the back of which he included a brief statement since famous as the first public reference to Imagism: "As for the Future, *Les Imagistes*, the descendants of the forgotten school of 1909, have that in their keeping." The conjunction of terms (*Les Imagistes* in French, a reference to "the future") made all too plain the provenance of Pound's new "school." Yet taken by itself, Pound's statement was little more than a cryptic hint, and his more definitive steps toward a reconception of art as public practice came only in the wake of three other events that occurred in the remaining months of 1912. In June, Margaret Cravens committed suicide, leaving Pound without the financial support that had sustained him for the last two years; in October the publishing firm that had guaranteed him £100 per year also collapsed; and just a few weeks before he had learned that Edward Marsh was assembling an anthology to present the recent work of younger poets as a collective project, the Georgians, a volume whose future success was already apparent to discerning observers by December of 1912.[11] These developments account for Pound's subsequent actions. In August and October 1912 he sent off poems by himself and H.D. to *Poetry* magazine in Chicago, characterizing them as "Imagiste." In December he wrote an essay containing the second public reference to Imagism, two paragraphs which asserted that Imagism was "the youngest school here that has the nerve to call itself a school." The aggressive tone was at odds with the tentative statements that followed, formulations designed to underscore the difference between Imagism and Futurism. Whereas Futurism emphasized collective identity, Imagism was more casual and individualistic, the fortuitous outcome of "two or three young men agree[ing], more or less, to call certain things good." Futurism issued comprehensive theoretical programs, but Imagism shunned such ambitions: "a school does not mean in the least that one writes poetry to a theory." (This claim echoes contemporary reviewers who charged that Futurist paintings were "rather a theoretic extension than a spontaneous development.") And whereas Futurism was based on a systematic interpretation of modernity, Imagism was purely a matter of writerly technique: "Their watchword was Precision," and they opposed only "interminable effusions."[12] These features were accentuated in subsequent pronouncements. In March 1913 Pound published an essay that explicitly posed an opposition between Imagism and Futurism: "The *Imagistes* admitted that they were contemporaries of the Post Impressionists and the Futurists; but they had nothing in common with these schools. They had not published a manifesto. They were not a revolutionary school . . ." Accompanying this was a second essay also by Pound, "A Few Don'ts By An Imagiste," its very title implicitly repudiating the manifesto genre.[13] Imagism, though commonly treated as the first avant-garde movement in English literature, was something quite different – it was the first anti-avant-garde.

Imagism was being overtaken by events before its antiprogram was fully formulated, a result of its failure to address the complications and unexpected consequences entailed in Marinetti's novel use of publicity and theatricality for culture. Marinetti's activities were eliding the boundaries that separated different spheres of cultural production; it was no longer the "private gallery," the polite salon, or the genteel review, but the concert hall and the mass-circulation newspaper that would serve as the new agora of cultural debate. Theoretical consequences were also entailed, and in the months that followed his talk at Bechstein Hall Marinetti elaborated them in a series of four manifestos: "The Technical Manifesto of Futurist Literature" (May 1912), "The Supplement to the Technical Manifesto" (August 1912), the famous "Destruction of Syntax – Wireless Imagination – Words-in-Freedom" (June 1913), and the ambitious "The Variety Theatre" (August 1913). Already in the first of these he broke new ground by launching a violent assault on the notion of aesthetic autonomy, the very concept of art. "Courageously let us set about making the 'ugly' in literature, and let us kill solemnity everywhere. Go away! don't listen to me with the air of great priests! Every day it is necessary to spit on the *Altar of Art*!" By November 1913, when Marinetti was again in England and giving lectures to packed houses, he was quoted as saying, "Art is not a religion, not something to be worshipped with joined hands." Instead it "should express all the intensity of life – its beauty . . . sordidness," and "the very complex of our life to-day."[14]

These developments were closely followed by London observers of the cultural scene, and English readers were kept abreast. In September 1913 the journal *Poetry and Drama*, edited by Harold Monro, devoted an entire issue to examining Futurism. (Its previous issue had granted only a paragraph to Imagism.) It included a translation of "The Destruction of Syntax" and thirty pages of poems by Marinetti and his colleagues. In a prefatory editorial, Monro praised Marinetti warmly, hailing him for dissolving the distinction between poetry and popular culture, art and life. Marinetti had gained "22,000 adherents" and his book *The Futurist Poets* had sold 35,000 copies, a fact that in itself constituted "Marinetti's most interesting attitude." Here was poetry no longer written "for. . . close and studious scrutiny by the eye" and "no longer. . . withheld from the people" by "educationalists" or "intellectuals." Here, instead, was poetry intended "for the ear" and "for immediate and wide circulation," poetry "regaining some of its popular appeal." Marinetti was restoring poetry to its status in an earlier era, an age when "the minstrel and the ballad-monger then represented our modern Northcliffe." It was a telling reference. Northcliffe, the greatest of the early modern press barons, was famous for having created the *Daily Mail* in 1896, a newspaper whose sales topped 1,000,000 a day in 1902 and achieved the largest circulation in the world, addressing a mass audience with a mix of arresting stories, appealing format, and attractive competitions. Northcliffe, in short, had blurred the distinction between news and entertainment, turning the news into a species of diversion. Monro's remark hinted at tensions latent in the collapse of life and art he wished to celebrate: for now there was no longer a meaningful distinction between poetry and the most ephemeral of all commodities, the daily newspaper.[15]

Marinetti returned to London two months after the publication of Monro's special issue, the object of unprecedented media attention. His daily lectures were carefully reported and attentively analyzed by the press, and on 21 November 1913 he published his most recent manifesto, "The Variety Theatre," in Northcliffe's *Daily Mail*. The new work attempted to draw out the institutional and generic consequences of his previous attacks on the concept of aesthetic autonomy, doing so by an intransigent vindication of a despised and popular cultural form. The music hall, wrote Marinetti, "is naturally anti-academical, primitive, and ingenuous, and therefore all the more significant by reason of the unforeseen nature of its fumbling efforts and the coarse simplicity of its resources . . . [It] destroys all that is solemn, sacred, earnest, and pure in Art with a capital *A*."[16] Six months later, Marinetti returned to England again, and now he was given a chance to put his theories into effect, booked to appear at the largest music hall in London, the Coliseum, for an entire week (twice daily, Monday to

Saturday, 15–21 June). By this time Marinetti had acquired an extraordinary stature in the life of the popular press. His self-portrait appeared on the front cover of the weekly *Sketch*; his views on "Futurist" clothes made headlines; his every lecture was respectfully chronicled and analyzed; and major newspapers competed for advance stories about the "Futurist Music" to be presented at the Coliseum.[17] When Marinetti strode across the stage to deliver his prefatory comments to a concert of Futurist noise-tuners, his every step betokened a momentous event – a crossing of cultural boundaries, a passage into a new realm of cultural practice.

The Coliseum, however, was not an ordinary music hall. Its planning and construction had epitomized new developments that were transforming the world of Edwardian entertainment. Its site had been selected because it stood opposite the exit of Charing Cross station, addressing the crowds of prosperous and respectable suburbanites who poured into the metropolis for a day's shopping. They were "middle-class people for whom a visit to a serious play might seem too ambitious and a visit to a music-hall too racy." The Coliseum, in other words, offered a version of music hall that was sanitized, deracinated from the culture of the working and lower middle classes and assimilated instead to the tastes of a middle class increasingly defined by consumerism. Marie Lloyd, the music-hall star whose *risqué* lyrics and *double entendres* had won an adoring audience, never performed at the Coliseum: she was too vulgar. Opened in 1904, it was the most lavish music hall in London: its seating capacity was 4,000, its stage and proscenium the largest ever built, its architecture distinguished by a massive tower that held a revolving globe with the name "COLISEUM" in electric lights. Here was something "to catch the attention of those prosperous shoppers" – culture as consumption, art as entertainment.[18] Here was the site of Marinetti's last theatrical venture in England.

It proved to be a failure, and contemporaries understood the reasons immediately. Reviewing the première performance, *The Times* wrote:

> Signor Marinetti rather mistook his audience yesterday afternoon, when he tried to deliver an academic exposition of Futurist principles at the Coliseum, and he had, in consequence, to put up with a rude reception from a gallery which seemed fully qualified to give him a lesson in his own "Art of Noises."[19]

Marinetti indeed "mistook his audience," for he had badly gauged the changes that were overtaking the music halls. His sense of the music hall derived from his observations in Italy, where it was still a vital if troubled genre of urban popular culture, a hybrid form that addressed a public still making the transition from a largely agrarian to a more urban lifestyle, a form that adopted motifs of the village carnival in order to treat the dislocations of metropolitan experience. In England, however, the music hall was dying – indeed, already dead. It was a corpse that was experiencing a spurious afterlife through its incorporation into the "Palace of Variety," the new institution of an advancing consumer economy; no longer the hybrid creation of popular experience, it was a prototype of mass commodity culture. After World War I it would be swept away by Hollywood cinema.

Marinetti's failure only makes more ironic the fate of the second endeavor that was planned by Pound and his colleagues in answer to the success that Marinetti had been enjoying in late 1913 and early 1914 – the invention of a new movement named Vorticism that was to be embodied in a review called *Blast*. The journal appeared scarcely two weeks after Marinetti's fiasco at the Coliseum. Filled with belligerent manifestos and a typographical style that signaled its origins all too plainly, the journal was virtually a graphic counterpart to a music hall performance. *Blast* was greeted with a revealing lack of critical acceptance; contrary to what later critics have urged, contemporaries were neither shocked nor provoked by it, but simply bored – and not because it represented an incomprehensible novelty, but because it was all too familiar:

> Almost all the pictures reproduced are (like the typesetting of the first pages), Futurist in origin, and nothing else. And as for the productions of the literary Vortices, these are not even so fresh as that . . . All it really is is a feeble attempt at being clever. *Blast* is a flat affair. We haven't a movement here, not even a mistaken one.

And in perhaps the most cutting words of all, the same reviewer remarked:

> Mr. Pound used to be quite interesting when he was a remote passéeist and wrote about the Provençal troubadours; but as a revolutionary I would rather have Signor Marinetti, who is at any rate a genuine hustler, whereas Mr. Pound assuming violence and ruthlessness is as unimpressive in his movements as a man who is trying to use someone else's coat as a pair of trousers.[20]

Blast was indeed a dull affair, also yielding poems that are among the dreariest that Pound ever produced. His attempt to address and provoke an audience through a programmatic polemical onslaught had proved a failure in economic, intellectual, and critical terms.

Initially, then, Marinetti's practical and theoretical activities in London during the period 1912–14 had two related effects on Pound and what has come to be termed the Anglo-American avant-garde. One was to reconfigure the relations among the institutions in which the discourse of art and poetry were produced, forcing intellectuals and artists to assay the potential role of new institutions of mass culture and their bearing on the place of art in a cultural marketplace being radically transformed. The other was to precipitate a collapse of the entire set of distinctions between art and commodity, to effect a perceptible, irreversible leveling of both within the single and amorphous category of the commodity. Further, by late 1914 it was clear that the principal attempts to address or resolve these dilemmas had been failures, whether it was the rearguard restoration effort of Imagism or the imitative gesture of *Blast*. But if one could neither go back to reconstruct the aristocracy of the salon nor rush forward to embrace the egalitarianism of the commodity, what solution was there? The answer, paradoxically, was to do a little of both – to reconstruct an aristocracy, but to reconstruct it within the world of the commodity. To accept, in other words, the status of art as a commodity, but simultaneously to transform it into a special kind of commodity, a rarity capable of sustaining investment value. Or to reformulate this, the answer to the leveling effect precipitated by a consumer economy was to defer consumption into the future, to transform it into investment; which is to say, to encourage or even solicit the ephemeral allure of the consumer economy, acknowledging the status of art as commodity, but to postpone and sublimate its consumption by turning it into an object of investment whose value will be realized only in the future. "Art," we might say, becomes "news that stays news."

In concrete terms, this meant that what had once been an aristocracy of patron-saloniers would now be replaced by an elite of patron-investors. For the Anglo-American avant-garde, the future lay in the new patronage provided by a small group of people such as John Quinn, Harriet Shaw Weaver, Scofield Thayer, and James Sibley Watson, Jr. The actualization of this new space within the commodity economy was achieved primarily through the new and unprecedented use of two institutions which had already existed for some time, but which now became central to an emerging apparatus of cultural production: the little review and the limited or deluxe edition, venues located in a profoundly ambiguous social space, simultaneously sequestered and semi-withdrawn from the larger institution of publishing, situated instead within a submarket of collecting. It was in the little reviews – among them the *Little Review*, the *Egoist* and the *Dial* – that the principal masterpieces of the Anglo-American avant-garde would first be published. Likewise, their second appearance was almost uniformly in limited editions – 200 copies of Hugh Selwyn Mauberley, or the 254 copies of Eliot's *Ara Vos Prec*, or the 1,000 copies of *Ulysses* – editions at the farthest possible remove from the 35,000 copies of *The Futurist Poets*. And in this new social space, the kind of publicization that had once been aimed at a mass audience along the lines pursued by Marinetti and imitated by *Blast* was no longer of use. Asked by Margaret Anderson in 1917 how best to announce his collaboration on the *Little Review*, Pound now replied: "IF it is any use for advertising purposes, you may state that a single copy of my first book has just fetched £8 (forty dollars)." Similarly, seven years later when William Bird was drafting the prospectus for the first edition of *A Draft of XVI. Cantos* (a limited edition of 90 copies), Pound would urge the same argument: "Your best ad is the quiet statement that at auction recently a copy of Mr. P.'s [first book] 'A Lume Spento' published in 1908 at $1.00 (one dollar) was sold for $52.50."[21] These remarks, far from advancing assertions of intrinsic and autonomous aesthetic value, offer straightforward claims about the performance record of investments within a commodity economy: by 1917 *A Lume Spento* has been increasing in value at more than 50 percent a year, by 1924 at 28 percent a year, and the same should now prove true of the *Little Review* or *A Draft of XVI. Cantos*. The reason to buy these is not necessarily to read them, but to be able to sell them – perhaps at a substantial profit. Readers, in short, are giving way on an uneasy mixture of patron-investors, collectors, speculators on the rare book market, all situated within a complex and highly unstable institutional space.

What the patron-investors provided with their subsidies and endowments was an institutional space momentarily immune to the pressures of the larger market economy, partially removed from the constraints of an expansive and expanding mass culture. Yet that same space was simultaneously being transformed by its proximity to the small (and hence malleable) submarket for rare books and deluxe editions, a submarket just then being "modernized," just then becoming aware of the potential value of works by authors still living, in part as a result of its own interconnections with collecting in the visual arts. Accepting the collapse of art and the triumph of commodity culture, Modernism created a new distinction within commodity culture itself, distinguishing between commodities whose value is exhausted in immediate consumption and those whose worth is deferred or sublated into the future as investment. Doing so, Modernism gained for itself – for an evanescent moment – a breathing space within the present, a space from which it could formulate its often powerful critique of commodity capitalism, even as – and at the same time as – it mortgaged that critique in the future, mirroring the very system that it damned. But the consequences of this precarious and unstable compromise could not be forever deferred. For it was an inevitable outcome of this situation that the avant-garde's distaste for the dictates of the marketplace should ultimately be revealed as disingenuous precisely because, and insofar as, the works of the avant-garde began to command ever more significant prices within the larger open market. After that it was only a matter of time before we should see the emergence of forms of art that were already "precommodified," art that ironically and even nostalgically acknowledges its own exchange function, art that finds its richest moments – in several senses – in the works of Andy Warhol. Here the dwindling isles of authenticity welcome their own commodification as objects of tourism, producing the ennui of "postmodernism."

Early in January 1922, T. S. Eliot brought a disorderly sheaf of manuscripts to Paris, planning to ask his colleague Ezra Pound for a critical assessment of his work in progress. Leaving Paris a few weeks later, his manuscript now heavily marked by Pound, Eliot departed with the poem that we know as *The Waste Land*, a work that not only differed from what he had originally brought, but that would soon require an institutional venue through which to address a public, however defined. In the next eight months, from February to September, Eliot and Pound would engage in elaborate negotiations with the editors of three US periodicals, or in some cases with their friends or associates, in the hope of finding an appropriate American publisher.[22] (Evidently they assumed that the poem would appear in Britain in Eliot's own journal, later the *Criterion*, although in January of 1922 it had neither acquired a name nor announced a publication date.) Taken together, the three journals represent the spectrum of modernist publishing and trace the contours of an institutional structure crucial to Modernism's success, an ensemble of agents, practices, and protocols that gave Modernism its distinctive character.

The three journals that were candidates to publish *The Waste Land* in the US were the *Little Review*, the *Dial*, and *Vanity Fair*. Undoubtedly the easiest way to distinguish them is by the size of their readerships: the *Little Review* had the smallest circulation; the *Dial* was a significantly larger concern; and *Vanity Fair* was the largest of them all. But however useful as a mnemonic device, circulation was only one aspect within a much larger complex of features that made up these journals' identities.

The *Little Review* was founded in March 1914 in Chicago by Margaret Anderson. In late 1916 she moved the journal to New York, where it would remain until 1922 when Anderson moved to Paris. Also in late 1916, Anderson received an offer of collaboration from Ezra Pound, who proposed that he be allowed to edit at his discretion a certain number of pages per issue; contributors to these pages would be paid from a fund of £150 ($750) per year provided by John Quinn, a prominent New York corporate lawyer and cultural patron, with Pound himself distributing the funds, including a small allotment for his own salary (£60 per year). Anderson agreed and the new section appeared for the first time in May 1917 and continued until March of 1919; among other works, it contained the serial version of *Ulysses*. It was not long before Quinn's role in supporting the *Little Review* expanded to include an additional subsidy of $1,600 per year ($1,200 provided by a coterie of donors who were his friends). Pound ceased collaborating with the *Little Review* in early 1919, going on to become Paris correspondent and talent scout for the *Dial* in 1920.[23] The *Little Review*, meanwhile, continued publishing episodes of *Ulysses* until the number for July–August 1920, which was seized by US postal authorities and charged with obscenity in September. Five months later the journal was convicted. Lacking further support from Quinn, it was forced to cut back from monthly to quarterly publication. After 1923 even its quarterly appearances grew irregular, though with occasional subsidies it continued to publish until 1929.

The ongoing support of Quinn and his coterie of patrons meant that the *Little Review* existed in a special space that was semi-isolated from the direct demands of the larger market economy. Though Pound and Quinn repeatedly urged that the journal be more careful in its bookkeeping, no one truly expected the *Little Review* to be profitable and its editors remained largely indifferent to such issues. The total circulation of the *Little Review* was just over 3,000. Of this figure, 2,500 were subscribers, while 500–600 copies were sold at a handful of retail outlets – in New York, for example, at the Washington Square Bookshop, the Sunwise Turn, and Brentano's.[24] These stores, however, sold the journal less as a periodical competing with others available in the wider marketplace, more as a rarity complementing a collection of contemporary literature and art, one that might also prove a good investment. As we have seen, when Anderson asked Pound how best to announce his collaboration with the *Little Review*, he advised her to cite the increase in value likely to accrue to each issue of the journal in the years ahead. The *Little Review*, in other words, cannot really be viewed as a form of publication opposed to the dominant magazines of the mass market, for in practice it did not compete within that market, but bypassed it. Instead, it was the periodical counterpart to the deluxe edition, a rarity potentially liable to rise in value on the collectors' market, a market just beginning to view contemporary literature as a field of interest.

The role of the patron, therefore, became radically more ambiguous, ambiguity reflected in Pound's uncertainty concerning which noun to use when describing those whose money would underwrite the modernist venture. Corresponding with Margaret Anderson, for example, he oscillated between "guarantors" and "investors."[25] The terminological uncertainty merely recapitulated a confusion already epitomized in the little review: presented as "pure" art inimical to the demands of the marketplace, it was also being resituated within the economy of rare book collecting, a world of deluxe editions and little reviews that increasingly overlapped with the domains of art galleries and dealers.

The interconnections linking this intricate network are mapped out in an almost casual suggestion by Pound, delivered to Margaret Anderson in 1917, concerning an advertiser in the *Little Review*: "If I didn't say so before, I will say now, that the Mod. Gallery ought to pay for half a dozen reproductions a month, simply cost of blocks and printing. It would add to us, and advertise their painters." Pound was referring to the Modern Gallery, which first opened in 1916 and lasted until late 1921. Marius de Zayas, its owner, was a minor artist and journalist who had previously been associated with Alfred Stieglitz and the "291" Gallery; but whereas "291" had provided only an exhibition space, de Zayas opened his new gallery in order, as he put it, "to do business."[26] The gallery's principal clients were Eugene and Agnes Meyer, Arthur B. Davies, Walter Arensberg, and John Quinn. Few indeed, though fit enough. In 1920 alone Quinn purchased nearly $24,000 worth of works from de Zayas, and even after returning two paintings in early 1921, the sum of his 1920 purchases totaled almost $13,000. The figure should not be underestimated. Throughout the 1920s, for example, the executive secretary to Frank Crowninshield, editor of *Vanity Fair*, earned but $1,144 per year; if the same position today would earn roughly $35,000, Quinn's purchases would equal a figure around $390,000.[27] Quinn, of course, was also the primary guarantor of the *Little Review*. Thus, it is Quinn who buys the paintings from the gallery that advertises in the journal which, also supported by Quinn, writes the art criticism that praises and increases the value of the paintings purchased . . . well, by Quinn. Success, even survival, could depend on a small nucleus of patron-investors of just this sort.

The *Little Review* maintained a low ratio of advertising to circulation revenues, roughly 1:10.[28] This figure is important because it flew in the face of conventional wisdom in periodical publishing as it had evolved between 1890 and 1910, the period when it was first appreciated that one could sell a magazine for less than it actually cost to produce it by shifting the cost away from subscribers and on to advertisers. To do so, however, required a mass audience whom advertisers would pay to address. The *Little Review*, instead, earned the bulk (89 percent) of its revenues from circulation (apart from its subsidies, of course), and above all from subscriptions, which means that it survived by maintaining a direct rapport with a restricted group of readers. To put it differently, the *Little Review* represented a return to the kind of direct relationship with readers that had typified literary magazines in the genteel tradition of elite bourgeois readership.

The *Dial* was in some respects a publication quite different from the *Little Review*. Its two owners and coeditors were both from wealthy backgrounds. Scofield Thayer was heir to a fortune made in the manufacturing of woolens in Worcester, Massachusetts, while James Sibley Watson, Jr., was the scion of families who were among the original investors in the Western Union Telegraph Company. The two men had purchased the *Dial* in late 1919, a journal that came with a venerable history but troubles in its recent past. Begun in Chicago in 1880 and unaltered until 1913, when its founder and first editor died, the *Dial* had at first been continued by the founder's sons (1913–16), then purchased and managed by Martyn Johnson (1916–18), who had enlisted financial backing from Thayer in late 1918 in order to expand the journal and move it to New York. Finally it had been purchased outright by Thayer and Watson, who published their first issue in January 1920, issuing it monthly until 1929.[29]

The wealth of Thayer and Watson enabled them to support the *Dial* with patronage that was truly massive. From 1920 to 1922 the journal's annual deficits were respectively $100,000, $54,000, and $65,000, a cumulative shortfall of $220,000 that Thayer and Watson each supplied at the rate of $4,000 per month. (Recall the $2,350 per year that John Quinn and his syndicate provided the *Little Review*.) Not surprisingly, the *Dial* was also a significantly larger operation. Its total circulation in 1922 was 9,200, and its number of subscribers was two and a half times larger than the *Little Review*'s: 6,374, compared with 2,500 for the *Little Review* in 1917. Its ratio of advertising to circulation revenues was not 1:10, but 1:3 (specifically, $9,320 to $31,400) – to be sure, a figure still below that expected of a commercial periodical, but significantly above the level reached by the *Little Review*.[30] In this regard, as in many others, the *Dial* stood midway between the *Little Review* and *Vanity Fair*, and in its efforts to break even it consistently imitated the practices of both its rivals. Thus, throughout the early 1920s Thayer and Watson discussed plans for what they termed a "millionaires' number" of the *Dial*, one to be printed on special paper as a deluxe or limited edition of the journal itself, an issue that they planned to circulate among potential patrons in order to raise funds and reduce the *Dial*'s deficit.[31] Yet simultaneously they insistently pursued a campaign of publicity and struggled to increase retail sales in order to raise circulation and hence advertising revenues. The *Dial*, in other words, remained perennially uncertain about its status and aims: was it a commercial publisher seeking profitability or a vehicle of disinterested patronage free of commercial considerations? This was also the question that haunted the journal's discussions with Eliot over *The Waste Land*. When Eliot learned that another author had recently received a payment much higher than the figure offered to him, he withdrew the poem. As Pound explained to Thayer:

> That being the case I can hardly reprove Eliot – if you have put the thing on a commercial basis, for holding out for as high a price as he can get. [Added in autograph in margin:] (*i.e. if The Dial is a business house, it gets business treatment. If The Dial is a patron of literature T. contends it should not pay extra rates for "mere senility" . . .*)[32]

In many respects, the *Dial* mediated between the *Little Review* and *Vanity Fair*. The *Dial*, for example, repeatedly published material that had previously appeared in the *Little Review*, such as Wyndham Lewis's painting *Starry Sky* or a photo of Ossip Zadkine's *Holy Family*.[33] Indeed, at times all three journals were publishing the same material: the spring 1922 issue of the *Little Review* was devoted to works by Brancusi, the May number of *Vanity Fair* showed photographs of the same works, while the November issue of the *Dial* reproduced Brancusi's *Golden Bird* for the third time in the same year. Its mediating role was also apparent in editorial policy. While the *Little Review* boasted its intransigent aestheticism on the masthead ("no compromise with the public taste"), the *Dial* was more cautious: in a letter of November 1922 Thayer told his managing editor that he wished to publish works that "have *aesthetic value* and are not *commercially suicidal*" (author's italics). "Not commercially suicidal," when translated into ordinary prose, means *might be successful*. Its official policy was also a compromise: it invoked the philosophical idealism of Benedetto Croce to justify eclectic aestheticism and patrician urbanity, the conviction that "one must confine one's self to works of art" independent of social or moral considerations.[34] The *Dial*, differed from the *Little Review* and *Vanity Fair* not in substantive ideology, but in its tone of gravity.

Yet the *Dial* did not just borrow from the *Little Review*. In other respects it strove to imitate *Vanity Fair*, owned by Condé Nast. Editorially it copied *Vanity Fair*'s practice of offering a regular "London Letter" and a "Paris Letter," and it imitated *Vanity Fair*'s institution of so-called "service departments," which offered the reader advice and arrangements for the purchase of books and travel. Its layout and design were also conspicuously similar, and by 1922 the *Dial* was even sharing the same printing operations. It also attempted to integrate editorial and advertising functions in ways reminiscent of *Vanity Fair*: its monthly listing of gallery exhibitions took pains to praise its own advertisers. And like *Vanity Fair*, too, its management stressed publicity, advertising revenues, and street sales (as opposed to subscriptions). It developed displays to be set up at newstands, and it aggressively cultivated a larger metropolitan public. (Eliot counseled Thayer to pursue the same course in Britain, urging him to "arrange for the paper to be visible and handy on every bookstall, at every tube station."[35]) Again, when the *Dial* published *The Waste Land* and announced that Eliot would receive the journal's annual Dial Award, Thayer ordered the staff to keep track of every reference to these events in the press, an early form of market testing.[36] Above all, the *Dial* imitated the central principle which lay behind the success of *Vanity Fair* and its sister journal *Vogue*: in an era when most publishers were attempting magazines aimed at a mass market, Condé Nast and *Vanity Fair* deliberately appealed to a select, restricted audience.

Indeed, the *Dial* was acutely conscious of its competition with *Vanity Fair*, a theme that recurs in letter after letter by Thayer. To his mother he complained that contributors and staff members of the *Dial* were writing too frequently for *Vanity Fair*. To his managing editor he lamented, "If we have no aesthetic standards whatever, in what respect are we superior to Vanity Fair which in other respects gives more for the money?" A month later Thayer urged him to hasten the printing of a new photograph "lest 'Vanity Fair' get ahead of us on this point too." And four months later he ordered him to secure rights to a new painting by Picasso: "Otherwise Vanity Fair will be getting it." How closely the market for the two journals overlapped became clear when the *Dial* issued its special art folio in mid 1923. Eager to stimulate sales, Thayer begged Seldes to intervene: "Cannot you get Rosenfeld to write the thing up for Vanity Fair, which is our most important selling possibility?"[37]

To be sure, the *Dial* and *Vanity Fair* were not twins. By comparison the *Dial* was a modest operation. Its $9,320 in advertising revenues was tiny when compared to the $500,000 per annum generated by *Vanity Fair*. Paid advertising also occupied less space: in the November 1922 issue which printed *The Waste Land*, $27\frac{1}{2}$ of the 156 pages (or 18 percent) were taken up by advertising. Compare this with the July 1923 issue of *Vanity Fair*, which contained a selection of Eliot's earlier poems: here 76 out of 140 pages were devoted to paid advertising (54 percent), and many articles offered fashion and automobile reviews that were advertising thinly disguised. In 1922 the *Dial's* circulation stood at 9,200 copies per month; in the same year *Vanity Fair's* reached 92,000.[38]

Yet this latter figure should not mislead us into confusing *Vanity Fair* with mass-circulation periodicals such as the *Saturday Evening Post* or *McClure's*, whose circulations were numbered in millions, not thousands. *Vanity Fair* shared with those magazines a recognition of the primacy of advertising, but it adapted that principle to different ends. Condé Nast, *Vanity Fair*'s owner and publisher, was a pioneer in what is now called niche marketing. He recognized, in other words, that a variety of luxury consumer goods required not a mass audience, but a more select one of well-to-do readers. His task was to capture that audience and sell its purchasing power, its large amounts of disposable income, to advertisers, "Anything high-priced," Nast contended, "is better advertised in a periodical with readers of a special type – people of breeding, sophistication and means."[39] Nast began *Vanity Fair* after he had already been successful with magazines covering fashion (*Vogue*) and interior decoration (*House and Garden*), and in his third venture he adopted the same approach to the topic of arts and leisure: ideas were to be treated as matters of style, as intellectual fashions, not as eternal verities. *Vanity Fair*, whose first issue appeared in September 1913, might well be defined as a periodical counterpart to the Coliseum: it appealed to the same audience increasingly defined by consumption, by the purchase of luxury consumer goods, and by stylishness in all things.

Eliot, as we know, elected to publish *The Waste Land* not in the *Little Review* or *Vanity Fair*, but in the *Dial*. There were several reasons for this. One was a simple matter of personal finances. The *Dial* offered to give Eliot the annual Dial Award of $2,000 as a price for the poem, even though officially it would pay only its standard rate of $150.00. And because Eliot had already reached an agreement for the book publication with Horace Liveright, raising the possibility that sales of the *Dial* might detract from sales of the book version, the *Dial* also agreed to purchase 350 copies of the first printing. *Vanity Fair* could not match such sums; the highest price it ever paid to any contributor was $100, given to F. Scott Fitzgerald for a short story. The *Little Review*, cast adrift by Quinn, could no longer pay contributors at all. The massive patronage provided by Thayer and Watson created an artificial space in which it was possible, on some occasions, to earn more money by publishing for fewer readers. Another reason, no doubt, was the intangible issue of status and popularity. *Vanity Fair* was not a popular magazine of the same sort as the *Saturday Evening Post*, but its substantial circulation and light-hearted tone could not sound the note of aesthetic gravity associated with the *Dial*. Eliot wanted his poem to be successful, but not too successful.

The relationship between the three journals was partly a synchronic or structural one, partly a diachronic or temporal one. Each represented a moment in the growth and triumph of Modernism. When Eliot suggested the *Little Review* as a potential publisher in early 1922, his proposal looked back to the world of Modernism's past, to its origins in an exiguous coterie and the heady days of 1917–18, when his poems and articles had appeared in the rebellious journal. When Pound suggested in mid-summer 1922 that *The Waste Land* be published by *Vanity Fair*, his proposal looked forward to Modernism's future, to the ease and speed with which a market economy, and in particular an economy of luxury consumer goods, could purchase, assimilate, commodify, and reclaim as its own the works of a literature often deeply inimical toward its ethos and cultural operations. The *Dial*, in 1922, represented Modernism's present. Yet the future was fast approaching, as is illustrated by the fate of Eliot's own work shortly after the publication of *The Waste Land*. Only seven months later, in June of 1923, *Vanity Fair* devoted an entire page to reprinting earlier poems by Eliot: among them were "Sweeney Among the Nightingales" (first published in the *Little Review* in 1918), "A Cooking Egg" (first published in a tiny journal named *Coterie* in 1919), and "Burbank with a Baedeker" (first published in the short-lived *Art and Letters* in 1919). Linking the poems was an editorial box in the center of the page, presumably composed by Edmund Wilson (*Vanity Fair*'s managing editor), which lucidly articulated the journal's assumptions and aims:

> Since the publication of *The Waste Land*, Mr. T. S. Eliot has become the most hotly contested issue in American poetry. He has been frequently attacked for his unconventional form and what many readers consider his obscurity. But if one has read Mr. Eliot's earlier poems . . . from which the present selection is made, one gets the key to both his technique and his ideas.

In subsequent months *Vanity Fair* conducted an intense campaign, printing essays by Eliot in July 1923, November 1923, and February 1924; while in September 1923 it published a study of Eliot's work by Clive Bell. Eliot had indeed become "the most hotly contested issue in American poetry" – *Vanity Fair* and the *Dial* had said so themselves.[40]

Despite their diversity, one set of interests did bind together the *Little Review*, the *Dial*, and *Vanity Fair* – their involvement with the visual arts. All three journals were copious in publishing photographs of contemporary painting and sculpture. More important, however, was the affiliation that this signaled with the world of contemporary art collecting. John Quinn, who was patron of the *Little Review*; Scofield Thayer, who was co-owner, patron, and editor of the *Dial*; and Frank Crowninshield, who was the editor of *Vanity Fair* – all were major buyers of contemporary art. Quinn's purchases, as we have seen, totaled $24,000 in 1920 alone. In 1923, to give only one example, he purchased Cézanne's portrait of his father; a huge still-life interior by Matisse, six by eight feet; *The Jungle* by Rousseau; five Picassos, including the magnificent *Portrait of William Uhde*; two small works by Braque; and three major works by Brancusi. Thayer was almost as active: after residing in Paris, Vienna, and Berlin, and acting under the influence of Herwarth Walden, owner of the famous *Der Sturm* gallery, Thayer gathered a judicious collection of prewar German expressionists, including Kokoschka, along with a substantial number of works by Picasso, Matisse, and others, and at his instigation the *Dial* published a lavish collection of contemporary art reproductions entitled *Living Art*. Frank Crowninshield was also a collector: his penthouse flat housed eighteen paintings by Segonzac, five Modiglianis, seven Pascins, a large collection of African art, and one work by virtually every major painter in Paris. Often he drew upon his own collection for works to be reproduced in the magazine, also writing captions for photographic art features himself.[41] In 1929 he became one of the original seven-member board of the Museum of Modern Art, and when Alfred Barr first announced the formation of the museum in 1929, he did so, revealingly, with an essay in *Vanity Fair*. Quinn himself also published two essays in *Vanity Fair*, one on the sculptor Jacob Epstein and another on Joyce, a selection that suggests the extent to which contemporary art and literature might be paired. And when Quinn held a private party in 1923 to unveil his new Seurat, the great *Le Cirque*, he invited only his immediate family and Frederick James Gregg, the lead writer on art for *Vanity Fair* and an old friend.[42]

These patterns of collecting and patronage can help us better understand the rationale that informed the discussion about where to publish *The Waste Land* – and a pattern that emerges in the publishers' deliberations for the poem. When one emissary from *Vanity Fair* wrote from Paris to urge that the New York office acquire the poem, he had not yet read a word of its text. "Pound says they [i.e. *The Waste Land*] are as fine as anything written in English since 1900," wrote the agent. When Horace Liveright first advanced his offer to publish the poem in book form in January 1922, he too had not read a word of the poem; he based his decision on Pound's judgment that, "Eliot's *Waste Land* is I think the justification of the 'movement,' of our modern experiment, since 1900." And in an especially arresting formulation, Pound urged Scofield Thayer to acquire the poem for the *Dial* on the grounds that it was "as good in its way as Ulysses in its way."[43] To Thayer, these were resonant terms, for the *Dial* office had ordered nine copies of the first edition of *Ulysses*, Thayer himself taking two of the most expensive copies. Likewise, when his coeditor Watson visited Pound in Paris in mid-July, he was treated to the same arguments just at the moment when the first edition of *Ulysses* had sold out. Little wonder that Watson and Thayer should decide, one week later, to pay Eliot more than $2,000 for a poem that neither of them had yet read. For Watson and Thayer, acquiring *The Waste Land* was essential to their battle to secure the hegemonic status of the *Dial*. The announcement of the award would constitute the poem's status, which in turn would redound to the credit of the *Dial*. Their decision was based on a shrewd assessment of the interaction between aesthetic value, publicity, and money in a market economy.

In an important sense, the question of aesthetic value is inseparable from commercial success in a market economy, a difficulty that beset every argument for the intrinsic merit of literary Modernism. By 1922, literary Modernism required a financial–critical success that would lend it the kind of prestige already acquired by modernist painting; yet every step in this direction was hampered by market constraints less amenable to the kinds of pressures from elite patronage and investment that crystallized in the collections of Quinn, Thayer, or Crowninshield. The legal definition of intellectual property – it continues to belong to the author after its purchase by the consumer, in contrast to a painting or statue, which becomes the property of the purchaser – posed a series of intractable dilemmas. Patronage could nurture literary Modernism only to the threshold of its confrontation with a wider public; beyond that it would require commercial success to ratify its viability as a significant idiom. That was the question that haunted discussions about *The Waste Land*: assuming that the poem epitomized the investment of twenty years in the creation of a collective idiom – "our modern experiment, since 1900" – the protagonists were obliged to find a return on their investment in modernity.

The ambiguity of the *Dial*'s position is revealing here. For while Thayer scorned *Vanity Fair* and its apparent commercialism, he too was actively engaged in purchasing works of modern art and sculpture, and he too was an investor in a market commodity whose value was rapidly rising in large part through the efforts of the publicity apparatus he himself owned and controlled. Literary Modernism, by analogy, was now courting the risk of becoming "smart art," an investment that might pay and pay well if successful in the expanding market for modernity. But pay whom?

When *The Waste Land* was published, it did not enter a conduit that received and reproduced a neutral image of its original, but a multiplicity of social structures driven by conflicting imperatives: it became part of a social event in a discontinuous yet coherent process, an unprecedented effort to affirm the output of a specific marketing–publicity apparatus through the enactment of a triumphal and triumphant occasion. It was not simply the institutions that were the vehicle of the poem, but the poem that became the vehicle of the institutions – inseparable, finally, from the contradictory utilizations that had constituted it historically.

T. S. Eliot, we recall, had arrived in Paris on 2 January 1922. One month later, at 7 o'clock in the morning, Sylvia Beach hurriedly took a taxi to the Gare de Lyon to greet the morning express train from Dijon. As it slowed beside the platform, she later recalled, a conductor stepped down and handed her a small bundle that contained two copies of the first edition of *Ulysses*. Beach, proprietor of an English-language bookshop in Paris named "Shakespeare and Company," was elated. She hastened to the hotel at which Joyce was residing and personally handed him his own copy, a present for his birthday; then she hurried back to her store and placed the second copy in the window. Soon a crowd of onlookers gathered to celebrate the august event and admire the volume's handsome blue cover.[44]

This account, Beach's own, confirms widespread if unstated assumptions about the publication of *Ulysses*, and so also about literary Modernism. Joyce and Beach are cast into saintly roles, heroes who succeed despite a benighted legal system and the philistine masses; and their efforts are promptly appreciated by a small yet discerning circle of readers whose insight will later be confirmed by critics and scholars, eventually resulting in the book's canonical status. In reality, however, individual readers played only a limited role in shaping the success that greeted the first edition of *Ulysses*; on the whole, their importance was slight, and it remained decidedly secondary to that of another group, the dealers and speculators in the rare book trade, who bought the overwhelming majority of copies of the first edition. Paradoxically, the publication of *Ulysses* had the effect not of confirming the importance of discerning readers, but of demonstrating that readers might be superfluous. How did such a state of affairs come about, and what does it tell us about the ambivalent question of Modernism and its public?

Plans for the first edition of *Ulysses* were made in April 1921, days after Joyce learned that the *Little Review* had been convicted in New York of publishing obscenity for having issued the Nausicaa episode, an outcome that effectively eliminated any chance of finding an American publisher to undertake the book. Joyce and Beach agreed swiftly on the kind of publication they wanted. It would be a deluxe edition of 1,000 copies to appear in three issues, that is printed on three different grades of paper with corresponding prices.[45] Each copy would be numbered, with copies of the most expensive issue autographed by Joyce. Beach was acting partly under the guidance of Adrienne Monnier, the proprietor of a French bookstore located near her own. Monnier, who deemed her shop a "half convent" and herself a "nun of other times," had already published five deluxe editions, and, as Beach later recalled, she now "initiated me into the

Table 1. *The first edition of "Ulysses" (1922)*

issue	type of paper	price in francs	pounds sterling	US dollars
copies 1–100	Holland handmade	350 francs	£7 7s	$30.00
copies 101–250	Vergé d'Arches	250 francs	£5 5s	$22.00
copies 251–1000	linen paper	150 francs	£3 3s	$14.00

mysteries of limited editions."[46] The difference between a limited and an ordinary edition was more than a matter of paper quality. It extended to every feature of the book: price, royalties, discount structure, audience, and authorial control. The cheapest issue of the deluxe edition was priced at five to seven times the normal book price. Royalties, too, were arranged differently. An ordinary edition would have given Joyce royalties of 15 to 20 percent on gross sales; the royalties on a deluxe edition were much larger, typically 50 percent, and Beach herself proposed that Joyce receive 66 percent of net profits. Equally notable were differences in the discount structure. An ordinary edition was normally offered to booksellers at a discount of roughly 30 or 33 percent. A deluxe edition, in contrast, had an extremely modest discount, typically around 10 percent. The small discount was a direct function of another, more important difference – a change in audience. While an ordinary edition was primarily addressed to individual readers, a deluxe edition was directed partly to a small corpus of well-to-do collectors, but principally to dealers and speculators. Dealers, in other words, were more than simple conduits who sold whatever they had in stock to collectors upon demand: they were also active participants in shaping the market for a specific title; they would sell some copies to preferred clients, but they would also hold others until an edition was exhausted and its value on the collector's market had doubled or trebled.

Beach, following Monnier's lead, conceived her edition along lines that followed protocols of the Parisian trade in deluxe editions. But the circumstances surrounding *Ulysses* were different. The principal audience for the book was located in the US and the UK, rather than in France; and while Britain had a highly developed infrastructure of export agents who catered to the US book markets, France possessed nothing of comparable capacities. Beach, therefore, needed access to the UK market in order to reach the US market. Moreover, Beach and Joyce had first conceived her edition in response to the collapse of plans for American publication, leaving unresolved the question of a potential British edition. That presented a special problem because Joyce's publisher in the UK was Harriet

Shaw Weaver, and Weaver was also Joyce's patron, furnishing him with his only regular income. Weaver had long assumed that she would be publishing an ordinary edition to be released in the UK in tandem with an American edition, just as she had done earlier with *A Portrait*; already in late 1920 she had announced such an edition and by January of 1921 she had collected more than 150 orders for it.[47] When plans for Beach's edition were announced in April of 1921, and described to her solely as a replacement for the American edition, Weaver assumed that she was still free to proceed with her own edition. But a British ordinary edition posed an insuperable obstacle to Beach's project. No one, after all, would want to pay the hefty price of the deluxe edition when a few months' wait would procure the same book at one-fifth or one-seventh the price. By July of 1921 Beach was forced to ask Weaver to cancel the projected UK edition in order to stop the loss of potential orders. Weaver reluctantly agreed.[48] Though she probably thought that she was doing a personal favor for Beach, or for Beach and Joyce, she was also acknowledging the inalterable logic that structures a limited edition. For a limited edition is inherently monopolistic: it presupposes that one can exploit a market by manipulating the ratio of supply and demand, and its fundamental premise is that supply be issued from one source alone. Only thus can its price be in balance with the modest demand to which it appeals.

A second problem soon arose, again in connection with Weaver. Though Weaver herself was a publisher who had issued seven books between 1916 and 1919, she was wholly ignorant of limited editions, and when she learned that Beach was planning to allow a discount of only 10 percent to booksellers she was shocked: "I have had no experience of limited expensive editions and it had not occurred to me that booksellers make a practice of buying copies to hold up and sell at double or treble the original price." Reluctantly, Weaver again assented to Beach's proposal, but in the months that followed she repeatedly begged her to make exceptions for particular stores or agents who were "not the kind of firm which would be likely to buy copies to hold up and sell at an advanced price."[49] By midsummer of 1921, as Beach was growing increasingly nervous about the paucity of advance orders – at the same time she was persuading Weaver to cancel plans for the ordinary edition – she at last relented and increased the discount to 20 percent. Her decision had a paradoxical effect: it made the edition more accessible to a wider audience, enabling a modest number of bookstores to place orders on behalf of individual readers; but it also made the edition far more attractive to speculative booksellers, who could now rest assured of a small profit even if they sold it only at the published price, rather than holding the edition in the hope of greater profits.

Orders from dealers and agents soon mounted. Consider only the London firm of William Jackson.[50] On 7 July 1921 the firm ordered 8 copies. In August its order was increased to 20 copies, accompanied by a note from Mr. Jackson, adding, "I shall probably want more yet." In September the order was increased again to 35 copies; and in early January 1922 to 70 copies. On 19 January, Jackson wrote to inquire "when the book will be ready," and after learning that copies would be available in two weeks, he increased his order to 80 copies. Finally, on 1 February, he raised his order to 100 copies. It is an astounding figure, accounting for 10 percent of the entire edition, and for 13 percent of the issue at 150 francs. Of the cheaper copies most likely to be purchased by ordinary readers, nearly 1 in 7 was purchased by a single dealer.

The purchases by Jackson were representative of a broad trend. Of the 1,000 copies of the first edition, 59 percent were purchased by dealers, agents, and stores, while only 41 percent were purchased by individual buyers. Moreover, many of those individual buyers were publishers, journalists, or individual booksellers who also received a 20 percent discount extended to "members of the trade." When these are subtracted, it turns out that only some 35 percent of the first edition was actually purchased by ordinary readers.[51] Indeed, dealers consumed such a large proportion of the first edition that individual readers could scarcely learn that the book was published before it was sold out. On 5 March 1922, only four weeks after the book's publication date, Sisley Huddleston published a glowing review of *Ulysses* in the *Observer*, a Sunday newspaper with 200,000 subscribers which appealed to a cultivated audience of upper middle-class readers. Two days later Beach received orders for 136 copies, and by 14 March she had exhausted the entire supply of cheaper copies at 150 francs.[52] Thereafter readers were obliged to buy the more expensive copies, whether they wished to or not. Many, quite simply, could not afford them. By 16 June the entire edition was sold out, eighteen weeks after publication.

The market dynamics of the limited edition, while forging an opposition between dealers and ordinary readers, also worked to transform the role of the common reader, who was invited to take on some of the functions of the collector and patron. Because the author received 50 percent of the book's sale price (or in Joyce's case 66 percent of net), buyers were effectively turned into patrons directly supporting the artist, a new rapport of seeming immediacy that was restaged in the book itself, which embodied authorial presence in its every feature. Joyce controlled every aspect of the book's production: his approval was required for decisions about paper, typography, cover design, color, even the choice of printing inks. The book was no longer an industrial product shaped by publisher's conventions and production considerations; it was a token of the authorial self.

The market dynamics of the limited edition also worked to transform the reader into an investor of sorts. For a reader of moderate incomes especially, to purchase the first edition required a considerable aesthetic investment, an assent to strong claims about the work's value. Yet insofar as those claims seemed to be contradicted by a substantial body of critical and public opinion, buyers inevitably appealed to the workings of the marketplace as the final arbiter and guarantor of values in a capitalist economic order. "Most of those who are troubling to seek it out," wrote an anonymous critic in April 1922, "are buying it as an investment – they flatter themselves that a first edition of this remarkable author will bring them a handsome profit within a few years."[53] It was a deliberately harsh assessment, but it identified a mode of thinking made all but inescapable by the logic of the deluxe edition. That thinking, in turn, bore witness to a much broader phenomenon, the collapse of shared confidence in the notion of aesthetic autonomy and the independent coherence of aesthetic value – a collapse that had been precipitated partly by the theoretical and institutional onslaught that Marinetti and the avant-garde had launched, and partly by the relentless and ever-increasing penetration of capitalist relations into every dimension of life, including the aesthetic. Readers, no longer confident that they could appeal to the public sphere in support of their assertions about the aesthetic value of *Ulysses*, turned to the workings of the market itself, taking its outcomes to be confirmations, even justifications, of their claims.

In a most immediate sense, the market resoundingly gave them its approbation. The price of *Ulysses* soared in the months that followed its publication. In April 1922, copies of the cheapest issue were already circulating in New York at $20.00, a significant jump from the official price of $14.00 or $15.00. By mid June, Adrienne Monnier was selling copies of the 150-francs issue for 500 francs. By 5 August the price of the cheapest issue in London had risen to £10 (compared with the original selling price of £3 3s); by 15 August the price had doubled yet again to £20; and by October copies were selling in London for £40.[54]

Participants in the making of the first edition hailed these results as a victory. "Many congratulations on your success as a publisher," Harriet Shaw Weaver wrote to Sylvia Beach when she learned that the cheapest issue was sold out. "*Ulysses*," Ezra Pound declared to an acquaintance, "is . . . 'out' triumphantly."[55] Yet the triumph may have been more ambiguous than such statements suggest – indeed, it may have been a Pyrrhic victory of sorts. For in forfeiting demands for public justification to the operations of the marketplace, the participants in the first edition of *Ulysses* encouraged a misunderstanding that has continued to reverberate in debate about the avant-garde and its public. For the marketplace is not, and never can be, free from systemic distortions of power, and its outcomes cannot be equated with undistorted participation in practices of justification, or with norms of equal and universal participation in discussions about cultural and aesthetic value. The operations of the market are not an adequate substitute for free agreement; indeed, they are not a substitute at all, insofar as they are operations of an entirely different order. The invisible hand of Adam Smith is not a moral or rational agent, nor can it be an aesthetic agent. It can never be a substitute for processes of mutual intelligibility and critical justification.

Strangely, and yet appropriately, it was the person who first "initiated" Sylvia Beach "into the mysteries of limited editions," Adrienne Monnier, who alone among the original participants in the first edition of *Ulysses* came to perceive the immense tragedy that had occurred. Monnier was writing in 1938 and reflecting on the causes of what she now called "the scourge," the devastation that had followed when the fragile economy of patron-investors lay in ruins and the modernist experiment was now past.[56]

> I have said that the scourge was just and it is true that for several years, even the ones called the years of "prosperity," we all behaved ourselves rather badly. We made books objects of speculation; we made or let be made a *stock exchange* for books . . . Myself, did I not often propose books, saying that in a month the price would have at least doubled? And it was true. And it was so easy to sell under those conditions. Now, repentance! Ah, it was well done!

Despite the apocalyptic note derived from the mystical vocabulary that Monnier loved, she had accurately identified key characteristics in the cultural economy of literary Modernism. It is a commonplace of cultural history that literary patronage gradually vanished in the eighteenth century due to changes in copyright laws, the spread of literacy, and the steady emergence of a popular market. Yet it is a fact that much of the literature that we now designate under the notion of Modernism was produced under the aegis of a revived patronage that flourished on a remarkable scale. For several reasons, however, the patronage of literary Modernism was rarely the pure, unqualified, or disinterested support that we typically associate with notions of patronage. The extension of capitalist relations into every dimension of life meant that both writers and patrons were uneasy about an institution so clearly at odds with the work ethic, the meritocratic ethos that subtends market relations. As Robert Louis Stevenson put it already in

1881, he would agree to forego writing popular fiction provided that someone "give me £1,000 . . . and at the same time effect such a change in my nature that I shall be content to take it from them instead of earning it."[57] Though Quinn quite plainly served as patron to Pound, he always arranged it in such a way that Pound was receiving a salary for some editorial function, whether as foreign editor of the *Little Review* or correspondent and agent for the *Dial*. Because patronage was essentially a premodern form of social exchange, it had to be disguised as something else if it were not to seem too at odds with the modern world.

One mask that it adopted was the concept of "investment." Patrons were not just giving away money in misguided sentimentalism about the arts, they were investing in something that would increase in value in the future. But for literature, the question remained: what *was* that something? In March 1922, only days after learning of the success that was greeting the first edition of *Ulysses*, Pound devised the Bel Esprit project, a proposal that thirty people agree to guarantee £10 (or $50.00) per year to T. S. Eliot, so providing him with a guaranteed income of £300 year. Bel Esprit, he explained to readers, was needed "because the individual patron is nearly extinct."[58] But although conceived as a replacement for patronage, Bel Esprit was not merely patronage in a new form, a point that Pound stressed to John Quinn:

> I can't come back too STRONGLY to the point that I do NOT consider this Eliot subsidy a pension. I am puke sick of the idea of pensions . . . For me my £10 a year on Eliot is an investment . . . I put this money into him as I would put it into a shoe factory if I wanted shoes. Better simile, into a shipping company, of say small pearl-fishing ships, some scheme where there was a great deal of risk but a chance of infinite profit.[59]

Yet the metaphor of investment was only partially applicable to literature: normally one's return on a successful investment results in an increase in one's own wealth or property; but since literary property remains the author's, investment could hardly characterize the process Pound wished to describe.

To achieve more congruity between the metaphorics of investment and the dilemmas posed by intellectual property, it was necessary to concretize the literary, to turn it into an object. Which is why the deluxe or limited edition acquired such prominence: it transformed literary property into a unique and fungible object, something that more nearly resembled a painting or an *objet d'art* with auratic presence, a "something" that could genuinely rise in value, at least on the collectors' market. Literary Modernism constitutes a strange and perhaps unprecedented withdrawal from the public sphere of cultural production and debate, a retreat into a divided world of patronage, investment, and collecting. Uneasiness concerning the ethical legitimacy of patronage, corresponding efforts to assimilate patronage to concepts of investment and profit, and the concomitant attempt to objectify literary value in the form of the rare book or deluxe edition – all these register a profound change in the relations among authors, publishers, critics, and readers. To a remarkable degree, modernist literature was an experiment in adopting exchange and market structures typical of the visual arts, a realm in which patronage and collecting can thrive because its artisanal mode of production is compatible with a limited submarket for luxury goods. Perhaps it is no accident that paintings repeatedly figure as metaphors for the literary work in this period, from *A Portrait of the Artist* to Lily Briscoe's abstract portrait of Mrs. Ramsay in *To the Lighthouse*. A submarket of this sort is extremely responsive to pressures from a small nucleus of patron-collectors: even a single figure or institution can alter its dynamics, as attested by the effects of the Getty Museum in the market for old masters. Modernism required not a mass of readers, but just such a corps of patron-collectors.

The Great Depression devastated the fragile economy of Modernism, and in the absence of the patron-investors who had sustained it during the teens and twenties, Modernism turned to the university, welcoming its direct support (T. S. Eliot gives the Clark lectures at Cambridge in 1926, the Norton lectures at Harvard in 1933) or assenting to its canonization, so guaranteeing a new market of pliant students, rather than unruly general readers. That protracted process has often been noted, usually in the form of a sardonic narration that depicts the academy as a site in which "the subversive, experimental energies of the avant-garde culture of the early part of the century have been formulated, controlled, contained, marketed and cancelled."[60] Yet one may have doubts about the postulate of a golden age of "subversive, experimental energies" that are only belatedly ensnared in a postlapsarian world of containment and marketing. Modernism's traffic with the emerging world of consumerism and fashion was more complicated, more ambiguous than such narrations tend to assume – ambiguity that may itself account for Modernism's uncertainty regarding the nature of representation in art, its stress on the means by which illusions and likenesses are made. Its radical interrogation of the cultural repertoire, which permanently altered the relations of the arts with society at large, may owe much indeed to its equivocal status as an institution that was simultaneously half withdrawn from yet half nestled within, the larger apparatus of cultural production. Academics of today, in presupposing a schematic opposition between "subversion" and "containment," bear witness only to the poverty of historical imagination with which they address the past. They may well believe that Modernism was once "subversive," just as *The Times* of London once thought Marinetti guilty of "anarchical extravagance." But Marinetti himself knew better: "In London," he wrote to a friend, "our success has been colossal, increasing in a truly fantastic fashion !"[61]

NOTES

1 Charles Dickens, in K. J. Fielding, ed., *The Speeches of Charles Dickens* (Oxford: Clarendon Press, 1960), p. 155.

2 Andreas Huyssen, *After the Great Divide: Modernism, Mass Culture, Postmodernism* (Bloomington: Indiana University Press, 1986), pp. 47, 161, 163. See also James Naremore and Patrick Brantlinger, eds., *Modernity and Mass Culture* (Bloomington: Indiana University Press, 1991); Thomas Crow, "Modernism and Mass Culture" in Benjamin Buchloh, Serge Guilbaut, and David Solkin, eds., *Modernism and Modernity* (Halifax: Nova Scotia College of Art and Design, 1983), pp. 215–64.

3 On Pound as "troubadour" see Omar Pound and A. Walton Litz, eds., *Ezra Pound and Dorothy Shakespear: Their Letters 1909–1914* (New York: New Directions, 1984), p. 70; hereafter cited as *EP/DS*. On Cravens see Omar Pound and Robert Spoo, Introduction to their *Ezra Pound and Margaret Cravens: A Tragic Friendship, 1910–1912* (Durham, NC: Duke University Press, 1988), hereafter cited as *EP/MC*. Income figures are from Arthur Marwick, *The Deluge* (Boston: Little, Brown, 1965), pp. 23 and 20.

4 Pound to Henry Hope Shakespear, [12 March 1912], in *EP/DS*, p. 87. Also in March 1912, Dorothy Shakespear notes that Selwyn Image, Slade Professor of Art at Oxford, earns £400 per annum, in *EP/DS*, p. 94.

5 See *EP/DS*, p. 89, for the lecture program, and p. 349, for Lady Low.

6 On the Tennant dynasty see Simon Blow, *Broken Blood: The Rise and Fall of the Tennant Family* (London: Faber and Faber, 1987). On Pamela Wyndham and her family see Caroline Dakers, *Clouds: The Biography of a Country House* (New Haven: Yale University Press, 1993), pp. 160–76; on the Tennants' country house see Clive Aslet, *The Last Country Houses* (New Haven: Yale University Press, 1982), pp. 245–55. On Queen Anne's Gate see *The Survey of London*, eds. Montague H. Cox and Philip Norman, vol. x, *The Parish of St. Margaret, Westminster*, part 1 (London: London County Council, 1926), pp. 78–81, 101–3, 128–31. On 34 Queen Anne's Gate see the Department of the Environment, *List of Buildings of Special Architectural or Historic Interest: City of Westminster, Greater London*, part 5 "Streets Q–S," pp. 1333–7. For the collection of paintings housed in the "private gallery," see the catalog ascribed sometimes to Edward, sometimes to Pamela Tennant, *Catalogue of Pictures in the Tennant Gallery, 34, Queen Anne's Gate, S.W., . . . Compiled From Various Sources by Various Hands* (London: privately printed, n.d. but 1910); and W. Roberts, "The Passing of the Tennant Collection," *Queen*, 154 (18 October 1923): 470–1. American libraries catalog Pamela's works under the name Grey, because of her later marriage to Sir Edward Grey; British under Tennant. Her chief works through 1912 are *Village Notes, and Some Other Papers* (London: W. Heinemann, 1900), a collection of essays; *Windlestraw*

(London: printed at the Chiswick Press, 1905), a collection of her own poems; and *The Children and the Pictures* (London: W. Heinemann, 1907), a work of prose fiction. On Pamela's place in London Society, see Anonymous, "In the Great World: Lord and Lady Glenconner," *Sketch* (10 December 1913): 298.

7 Ezra Pound, "Psychology and Troubadours," *Quest*, 4.1 (May 1912): 37–53, reprinted in Lea Baechler, A. Walton Litz, and James Longenbach eds., *Ezra Pound's Poetry and Prose: Contributions to Periodicals* (New York: Garland Publishing 1991), vol. I, pp. 83–99, here at p. 86, hereafter cited as *EPPP*.

8 See advertisements in *The Times*, 19 March 1912, p. 1 col. 6, and in the *Pall Mall Gazette*, 19 March 1912, p. 4 col. 3. Tickets, in four price categories (10s 6d, 5s, 2s 6d, and 1s) could be purchased at Bechstein Hall or the Sackville Gallery.

9 "A nation of sycophants" is quoted from Anonymous, "'Futurist' Leader in London," *Daily Chronicle*, 20 March 1912, p. 1 col. 3; "rewarded him" is from Anonymous, "Futurism in Literature and Art," *The Times*, 21 March 1912, p. 2 col. 6; and "wildly applauded his outspoken derision" is from Harold Monro, "Varia," in *Poetry and Drama*, 1.3 (September 1913): 263. See also anonymous, "Futurism in London," *Morning Leader*, 21 March 1912, p. 7.

10 Dorothy Shakespear to Ezra Pound, 19 March 1912, in *EP/DS*, pp. 89–90.

11 Ezra Pound, perfatory note to "The Complete Poetical Works of T. E. Hulme" (first published at the end of *Ripostes* in October 1912, rev. edn (New York: New Directions, 1990), p. 266; and Christopher Hassall, *Edward Marsh: Patron of the Arts. A Biography* (London: Longman, 1959), pp. 189–93.

12 Ezra Pound to Harriet Monroe, [18] August 1912 and [October 1913], in D. D. Paige, ed., *Selected Letters of Ezra Pound, 1907–1941* (New York: New Directions, 1970; 1st edn, 1950), pp. 10, 11. "Editorial Comment. Status Rerum," dated 10 December 1912, in *Poetry*, 1.4 (January 1913): 123–7, reprinted in *EPPP*, vol. I, pp. 111–13; all quotations here are from p. 112. The hostile remark concerning Futurist theory is found in Anonymous, "Fine Art Gossip," *Athenaeum*, 4402 (9 March 1912: 289–90, here at 290.

13 F. S. Flint (though actually drafted by Pound and merely rewritten by Flint), "Imagisme," in *Poetry*, 1.6 (March 1913): 198–200, reprinted in *EPPP* vol. I, p. 119; and Ezra Pound, "A Few Don'ts By An Imagiste," in *Poetry*, 1.6 (March 1913): 200–6, reprinted in *EPPP*, vol. I, pp. 120–2.

14 F. T. Marinetti, "Manifesto technico della letteratura futurista," in Luciano De Maria, ed., *Teoria e invenzione futurista*, 2nd edn (Milan: Mondadori, 1983), pp. 53–4; or in English translation in R. W. Flint ed., *Let's Murder the Moonshine: F. T. Marinetti, Selected Writings* (Los Angeles: Sun and Moon, 1991; 1st edn, 1971), p. 97. Hereafter the Flint edition is cited as *LMM*. Anonymous, "Futurism in Poetry," *The Times*, 18 November 1913, p. 5 cols. 5–6.

15 Harold Monro, "Varia," in *Poetry and Drama*, 1.3 (September 1913): 263–5. On Northcliffe see Richard Bourne, *The Lords of Fleet Street: The Harmonsworth Dynasty* (London: Unwin Hyman, 1990). The classic text for the modernist distinction between poetry and journalism is Stéphane Mallarmé, "Crise de vers" and "Sur l'evolution littéraire" in *Œuvres complètes*, ed. Henri Mondor and G. Jean-Aubry (Paris: Gallimard, Bibliothèque du Plèiade, 1956), pp. 360–8 and 866–72.

16 "The Variety Theatre" is the title by which the manifesto has since become best known. Originally the English translation was titled, "The Meaning of the Music Hall. By the Only Intelligible Futurist," in the *Daily Mail*, (Friday) 21 November 1913, p. 6, col. 4. Page 6 also contained the lead editorial (cols. 2–3), giving the manifesto a prominent *mise-en-scène*

17 See *Sketch*, 1111, 13 May 1914, cover page; and "FUTURIST CLOTHES. Man's Suit in Single Piece. ONE BUTTON," in *Pall Mall Gazette*, 28 May 1914, p. 2, col. 3. The *Sketch* also reports that Marinetti "has been lecturing to very interested audiences." See Anonymous, "Futurist Music: 'Noisy Tuners' at a Rehearsal; Cracklers and Roarers," *Pall Mall Gazette*, (Friday) 12 June 1914, p. 1, col. 5.

18 See Felix Barker, *The House that Stoll Built: The Story of the Coliseum Theatre* (London: Frederick Muller, 1957), here quoting Stoll, p. 11. See also Victor Glasstone, *Victorian and Edwardian Theatres* (Cambridge, MA: Harvard University Press, 1975), here quoting Stoll, p. 116.

19 *The Times*, 16 June 1914, p. 5 col. 4, "ART AND PRACTICE OF NOISE. Hostile Reception of Signor Marinetti."

20 Solomon Eagle [i.e., J. C. Squire], "Current Literature: Books in General," *New Statesman*, 3.65 (4 July 1914): 406. Compare Anonymous, "The Futurists," *New Statesman*, 3.66 (11 July 914): 426:

> One can forgive a new movement for anything except being tedious: *Blast* is as tedious as an imitation of George Robey by a curate without a sense of humour . . . to make up of the pages of *Blast* a winding-sheet in which to wrap up Futurism for burial is to do an indignity to a genuine and living artistic movement. But, after all, what is Vorticism but Futurism in an English disguise – Futurism, we might call it, bottled in England, and bottled badly? . . . the two groups differ from each other not in their aims, but in their degrees of competence.

21 Ezra Pound to Margaret Anderson, 10 May 1917, in Thomas L. Scott, Melvin J. Friedman, and Jackson R. Bryer, eds., *Pound/The Little Review* (New York: New Directions, 1988), p. 46, hereafter cited as *P/LR*; and Ezra Pound to William Bird, 7 May 1924, in Bird Manuscripts, Lilly Library, University of Indiana.

22 On these negotiations see Lawrence S. Rainey, "The Price of Modernism: Publishing 'The Waste Land'" in Ronald Bush, ed., *T. S. Eliot: The Modernist in History* (Cambridge: Cambridge University Press, 1991), pp. 90–133.

23 See Ezra Pound to John Quinn, 8 February 1917, in Timothy Materer, ed., *The Selected Letters of Ezra Pound to John Quinn* (Durham, NC: Duke University Press, 1991), pp. 94–7, hereafter cited as *EP/JQ*. On Pound's relations with the *Little Review*, see Thomas L. Scott and Melvin J. Friedman, "Introduction," *P/LR*, pp. xiii–xxxiv; on the *Little Review*, see Frank Luther Mott, *A History of American Magazines*, vol. V, *Sketches of 21 Magazines, 1905–1930* (Cambridge, MA: Harvard University Press, 1968), pp. 166–78. On Quinn's syndicate, see B. L. Reid, *The Man From New York: John Quinn and His Friends* (Oxford: Oxford University Press, 1968), p. 343.

24 Mott, *A History of American Magazines*, vol. V, *Sketches*, p. 171, considers it "unlikely that the circulation ever rose to much over a thousand." His figure is intended to correct the earlier estimate of 2,000 given by Frederick J. Hoffman,

Charles Allen and Carolyn F. Ulrich, *The Little Magazine: A History and Bibliography* (Princeton: Princeton University Press, 1946), p. 57. However, Margaret Anderson in 1917 told Ezra Pound that the total circulation was 3,100, of which 2,500 were subscriptions. Her figures are reported in a letter from Pound to John Quinn, 8 February 1917, in *EP/JQ*, p. 95.

25 For example, Pound to Margaret Anderson, 30 December 1917 and [? January or February 1918], in *P/LR*, pp. 170–1, 202.

26 Ezra Pound to Margaret Anderson, [6 November 1917], in *P/LR*, p. 142. "Our object in opening a new gallery is to do business not only to fight against dishonest commercialism but in order to support ourselves and make others able to support themselves" (Marius de Zayas to Alfred Stieglitz, 27 August 1915; Alfred Stieglitz Archive, Beinecke Library, Yale University). See also Douglas Hyland, *Marius de Zayas: Conjurer of Souls* (Lawrence, KS: Spencer Museum of Art, University of Kansas, 1981), p. 46, who urges that de Zayas sought to make a gallery "which would be a commercial venture in a way that Stieglitz's had never been." On de Zayas's gallery see Hyland, *Marius de Zayas*, pp. 46–52, hereafter cited as Hyland.

27 On Quinn's purchases, see Hyland, p. 48, and Reid, *Man From New York*, pp. 471–2; for the salary of the executive secretary see Martha Cohn Cooper, "Frank Crowninshield and *Vanity Fair*," unpublished Ph.D. dissertation (University of North Carolina at Chapel Hill, 1976), p. 48.

28 One way of estimating this figure is by extrapolation from the *Egoist*, a comparable journal. In the second half of 1915 the *Egoist* earned £37 ($185) in sales and subscriptions, and one surmises that its advertising revenues were around £5; see Jane Lidderdale and Mary Nicholson, *Dear Miss Weaver: Harriet Shaw Weaver, 1876–1961* (New York: Viking Press, 1970), p. 99. Mott, *A History of American Magazines*, vol. V, *Sketches*, p. 171, estimates that advertising revenues for the *Little Review* "seldom or never exceeded $500 a year."

29 See Nicholas Joost, *Scofield Thayer and "The Dial"* (Carbondale: Southern Illinois University Press, 1964), pp. 3–20, and *"The Dial," 1912–1920* (Barre, MA: Barre Publishers, 1967).

30 All figures are from the annual financial reports of the *Dial*, conserved among "The *Dial* Papers," Beinecke Rare Book and Manuscript Library, Yale University.

31 Joost, *Scofield Thayer and "The Dial,"* pp. 39–40, briefly discusses "the millionaires' number." The topic recurs throughout the correspondence between Thayer and Watson in "The *Dial* Papers," Beinecke Library.

32 Ezra Pound to Scofield Thayer, 23 April 1922, "The *Dial* Papers," Beinecke Library, series 4, box 38, folder 1922.

33 Lewis appeared in the *Little Review* of November 1918 and the *Dial* of August 1922, Zadkine in the *Little Review* of December 1918 and the *Dial* of October 1921.

34 Scofield Thayer to Gilbert Seldes, 28 November 1922, in "The *Dial* Papers," Beinecke Library, series 4, box 40, folder 1922. See [Schofield Thayer], "Comment," *Dia,l*, 73.1 (July 1922): 119. Thayer draws on Joel Springarn, *Creative Criticism: Essays on the Unity of Genius and Taste* (New York: Henry Holt, 1917), a work that is dedicated to "to my friend Benedetto Croce, the

most original of all modern thinkers on Art." For Springarn's influence on the *Dial* see William Wasserstrom, *The Time of the Dial* (Syracuse, NY: Syracuse University Press, 1963), pp. 17–19.

35 T. S. Eliot to Scofield Thayer, 1 January 1921, in Valerie Eliot, ed., *Letters of T. S. Eliot*, vol. I *1899–1922* (New York: Harcourt Brace Jovanovich, 1988), p. 429.

36 Scofield Thayer to Gilbert Seldes, 12 October 1922, in "The *Dial* Papers," Beinecke Library, series 4, box 40, folder 1922. The practice was a regular one at the *Dial*, and newspaper clippings from 1920–29 fill three boxes: series 2, boxes 16, 17, and 18.

37 Scofield Thayer to Mrs. Edward D. Thayer, 16 December 1922, "The *Dial* Papers," Beinecke Library, series 4, box 43, folder 1922; and Scofield Thayer to Gilbert Seldes, 26 December 1922, "*Dial* Papers," series 4, box 40, folder 1922; in this letter Thayer also complains that "Mr. Burke's review [in the *Dial*] interested me, but I do not find it so good as his recent article developing more or less the same theme in Vanity Fair." Scofield Thayer to Gilbert Seldes, 18 January 1923; 28 May 1913; and 8 June 1923, "The *Dial* Papers," series 4, box 40, folder 1923.

38 See Kitty Hoffman, "A History of *Vanity Fair*: A Modernist Journal in America," unpublished Ph.D. dissertation (University of Toronto, 1980); and Cynthia L. Ward, "*Vanity Fair* Magazine and Modern Style, 1914–1936 (New York City," unpublished Ph.D. dissertation (State University of New York at Stony Brook, 1983). Also see Caroline Seebohm, *The Man Who Was Vogue: The Life and Times of Condé Nast* (New York: Viking Press, 1982). On the contemporary magazine industry see Theodore Peterson, *Magazines in the Twentieth Century* (Urbana: University of Illinois Press, 1964), who discusses *Vanity Fair*'s advertising revenues, p. 271. For the journal's circulation figures see *N. W. Ayer & Son's American Newspaper Annual and Directory* (Philadelphia: N. W. Ayer, 1922), p. 1225, reporting figures from the Audit Bureau of Circulation. On advertising as "an integral part of the magazine," see Cohn Cooper, "Frank Crowninshield and *Vanity Fair*," p. 42.

39 Condé Nast, quoted in Edna Woolman Chase and Ilka Chase, *Always in Vogue* (Garden City, NY: Doubleday, 1954), p. 66. Nast stated in the first issue of *Vanity Fair*: "Our ambition is not towards a popular magazine with a big subscription list. We don't expect everybody to be interested in *Dress and Vanity Fair* [the journal's name for its first four issues] and, frankly, we shall not try to interest everybody." Condé Nast, "In Vanity Fair," *Vanity Fair*, 1.1 (September 1913): 19.

40 "A Group of Poems by T. S. Eliot: A Selection from the Dramatic Lyrics of a Much Discussed American Poet" in *Vanity Fair*, 20.4 (June 1923): 67. The other articles by Eliot appeared in *Vanity Fair*, 20.5 (July 1923): 51, 98; 21.3 (November 1923): 44, 118; and 21.6 (February 1924): 29, 98.

41 On Quinn's collecting in 1920, see Reid, *Man From New York*, p. 594; less is known about Thayer's collecting, but see Joost, *Schofield Thayer*, pp. 23–36; on Crowninshield see Nicholas Fox Weber, *Patron Saints: Five Rebels Who Opened America to a New Art* (New York: Knopt, 1992), p. 56, and *The Frank Crowninshield Collection of Modern French Art*, auction catalog, Parke-Bernet Galleries, 20–21 October 1943.

42 Alfred H. Barr, Jr., "An American Museum of Modern Art," *Vanity Fair*, 33 (November 1929): 79, 136. John Quinn, "Jacob Epstein, Sculptor," *Vanity Fair*, 9 (1917): 76, 114; and "James Joyce, A New Irish Novelist," *Vanity Fair*, 8 (1917): 49, 128. On Crowninshield and MOMA, see Ward, "*Vanity Fair* Magazine and the Modern Style," pp. 91–2, 100–1; on Quinn and Gregg see Reid, *Man From New York*, pp. 580 *et passim*.

43 John Peale Bishop to Edmund Wilson [managing editor, *Vanity Fair*], 5 August 1922, Beinecke Library, Yale University, Edmund Wilson Papers, series 2; Ezra Pound to Felix Schelling, 13 July 1922, in D. D. Paige, ed., *Selected Letters*, pp. 178–9; Ezra Pound to Schofield Thayer, 8 March 1922, "The *Dial* Papers," box 40, folder 2019.

44 Sylvia Beach, *Shakespeare and Company* (Lincoln: University of Nebraska Press, 1980; 1st edn, 1956), p. 84. See also Noel Riley Fitch, *Sylvia Beach and the Lost Generation* (New York: Norton, 1983); and Lawrence Rainey, "Consuming Investments: Joyce's *Ulysses*," *James Joyce Quarterly*, 33.4 (September 1996 [but February 1997]): 531–67.

45 James Joyce to Harriet Shaw Weaver, 10 April 1921, in Stuart Gilbert, ed. *The Letters of James Joyce*, vol. 1 (New York: Viking Press, 1967), pp. 161–3.

46 Adrienne Monnier, quoted by Richard McDougall, ed. and trans., *The Very Rich Hours of Adrienne Monnier* (New York: Scribner's 1976), p. 13; also Beach, *Shakespeare and Company*, p. 48.

47 Lidderdale, *Dear Miss Weaver*, p. 176.

48 Harriet Shaw Weaver to Sylvia Beach, 8 July 1921, in Beach Papers, Princeton University, box 232, folder 2. "I am much concerned at hearing, first from Mr. McAlmon and then from you, that the announcement of the cheaper English ordinary edition of *Ulysses* has been affecting adversely the chances of the Paris limited edition." "The cheaper prospective edition," she now concedes, "is doing harm," and to redress it she would "send out to all shops on our lists (and to any people I hear of who are waiting for the cheaper edition) the notice" that the English edition was postponed "indefinitely."

49 Harriet Shaw Weaver to Sylvia Beach, 27 April and 19 July 1921, Princeton University, Beach Papers, box 232, folder 2.

50 Jackson's orders are in Princeton University, Beach Papers, box 132, folder 12.

51 Beach's sales records for *Ulysses* form an immense body of documentation. Most of the correspondence and order forms are housed at Princeton University, Beach Papers, boxes 132–3, but a small group of order forms (fifty-seven of them) are found at State University of New York at Buffalo, Capen Library, Poetry Collection, Beach Papers, folder "Ulysses Subscriptions, 1st Edition." In addition, Beach kept four different record books, now located in Princeton University, Beach Papers, box 63. Finally, Beach also maintained a "Calepin de vente," now in the Maurice Saillet Papers, Carlton Lake Collection, Harry Ransom Research Center for Research in the Humanities, University of Texas, Austin. I have collated the materials at Princeton, Buffalo, and Austin.

52 Sisley Huddleston, "Ulysses," the *Observer*, 5 March 1922; reprinted in Sisley Huddleston, *Articles de Paris* (London: Methuen and Co., 1928), pp. 40–47, and Robert Deming, ed., *James Joyce: The Critical Heritage*, (London: Routledge and Kegan Paul, 1970), vol. 1, pp. 213–16. Circulation figures for the *Observer* are from David Ayerst, *Garvin of the "Observer"* (London: Croom

Helm, 1985), pp. 70, 128, and 229, and David Griffiths, ed., *Encyclopaedia of the British Press* (London: Macmillan, 1992), p. 444. Ezra Pound to Homer Pound, [10 March 1922], Beinecke Rare Book and Manuscript Library, Yale University, YCAL 43.

53 Anonymous, "A New Ulysses," *Evening News*, 8 April 1922, p. 4; reprinted in Deming, ed., *James Joyce*, vol. I, p. 193.

54 Prices in the New York market are reported in John Quinn to Sylvia Beach, 27 March 1922; Buffalo, Poetry Collection, Beach Papers. The early August price in London is reported by Mitchell Kennerley to Sylvia Beach, [4 August 1922]; Princeton University, Beach Papers, box 132, folder 5. The London price from 12 August is from Mitchell Kennerley to John Quinn, reported in Reid, *Man From New York*, p. 533. The October price reported by Joyce is from James Joyce to Mrs. William Murray, 23 October 1922, in Gilbert, ed., *Letters of James Joyce*, vol. I, p. 190.

55 Hariet Shaw Weaver to Sylvia Beach, 17 March 1922; Princeton University, Beach Papers, box 232, folder 3; Ezra Pound to Alice Corbin Henderson, 12 March 1922, in Ira B. Nadel, ed., *The Letters of Ezra Pound to Alice Corbin Henderson* (Austin: University of Texas Press, 1993), p. 224.

56 Adrienne Monnier, *The Very Rich Hours of Adrienne Monnier*, trans. Richard McDougall (New York: Scribner's, 1976), p. 141.

57 Robert Louis Stevenson, quoted in Jenni Calder, *Robert Louis Stevenson: A Life Study* (Oxford: Oxford University Press, 1960), p. 172.

58 On Bel Esprit see Humphrey Carpenter, *A Serious Character: The Life of Ezra Pound* (Boston: Houghton Mifflin, 1988), pp. 409–12; *EP/JQ*, pp. 8–10. Ezra Pound, "Paris Letter," *Dial*, 73.5 (November 1922): 549–54; reprinted in *EPPP*, vol. IV, pp. 259–63, quotation, p. 261.

59 Ezra Pound to John Quinn, 4–5 July 1922, in *EP/JQ*, p. 213.

60 Steven Connor, *Postmodernist Culture* (Oxford: Basil Blackwell, 1989), p. 12.

61 *The Times*, 21 March 1912, p. 2, col. 6; and F. T. Marinetti to F. B. Pratella, 12 April 1912, in Drudi Gambillo, Maria, and Fiori, Teresa, eds., *Archivi del Futurismo*, 2 vols. (Rome: De Luca, 1959–62), vol. I, pp. 237–8: "A Londra, il successo colossale aumentò in modo fantastico."

3

DAVID TROTTER

The modernist novel

To write about the modernist novel, as opposed to the Victorian novel, say, or the Edwardian novel, is to write not only about the possibilities of the genre, but about its perceived impossibility. The possibilities were evident enough. From about 1890 to about 1930, the novel was as popular as it had been during the Victorian period, and newly diverse. According to Henry James, in 1899, it was a universally valid form, "the book *par excellence*"; according to Ford Madox Ford, in 1930, it was indispensable, "the only source to which you can turn to ascertain how your fellows spend their entire lives."[1] And yet there was also a feeling, more prevalent among writers than among critics, that the novel as traditionally conceived was no longer up to the job: that its imaginary worlds did not, in fact, correspond to the way one's fellows spent their entire lives. The feeling was most fully and influentially articulated by T. S. Eliot, when he argued, in "*Ulysses*, Order and Myth" (1923), that the novel had effectively "ended" with Flaubert and James: that the very formlessness which had once made it the adequate "expression" of a previous age, an age not yet formless enough to require "something stricter," now prevented it from expressing a modernity characterized above all by the loss of form.[2] Before considering Eliot's solution, it would be as well to examine further the dimensions of the problem. Those dimensions are most evident, I believe, in two novels which have always been regarded as quintessentially modernist: Ford's *The Good Soldier* (1915), and Wyndham Lewis's *Tarr* (1918).

The end of the novel: Ford and Lewis

Ford's book *par excellence* was not quite the same as James's. In his faith that novels produce knowledge, in his insistence that every last detail in a novel should be at once explicable and explanatory, Ford was entirely Jamesian, and Jamesian in a way that would not have offended Tolstoy or George Eliot. And yet he also claimed that he had always sought in his own writing to render "the impression not the corrected chronicle":[3] that is, experience as it happens, not as it is subsequently conceptualized. Experience as it happens cannot very well be said to amount to reliable knowledge about the way our fellows live their lives. Ford's Impressionism, a refinement of narrative techniques developed by his immediate precursors, James and Conrad, thus had radical implications for the novel's supposed intelligibility and usefulness.

Whatever is described in the most innovative fiction of the period is described in relation to, and only in relation to, a perceiving mind. James's later novels – *The Wings of the Dove* (1902), *The Ambassadors* (1903), *The Golden Bowl* (1904) – create centers of consciousness through which the apprehension of events is filtered. Joseph Conrad's *Lord Jim* (1900) and *Heart of Darkness* (1902) pair the narrator, Charlie Marlow, a much-traveled sea captain, with figures (Jim, Kurtz) whose volatile mixture of idealism and corruption at once fascinates him, and reveals the limitations of his own view of the world. Ford's *The Good Soldier* represents a further turn of the impressionist screw. Dowell, the narrator, is himself as volatile a mixture of idealism and corruption as his friend and rival Edward Ashburnham, whose serial philanderings have destroyed several marriages and driven a young woman mad. He says that he cannot help us to understand the sad story he has to tell because the "whole world" is for him like "spots of color" on an immense canvas; if this was not so, he would have "something to catch hold of" (a determinate identity).[4] Dowell, in short, suffers from Impressionism:[5] his inability to tell a straight story is an aspect of his inability to know and be himself.

Dowell has tried to reconstruct the sequence of events which makes up his narrative by talking to Edward Ashburnham and his wife, Leonora. As far as we can tell, however, he had no such talk with Nancy, the young woman seduced by Ashburnham, before she lapsed into madness. Some of his remarks about her conduct are accordingly circumspect. But he does presume to describe her most intimate thoughts ("Nancy had, in fact, been thinking" [195]), as well as one of her drunken fantasies about Ashburnham. This presumption leaves us in "an interpretative quandary to which the openly avowed speculations of Marlow produce no equivalent."[6] Dowell may have gone mad. His obsession with Nancy may have led him to invent her thoughts and feelings. The narrative's over-determination, at this point, inspires even less faith in Dowell than his own frequent admissions of uncertainty.

Marlow tells his tales to groups of men rather like those assembled at the beginning of Kipling's soldiering stories, James's *The Turn of the Screw* (1898), and H. G. Wells's *The Time Machine* (1895): men whose very unremarkableness, soon to be stimulated, perhaps, by exposure to the unknown, embodies a last hope for social and moral consensus. Dowell, by contrast, has only the eerily abstract "idea of being in a country cottage with a silent listener" (167). The silent listener (or silent reader) cannot very well hope to embody consensus of any kind. The Impressionism from which Dowell suffers threatened the genre's traditional claim to extend and revise a shared knowledge of the world which might yet constitute the basis for community.

There was another threat to the novel's intelligibility and usefulness, the most absolute then and least understood now. This was the threat posed by Futurism's advocacy of modernization in all its forms (economic, technological, social, political). F. T. Marinetti, the futurist poet and theorist, rejected literary tradition in the name of the dynamism and inhumanity of the machine age. Marinetti's proselytizing visits to London between 1910 and 1915 provided the catalyst for Anglo-American Modernism. To his dissemination of energies, Ezra Pound and Wyndham Lewis opposed the Vortex, an energy articulated by form; to Marinetti's hatred of the past, they opposed the distancing effect of temporal disjunction (the layering of historical moments); to his belief in technology, they opposed a belief in art.[7] Such formulations, it is generally assumed, soon saw off the excitable Italian. Less often noticed is Marinetti's return, in Lewis's Time and Western Man (1927), to haunt the very idea of a modernist fiction.

Time and Western Man is, among other things, an attack on "the whole 'revolutionary' position" in contemporary politics and culture: "however 'revolutions' may begin," Lewis argued, "they always end in what Marinetti termed passéism." Marinetti's amnesiac Futurism is used as a stick with which to beat representation itself. Even the most original ideas, Lewis seems to say, become imitations as soon as they are represented (in words, images, deeds). The passéism of representation itself is the main obstacle to the artist or writer who would "make it new." Lewis was particularly hard on Joyce. The main "figures" in Ulysses are all "walking clichés," he maintained, and the narrative technique which renders them is primly orthodox, for all its evident virtuosity. Stephen Dedalus is a "lifeless" prig, while Leopold Bloom possesses "all the recognized theatrical properties of 'the Jew' up-to-date."[8] That Lewis misconstrues Joyce's method should not be allowed to conceal the radical implications of what is in effect a critique of the novel as a genre. Figures in narrative fiction do tend towards cliché because they have to be made continuously recognizable despite internal and external alterations.

The opening chapters of Tarr (1918), in which the hero, an English artist in Paris, challenges and insults the walking clichés who pass for his friends and colleagues, are Lewis's most raking assault on the genre which was to sustain his career as a writer. What Tarr loathes in them is their instant and unbroken recognizability. But there are limits to his own ability to avoid recognition. Tarr puts all his asceticism (that is, his imagination, his resistance to cliché) into his art; his taste in women remains, as a consequence, thoroughly derivative. Having trashed enough cliché for one morning, he visits his mistress, Bertha Lunken, only to discover that he himself has become something of a cliché in the eyes of at least one person. "This familiar life, with its ironical eye, mocked at him, too." Bertha and Tarr mirror each other. "Bertha's numb silence and abandon was a stupid *tableau vivant* of his own mood. In this impasse of arrested life he stood sick and useless."[9] Arrested life is precisely what Lewis was later to find, and deplore, in Stephen Dedalus. Arrested by sex, Tarr gradually becomes a figure in a novel. He puts more and more of his asceticism into sex, less and less into art. The novel's concluding paragraphs sardonically catalog a series of thoroughly novelistic impetuosities and entrapments.

After Tarr has been halted in his tracks by Bertha's silence and abandon, the focus shifts to Otto Kreisler, a German sculptor and bourgeois bohemian, who becomes his chosen antagonist. Kreisler puts all his asceticism into sex; his sculpture is correspondingly lifeless. A creature of representation, such originality as he can lay claim to lies in the vehemence of his gestures, his humiliations. In an essay on "Inferior Religions" published in the *Little Review* in 1917, Lewis argued that the "chemistry of personality" working deep within a person throws off "carnival masks" which we can "photograph and fix" into an identity.[10] Kreisler is a set of masks. Desire for the equally fixed and photographed Anastasya Vasek converts his customary "dullness" into "mechanical obstinacy." "He was a machine, dead weight of old iron, that started, must go dashing on" (100). And dash on he does, as wild a body as the "great comic effigies" hoisted in Lewis's early short stories, through flirtation, rape, accidental murder, and suicide. Kreisler's fate is to be a figure in a novel. Tarr, having set out to challenge and insult Kreisler, becomes more and more like him. Lewis set out to challenge and insult, through Tarr's asceticism, the novel as a genre. The genre won. His later remark that the book should have been called *Otto Kreisler* rather than *Tarr* was a confession that it was after all a novel.

It has been said that Lewis's work exists in a "special antagonism" to Ford's.[11] Ford threatened the novel with too much mind. Lewis threatened it with too much body. According to Ford, all that can be represented is the pattern of impressions striking a disembodied and isolated consciousness;

according to Lewis, all that can be represented is the sound of collisions, the impact made by one comic effigy upon another. Neither view does much for the novel's traditional claim to extend and revise a shared knowledge of the world. Yet Dowell, by identifying with Ashburnham, as Marlow identifies with Jim and Kurtz, at least recognizes his own desire for an identity based on moral choice, and so cancels his self-confessed "faintness." Furthermore, the punctiliously mimetic syntax with which Lewis renders Kreisler's death – "He hung, gradually choking, the last thing he was conscious of, his tongue" (301) – suggests that he was on occasion prepared to let a figure in a novel be a figure in a novel, if only at the moment of its vanishing.

The search for stricter form: Joyce and Lawrence

Eliot wanted to make the novel possible again by instilling into it a stricter form. He admired Joyce's use of Homeric myth as "a way of controlling, of ordering, of giving a shape and a significance to the immense panorama of futility and anarchy which is contemporary history."[12] The solution to literature's inadequacy in the face of futility and anarchy was *more* literature: the novel would render itself less "novel," less abjectly the expression of an abject age, if it began to associate with epic. This tendency in modernist theory and practice might be thought of, by analogy with Nietzsche's will-to-power and will-to-life, as a will-to-literature. Modernism was one of the fiercest campaigns ever mounted in favor of literature.

The terms in which Modernism's will-to-literature made itself known had been established in nineteenth-century debates about Naturalism and Symbolism. Emile Zola had sought to modernize literature by making it less literary: writers should not flinch from unpoetic subject matter, and should treat whatever they wrote about with scientific exactitude and objectivity. Symbolism, on the other hand, modernized literature by making it more literary. Symbolism's indeterminacies preserved literature from science and common sense. Literature, according to Arthur Symons's influential *The Symbolist Movement in Literature* (1899), had become a kind of religion, with all the duties and responsibilities of sacred ritual. Naturalism and Symbolism might be said to have embodied its most extreme tendencies, towards mimesis and towards poesis. Should the work of art be judged, as Roger Fry put it in *Vision and Design* (1920), by its "conformity to appearance" or by "purely aesthetic criteria"?[13] In modernist writing, mimesis is not so much an end in itself as an occasion for the triumph of poesis. Both novelists and poets invoked through their choice of subject matter and technique a resistance to literature which they knew would yield only to the excess literature at their command.

The dialectic between Naturalism and Symbolism is nowhere more apparent than in *Portrait of the Artist as a Young Man* (1916), which Eliot regarded as Joyce's farewell to the novel. Stephen Dedalus devises symbolist poems, and symbolist theories which have often been taken out of context as modernist doctrine. Having rejected the Church's sacred ritual, he makes a sacred ritual out of art. According to him, beauty precludes emotions such as desire and loathing which are kinetic rather than static, and directed towards a physical rather than a spiritual end. Yet his exposition of this theory, which takes the form of a dialogue with his friend Lynch, as they walk through the Dublin streets, is itself both kinetic and physical. One of his speeches is interrupted by a "harsh roar of jangled and rattling metal," when a dray laden with old iron turns the corner.[14] Stephen's response to interruptions is to evolve a literary style capable of abstract order. He derives less pleasure from the reflection of external reality in language than from "the contemplation of an inner world of individual emotions mirrored perfectly in a lucid supple periodic prose" (181). When, a few minutes later, he dedicates himself to the creation of beauty, he dedicates himself to a style, a theory, rather than to a subject matter, in a periodic prose which mirrors the emotion, and which we can sense him admiring. Joyce just as evidently does not endorse this rampant will-to-literature, since he punctuates the reverie with the sound of young men bathing: "O, cripes, I'm drownded" (183).

Stephen's devotion is rewarded, towards the end of chapter 4, by the sight of a young woman gazing out to sea: a figure his lucid supple periodic prose immediately converts into a symbol. Chapter 5 opens with Stephen's breakfast. "The yellow dripping had been scooped out like a boghole and the pool under it brought back to his memory the dark turf-coloured water of the bath in Clongowes" (188). The sentences which describe this scene are notably plain and notably faithful to appearance. Here, in the sad decline of the Dedalus family into squalor, is a story Zola might have written. In an early essay, Joyce had praised Henrik Ibsen for portraying "average lives in their uncompromising truth."[15] The Naturalism of *A Portrait*, its attention to the uncompromising truth of the lives which surround Stephen's, establishes a powerful resistance to literature. All five chapters conclude with a moment of self-transcendence; four times, the next chapter opens with a harsh reversion to squalor and to a plain style. The fifth and final chapter peters out in Stephen's inconsequential diary. Although the diary's conclusion invokes the promise of achievement encrypted in his surname, it can hardly be said to resolve the dialectic between Naturalism and Symbolism. *A Portrait* is Modernism in a state of suspended animation.

Curiously enough, the writer who most summarily resolved the dialectic was Joyce's antithesis, D. H. Lawrence, whose vitalist philosophy decreed that a work of art should be judged neither by its fidelity to appearance, nor by purely aesthetic criteria, but by its tendency to intensify or diminish the will-to-life. In a 1913 review of *Death in Venice*, Lawrence characterized Thomas Mann as the "last too-sick disciple" of Flaubert, a writer who had "stood away from life as from a leprosy."[16] His own work up to and including *Sons and Lovers* (1913) certainly did not stand away from the squalors and intimacies of a Midlands mining community. But the letters he wrote to his friend and mentor Edward Garnett in 1914 announced a change of emphasis. He now insisted that he was going "a stratum deeper" than anyone else had ever gone in writing that was "all analytical – quite unlike *Sons and Lovers*, not a bit visualised." Going deeper meant abandoning the "old stable ego," the traditional concept of character.[17] The first fruit of these labors, which are generally thought to have made Lawrence a Modernist, was *The Rainbow* (1915). In its portrayal of the impact of social change on a Midlands family, the Brangwens, *The Rainbow* is in fact quite extensively visualized. Furthermore, it invokes Naturalism as a way of seeing, indeed a way of living. The "homogeneous amorphous sterility" of the industrial landscape, its "Zolaesque tragedy," appalls Ursula Brangwen, but fascinates her corruptible companion, Winifred Inger.[18] By marrying Tom Brangwen, the colliery manager, Winifred chooses to live a Zolaesque tragedy. But mimesis, in this novel, is the occasion for the triumph of poesis. The marriage tests Ursula's will-to-life. It strengthens her determination not to succumb to the sterility of modern life. Zola, meanwhile, or Zola's shadow, tests Lawrence. Ursula owes her regeneration, at the very end of the novel, not to new thoughts or actions, but to a new sight, a sight seen, like Stephen Dedalus's sight of the young woman, through symbolist rather than naturalist eyes. "She saw in the rainbow the earth's new architecture, the old, brittle corruption of houses and factories swept away, the whole world built up in a living fabric of Truth, fitting to the overarching heavens" (459). The Truth emblazoned in the rainbow is a tribute as much to the reassertion of Lawrence's will-to-literature as to the reassertion of Ursula's will-to-life. Her brave new world fits not to the over-arching heavens gradually made visible by the development of the narrative, but to the overarching symbol incorporated from the outset in its title, and now, at last, understood. Rainbows of one kind or another were to arch over a number of novels published in the 1920s which have since become modernist classics.

Mythical methods: Lawrence, Fitzgerald, Woolf

In November 1915, in the middle of a catastrophic war, and after the suppression of *The Rainbow*, a defiantly optimistic novel, Lawrence gave up on England's "collapsing" civilization.[19] The book he embarked on in April 1916, *Women in Love*, a "potential sequel" to *The Rainbow*, was his most brutally apocalyptic (at one point he thought of calling it *Dies Irae*, "Day of Wrath"). Apocalypse was one of the things modernist writers imagined most fondly.[20] They saw themselves as inhabitants of a social and cultural system which had stagnated to the point where it was no longer susceptible to reform, but could only be renewed through total collapse or violent overthrow. Without apocalypse, Yeats, Eliot, and Pound would not have had careers. Yeats, Eliot, and Pound sit rather more easily together than the writers I shall consider in this section: Lawrence, Fitzgerald, and Woolf. But these, too, found in the literature of crisis a formula which enabled them to investigate at one and the same time a collapsing civilization and a collapsing genre.

Women in Love (1920), *The Great Gatsby* (1925), and *To the Lighthouse* (1927) share an interest not only in the continuous purposeful violence generated by an extraordinary event like the First World War, but in the random incidental violence sometimes shaken loose from ordinary existence. In a time of crisis, the fabric of meaning wears thin in places, and meaninglessness shows through: the stories we tell about experience, the symbols which offer themselves from within it, no longer suffice. Where meaninglessness does show through, it often takes the form of injury, because injury disturbs or negates the familiar shape human beings take. Injury was one of Lawrence's great subjects, and *Women in Love* is so full of it that it soon ceases to be incidental. When the Brangwens arrive for the water party at Shortlands, in chapter 14, they find that Gerald Crich has hurt his hand, which he carries, bandaged, in his jacket pocket. Gudrun Brangwen feels relieved that no one asks him about it (the routine explanations no longer seem adequate). By the time Winifred Crich's rabbit has got its claws into them, in chapter 18, they have become specialists in injury. In *The Great Gatsby*, it is people in motorcars who take the greatest toll, with people on foot a close second. Tom Buchanan breaks the arm of one mistress, when his car crashes, and the nose of another when he hits her. Ordinary violence arrives unannounced, and has gone before story or explanation can close around it ("Then there were bloody towels upon the bathroom floor, and women's voices scolding").[21] It is characteristic of Mrs. Ramsay, in *To the Lighthouse*, that she should take an interest in a one-armed bill-sticker, victim of a farming accident; but the circus his posters advertise soon makes her "forget her pity."[22]

The literature of crisis seeks out concentrations (it is often an urban literature, because cities compress both time and space by multiplying encounters). It finds in the nodes and clusters where rottenness accumulates the portents of the catastrophe which will validate its apocalyptic fantasies. Walking down the main street of Beldover, in the first chapter of *Women in Love*, Gudrun Brangwen wonders why she should have chosen to subject herself to "this amorphous ugliness of a small colliery town in the Midlands."[23] The chapter does not offer a description of Beldover which might enable us to identify the very specific ugliness she has in mind. In the absence of such information, the associations of intimacy and relatedness embedded in the demonstrative come into play. Suspending his narrative for a moment, with Gudrun immobilised by "revulsion," Lawrence summons us to inspect "this" particular concentration of rottenness, just as, in Eliot's *The Waste Land*, a voice calls the prophet in under the shadow of "this red rock" to witness fear in a handful of dust.

Gudrun's revulsion is the prelude to commitment (the story will soon advance her to a position already marked out by Lawrence's rhetoric). Chapter 9 describes her growing "nostalgia" for Beldover. "She felt herself drawn out at evening into the main street of the town, that was uncreated and ugly, and yet surcharged with this same potent atmosphere of intense, dark callousness" (116). The surcharge, indicating concentration, a saturated node, acquires, in Lawrence's description of the main street, narrative as well as rhetorical substance. Gudrun is drawn despite herself into the embrace of Beldover, and of Beldover's virtual owner, Gerald Crich, whom she first kisses under the bridge where the colliers kiss their sweethearts (330–3).

Gudrun and Gerald are specialists not only in injury but in fructifying revulsion. When Gerald dives again and again into the lake at Shortlands in a futile attempt to rescue his drowning sister, in chapter 14, Gudrun wants to plunge in with him, "to know the horror also" (181). When Gerald first comes to Gudrun, by way of his father's newly dug grave, whose cold and sticky clay repels him, he plunges and sinks into her soft warmth, burying his head between her breasts (344). Together, Gudrun and Gerald seek out surcharged concentrations of rottenness, until they themselves become surcharged concentrations: Gerald in suicide, Gudrun in subjection to the comprehensively rotten Loerke.

Ursula Brangwen and Rupert Birkin, on the other hand, live to a different rhythm, not that of fructifying revulsion, but that of desire satisfied, and thereafter at intervals lost and rediscovered. Ursula, unlike her sister, is "inured" to Beldover (12), as Birkin is to London Bohemia. It is Birkin who finally persuades Gerald to stop diving; like Ursula, he remains "callous" about the accident, unmoved, unabsorbed (190). For them, desire satisfied produces "anguish" that there cannot be some other kind of relationship, which in turn renews desire.

The division of attitude between the two pairs of protagonists divides the novel. Gerald and Gudrun inhabit a naturalist degeneration plot: progressive exposure of an inherent moral flaw drives them down through boredom and despair to subjection or death. They are described metonymically, as they would be in a Naturalist novel, by means of an inventory of dress, appearance, habit and occupation. Birkin and Ursula, on the other hand, inhabit what a symbolist regeneration plot would look like, if Symbolism had ever gone in for plots. They have no history (Ursula is barely recognizable as the forthright heroine of *The Rainbow*). Their only embodiment is metaphor (Ursula as a strange unconscious bud of womanhood, and so forth), and they renew themselves by yet further disembodiment (they quit their jobs). Ursula and Gudrun belong to different novels. When they go sketching by the lake, in chapter 10, Gudrun is both fascinated and repelled by the water plants: "she could feel their turgid fleshy structure as in a sensuous vision, she *knew* how they rose out of the mud." She has found a node of rottenness. Ursula, by contrast, "rose and drifted away, unconscious like the butterflies" (119).

At times, the two plots seem about to fuse, as Ursula is paired momentarily with Gudrun, Birkin with Gerald. But in the end they diverge, and Lawrence's inability to prevent this divergence does produce a certain strain: the naturalist degeneration plot proves such a stiff test for his will-to-literature that when it reasserts itself, as it must do if he is to finish his novel, it does so in a somewhat erratic fashion. The danger at such moments, David Bradshaw argues, is that the writer will impose his own anxieties and aspirations on the characters in a "coercive form of wishful or wilful thinking."[24] When Birkin looks at Gerald's corpse, he remembers "the beautiful face of one whom he had loved," and feels momentarily restored. "No-one could remember it without gaining faith in the mystery, without the soul's warming into new, deep life-trust" (471). Where, Bradshaw asks, does this restoration come from? Not from the narrative; since we have no idea which beautiful face Birkin, the man without a history, is talking about. It comes from Lawrence's own determination to warm at least one soul, if only for a moment, before the last day (and literature's last day) is finally done.

Tom Buchanan, in *The Great Gatsby*, has something of Gerald Crich's bull-like presumptuousness, and something of his gullibility where social theory is concerned. There are times, such as the description of the Valley of Ashes, when Fitzgerald seems to envisage a crisis novel on a Lawrentian scale. But Tom Buchanan is also an American "good soldier": like Edward Ashburnham, he is a "national figure in a way" (12), and one who gets caught in compromising situations with servant girls. When the rumor goes around that Tom's wife, Daisy, is a Catholic, we might almost suspect her of modeling herself on the staunchly Catholic Leonora Ashburnham. Nick Carraway makes a not un-Dowell-like narrator. Fitzgerald's affiliations were not with Lawrence, but with Ford and, especially, Conrad.

Carraway's first sight of the great Gatsby is of a man stretching out his arms to the "dark water" in a "curious way" (27). We have been here before. Gatsby is Kurtz or Lord Jim to Carraway's Marlow: a man at once stronger and weaker than his chronicler, potent in and through his dreams, but fallible. Carraway's tale, like Marlow's, is of Westerners going East into the heart of darkness. His last sight of Gatsby, a bright spot of color against white steps, dreamer still of an "incorruptible dream" (160), recapitulates Marlow's last sight of Jim, a white figure against a dark background, incurably "romantic." Not surprisingly, Fitzgerald found it harder to instil enigma into palpable wealth than Conrad had to instil it into the outposts of empire. When Carraway contrasts his own provincialism with the "vast carelessness" of the Buchanans (186), we may suppose that while Fitzgerald had seen the carelessness for himself, it was Conrad who made him think of it as vast.

Fitzgerald's first novel, *This Side of Paradise* (1920), was the story of a Stephen Dedalus-like "romantic egotist," Amory Blaine, who writes symbolist poems and assesses his Princeton acquaintances by inspecting their private libraries. It is Symbolism which renders (by failing to render precisely) the inexhaustibleness of the "inexhaustible charm" of wealth. Thus Carraway hears, beyond Gatsby's sentimentality, "an elusive rhythm, a fragment of lost words, that I had heard somewhere a long time ago" (118). Indeed, Gatsby's car, "terraced with a labyrinth of wind-shields that mirrored a dozen suns" (70), would not have been altogether out of place in a poem by Mallarmé. The problem, again, is wishful or willful thinking. Fitzgerald's yearning for a deep life trust is almost as urgent as Lawrence's. On his last night on West Egg, Carraway sits in the moonlight by Gatsby's empty house, and urges his soul into warmth: "I became aware of the old island here that flowered once for Dutch sailors' eyes – a fresh, green breast of the world" (187). Where does *this* come from?

It is a question that might also be asked about the "vision" which enables

Lily Briscoe to complete her portrait of Mrs. Ramsay, in *To the Lighthouse*, and, since it coincides with Mr. Ramsay's long-deferred arrival at the lighthouse, Woolf to complete her novel. "Yes, she thought, laying down her brush in extreme fatigue, I have had my vision" (281). Is the vision the product of abilities and experiences rendered in and by the narrative? Or has the author wished or willed it on Lily's behalf? Woolf, I think, anticipated the question. Lily, baffled by her inability to reimagine Mrs. Ramsay, warns herself against wishful or willful thinking. "But one got nothing by soliciting urgently" (261). Woolf's answer to the question lies in the structure of her novel.

Part I of *To the Lighthouse*, "The Window," takes place on a September evening at a holiday home in the Hebrides, and describes the various activities and preoccupations of the Ramsays, their eight children and six guests. The main focus is on the family as an institution whose stability is at once creative and constricting. Families guarantee personal immortality through lineage and affiliation. But the centrality of this institution in society's self-furtherance has led it to arrogate powers and values which do not necessarily belong to it. Established as the primary medium of symbolic exchange, it expands or reduces all anxieties and aspirations to its own size, converting any stray ambition into itself. Woolf's point seems to be that while everything in the family is reproduction (of powers, of values), not all reproduction is in the family. To the personal immortality made more likely by lineage, though not guaranteed, since children sometimes die young, Woolf opposed the personal immortality made more likely by art, though not guaranteed, since paintings sometimes get stuffed in attics.

The family's arrogation of powers and values encourages arrogance. The egotism displayed by Mr. and Mrs. Ramsay is insufferable, and compelling, because it is displayed on behalf of an institution. This impersonal egotism, behind which, or interleaved with which, the person occasionally appears, or can be made to appear by a hopeless love, manifests itself as an absurd reduction of everything to the family, on Mr. Ramsay's part, and an absurd expansion of the family until it becomes everything, on Mrs. Ramsay's part. Mr. Ramsay behaves to his wife, his children, his startled guests, as though he were a gallant soldier, a castaway, the leader of a doomed polar expedition. Observing him, the resolutely unfamilial Lily Briscoe and William Bankes wonder "why so brave a man in thought should be so timid in life" (62–3). Mrs. Ramsay, by contrast, turns bravery in life into thoughts which are timid because their only term is replication. She wishes to replicate her bravely fertile marriage by pairing off Lily and William, Minta Doyle and Paul Rayley.

In "The Window," powers and values are arrogated not only on behalf of the family, but on behalf of literature. There is a kind of literary mega-lomania in the imperiousness of the proliferating metaphors: "the beak of brass, the arid scimitar of the male" (53), and so forth. Some of these metaphors belong to the characters; others have been wished or willed on their behalf by the author (does James really see his father as a beak of brass?). In part I, *style* solicits urgently. That Woolf should so frankly summon poesis to the aid of mimesis would not have surprised her first readers. Her career had already included one decisive shift of emphasis, from the orthodox realism of *The Voyage Out* (1915) and *Night and Day* (1917) to the lyrical experimentation of *Jacob's Room* (1922) and *Mrs. Dalloway* (1925). On 27 June 1925, at a time when she was planning *To the Lighthouse*, she recorded in her diary an ambition to substitute poesis for mimesis. "I have an idea that I will invent a new name for my books to supplant "novel." A new —by Virginia Woolf. But what? Elegy?"[25] The new—by Virginia Woolf did indeed prove to be an elegy, for her father, Leslie Stephen, the literary critic and biographer, notoriously short-tempered and dependent on his wife, and for her mother, Julia, a legendary pre-Raphaelite beauty. The style of part I urgently solicits, through its elaborate expansiveness, elegiac feeling: it is already a elegy, long before anyone has died. If Joyce, in Eliot's eyes, renewed the novel by associating it with epic, Woolf renewed it by associating it with elegy.

The pivotal part II, "Time Passes," boldly reduces the crisis novel's crisis to parentheses embedded in a description of the house's abandonment and decay during a period of ten years. The parentheses flatly inform us of the deaths of Mrs. Ramsay, her daughter Prue (in childbirth), and her son Andrew (in battle): the predictability of the last two making the first even harder to explain and endure. Events no longer obtrude, to be enshrined in metaphor. "There was the silent apparition of an ashen-colored ship for instance, come, gone; there was a purplish stain upon the bland surface of the sea as if something had boiled and bled, invisibly, beneath." These apparitions do not flower into meaning. Indeed, they block meaning, disrupt, for the stroller on the beach, "a scene calculated to stir the most sublime reflections" (182). The narrative is now a counterelegy, to the extent that it can recall the past ("how once the looking-glass had held a face"), but not the future in the past. Seventy-year-old Mrs. McNab, creature of experience rather than aspiration, fingers the gray cloak which had once provoked sublime reflections about Mrs. Ramsay's beauty (184).

Part II hollows out the world constructed in part I: an empty house, an empty style. It is this emptiness which makes possible the redemptions of part III. Mrs. Ramsay is still loved, and greatly missed, but it is only in her absence that Mr. Ramsay can reach the lighthouse (he would surely not have gone except as reparation) and Lily Briscoe complete her painting. Only when Mrs. Ramsay has receded, only when her beauty has ceased to still and freeze life, only when she has been supplanted by the life which goes on without her, can she become the object of Lily's painting, of Lily's love. The steps where Mrs. Ramsay had once sat fill elegiacally and then empty again. Only when she convinces herself that they really are empty and will remain empty for ever can Lily complete her painting. "She looked at the steps; they were empty; she looked at her canvas; it was blurred. With a sudden intensity, as if she saw it clear for a second, she drew a line there, in the centre. It was done; it was finished" (281). By emptying the steps, Woolf emptied her own will-to-literature. Not completely, though. For, just as the shape of the person who once occupied the steps remains in Lily's memory, so the conclusion of the novel's other story, with Mr. Ramsay's arrival at the lighthouse, validates the hint of sacred ritual in its overarching title. Woolf thus belongs, at a slight distance, with writers like Lawrence and Fitzgerald, like Marcel Proust and Thomas Mann, who were moved by a formidable will-to-literature.

Scorch marks: Joyce and Faulkner

The most enduring of the mythical moments of origin proposed for Anglo-American Modernism is the first post-impressionist exhibition in London in December 1910. My (equally mythical) choice would be the June 1918 issue of the *Little Review*, which included "Calypso," the fourth episode of Joyce's *Ulysses*.

> Mr. Leopold Bloom ate with relish the inner organs of beasts and fowls. He liked thick giblet soup, nutty gizzards, a stuffed roast heart, liver slices fried with crustcrumbs, fried hencod's roes. Most of all he liked grilled mutton kidneys which gave to his palate a fine tang of faintly scented urine.[26]

Up to the moment when those inner organs appeared, it would have been reasonable to suppose that *Ulysses* was a sequel to *A Portrait*. The Stephen Dedalus of its first three episodes is recognizable as the Stephen Dedalus of *A Portrait*, now back from self-exile in Paris, and different only in the degree of self-doubt to which he is subject, and to which a new interior monologue technique gives us unprecedented access. The self-doubt makes him even *more* of a Prufrock, a symbolist *manqué*, than he was in *A Portrait*. However, readers turning the pages of the June 1918 issue of the *Little Review* would have encountered, in Mr. Leopold Bloom and his idiosyncratic palate, something else altogether. Bloom has a way of thinking, feeling, acting, and speaking every bit as distinctive, and every bit as compelling, as Stephen's. Joyce responded to Ezra Pound's suggestion that Stephen should be brought forward at Bloom's expense by saying that Stephen interested him less because his "shape" could not now be changed. The age of Prufrock was over.

The first six episodes of *Ulysses* ("Telemachus," "Nestor," "Proteus," "Calypso," "Lotos-eaters," "Hades") are written in what Joyce called, in a letter of 1919, an "initial style":[27] they combine third-person, past-tense depiction of events with first-person present-tense depiction of the thoughts of the two main characters. The initial style devotes itself, as few literary styles had ever done before, to the mimesis of individual acts of apprehension: what we "see" is in general what Stephen and Bloom are conscious of. This degree of identification was too good (too reassuring) to last. When Joyce revised the *Little Review* version of the seventh episode, "Aeolus," which brings Stephen and Bloom separately to the central Dublin premises shared by the *Telegraph* and the *Freeman's Journal*, he added a set of newspaper-style subheadings ("THE GRANDEUR THAT WAS ROME") whose trite phrases comment obliquely on the dramatic action and mock the eloquence of the pundits assembled in the editorial office. The arbitrariness of these subheadings disrupts an initial style patently and reassuringly motivated by fidelity to appearance. Bloom's palate may be the first real surprise in *Ulysses*, but it is by no means the last.

However, the initial style makes a rapid recovery, to render for us Bloom's search for an enabling lunch, in "Lestrygonians," and Stephen's search for an enabling aesthetic theory, in "Scylla and Charybdis." The honeymoon between author and reader resumes, as a glimpse into the Burton restaurant neatly epitomizes Naturalism – "Spaton sawdust, sweetish warmish cigarette smoke, reek of plug, spilt beer, men's beery piss, the stale of ferment" (215) – while Stephen's sardonic identification with "the druid priests of Cymbeline, hierophantic" (280) neatly epitomizes Symbolism. The first nine episodes of *Ulysses* consign *A Portrait* to history by invalidating its solipsism. But, despite the "Aeolus" subheadings, they have not yet consigned literature to history because they still operate within the limits marked by literature's alternating self-representations as Naturalism (or extreme mimesis) and Symbolism (or extreme poesis).

On the last page of the fair copy of "Scylla and Charybdis," Joyce wrote "End of the First Part of 'Ulysses.'" The next five episodes ("Wandering Rocks," "Sirens," "Cyclops," "Nausicaa," "Oxen of the Sun") reveal a significant change of emphasis, from a preoccupation with character and realistic detail to a preoccupation with symbolic correspondences and stylistic elaboration. In "Wandering Rocks," Joyce for the first time used the initial style to depict the thoughts of characters other than Stephen and

Bloom; in "Sirens," he distorted it beyond recognition by filtering it through a musical structure which reconfigures Bloom's stream of consciousness to fit its own patterns; in "Cyclops," he abandoned it altogether in favor of a narrative persona (a barfly) whose salty monologue is punctuated by parodies of various literary and subliterary styles; in "Nausicaa," it returns temporarily, although only in the context of a more extended parody (of popular fiction); in "Oxen of the Sun," parody (of English literary styles) becomes the book's exclusive narrative technique, a screen through which the dramatic action, set in a hospital ward, can dimly be perceived. Joyce referred to this rapid appropriation and abandonment of styles as his "scorching" method: "each successive episode, dealing with some province of artistic culture (rhetoric or music or dialectic), leaves behind it a burnt-up field."[28] The burnt-up field was the field of his own will-to-literature.

The definitions of modernist writing produced in Anglo-American criticism from the 1930s to the 1970s – from Edmund Wilson's *Axel's Castle* (1931) to Hugh Kenner's *The Pound Era* (1971) – were primarily literary–historical in emphasis: their purpose was to distinguish literature written during the first three decades of the century, in formal and philosophical terms, from what came before, and, to a lesser extent, what came after. The terms did not always stick. Was *Ulysses* the last word in modern novels? Or the first word in modern poems? Some critics regretted that as a novel it ends after "Scylla and Charybdis," others that as a poem it does not begin until "Wandering Rocks." Few of these literary–historical accounts acknowledged the full implications of Joyce's commitment to parody. In "Sirens," for example, which describes Bloom's late lunch in the Ormond Bar, the book begins to quote, or to parody, itself. "Leopold cut liverslices. As said before he ate with relish the inner organs, nutty gizzards, fried cods' roes" (347). *As said before*: few novels draw attention so brazenly to their own artifice, while few poems advance with such self-dismissiveness towards symbolism.

Since the 1960s, *Ulysses* has to a large extent been read not as a novel or a poem, but, in the wake of deconstruction, as a "text." Textual readings suggest that the stylistic elaborations developed in the middle episodes expose the limits, not of literary genre, but of the symbolic order in and through which identity is constructed. These readings derive from deconstruction's emphasis on the difference *within* a text, or a person's identity, rather than on the difference *between* texts or identities. Where modernist fiction is concerned, they might be said to work best, not when they substitute "difference within" for "difference between," as a definition both of the field of study and of aesthetic and political value, but when they set the two concepts in relation. For Modernism could be understood as an attempt variously to exclude either difference-within or difference-between from definitions of aesthetic and political value. Of the "Men of 1914," Eliot, Pound and Lewis all evolved doctrines whose main function was to convert difference-within into difference-between. Their insistence on impersonality, and on the primacy of the "world of objects," in Eliot's phrase, was an effort to control the unsettling drift of desire, and to preempt the messy sexual and political coalitions into which its compulsive mimeticism, its insatiable "herd instinct," might lead it: the autonomy of art would ensure the autonomy of the self. "The only way of expressing emotion in the form of art," Eliot argued, "is by finding an 'objective correlative'; in other words, a set of objects, a chain of events, which shall be the formula of that particular emotion."[29] Joyce's appeal, by contrast, is that he made the search for objective correlatives his subject matter rather than his doctrine: "Circe" exposes the differences-within which Anglo-Irish culture has repressed in order to construct differences between men and women, rich and poor, Catholic and Jew, Englishman and Irishman. To put it another way, deconstruction has shown that Joyce had good moral and political reason to disable through parody the genre whose conventions his book began by observing. Of the other writers who also made differences-within their subject matter, the most significant, Kafka apart, was William Faulkner.

Faulkner did not need to begin by writing about a symbolist poet. He *was* one (*The Marble Faun*, 1924). His decisive departure from literary tradition came with his fourth novel, *The Sound and the Fury* (1929), where he took the step Joyce had taken in the June 1918 issue of the *Little Review*: he placed his Stephen Dedalus figure, Quentin Compson, in relation to other consciousnesses. Indeed, this Prufrock ushers *himself* into history, by committing suicide on 2 June 1910: the rest of the story, narrated successively by his two brothers, Benjy and Jason, and an omniscient narrator, takes place on three days in April 1928.

The Sound and the Fury is framed by exclusions: to begin with, an impossible interiority which excludes all difference-between; to end with, an impossible exteriority which excludes all difference-within. Benjy converts externally differentiated time and space into internally differentiated mood. When a golfer cries "Here, caddie," he thinks only of his beloved lost sister, Caddy, feels sad, and starts to bellow. Benjy presses up against boundaries – the fence through which he watches the golfers, the gate where he waits for Caddy, the fence across which he delivers Mrs. Patterson's letter, the piece of wood Dilsey places down the center of Luster's bed, the fence along which he follows the girls going home from school – which have for him no meaning, indeed no reality. It is others who notice that his clothes have snagged on the fence, or tell him to keep his hands in his pockets in cold weather. His words brush against the world of objects without grasping the distribution within it of cause and effect, or of racial and social characteristics. His narrative, unlike those of the other protagonists, does not differentiate black speech from white by its use of idiom (Dilsey says "Yes, sir" to his father, not "Yessuh" or "Yes, suh"). Benjy, in short, is Eliot's worst nightmare: a gigantic, blubbering subjective correlative.

Quentin Compson is a student at Harvard, and roughly the same age as Stephen Dedalus. Unlike Benjy, he knows all about differences-between; but he cannot live them. His interior monologue, which occupies the day of his suicide, thus recurs incessantly to difference-within. Stephen Dedalus, in "Proteus," remembers a time in Paris when he tried on a woman's shoe, and muses about "Wilde's love that dare not speak its name" (62). Quentin finds in his friends' chaffing an insinuation about his own protean sexuality ("Calling Shreve my husband").[30] A ritualized exchange with a poor black man at a railway crossing in Virginia may confirm momentarily his identity as a privileged white man. But observation of the Deacon, at Harvard, who has one social and racial identity for his familiars – "See you again, fellows . . . glad to have chatted with you" – and another for new arrivals from the South – "Right dis way, young marster, hyer we is" (83) – only serves to confuse the issue. Confusion is worse confounded when a young boy he encounters while killing time on the day of his suicide says that he "talks like a coloured man" (103). Authority deserts him as surely as it deserts K., in Kafka's *The Trial* (1925), another man arrested for a crime he is not aware of having committed.

Jason Compson, who has never left the South, and who has acted as head of the family since his father's death, establishes *his* authority through reiterated paranoid assertions of the difference between himself and a series of rapidly conceived sexual or racial antagonists. His anti-Semitism, for example, is as blatant, and as abrupt, as that of Mr. Deasy, the headmaster of the school at which Stephen teaches, in the "Nestor" episode of *Ulysses*. What appalls Jason about Caddy's daughter, Quentin, is her promiscuity, her "slip[ping] around." In his eyes, to slip around is to behave like a "nigger wench" (163): to sacrifice racial as well as moral integrity. His interior monologue seeks out the objective correlatives which will secure forever the differences between black and white, men and women: "Once a bitch always a bitch, what I say" (155). It thus represents the speech of a black woman like Dilsey as densely idiomatic: "Can't you liv in de same house wid you own blood niece without quoilin?" (219)

Jason's efforts to impose himself fail miserably, and his failure appears to invoke, in the novel's concluding section, an exaggeratedly imposing omniscient narrator who harbors no illusions about the feebleness of those efforts. This omniscience forces us to acknowledge discrepancies between event and meaning. In the opening paragraph, we encounter, not Dilsey's words, as in the previous sections, but her flesh, as the wind needles laterally into it, "precipitating not so much a moisture as a substance partaking of the quality of thin, not quite congealed oil" (229). The words which needle this flesh as emphatically as the wind does, tattooing it with discursive elaboration, are evidently the narrator's. What does Dilsey know about precipitation? Luster, carrying a pile of logs, is invisible "within and beyond his wooden avatar" – but not to Dilsey, who, unmindful of symbolism, guides him across the kitchen with a firm hand. As the flesh weakens, in this final section, blundering to a halt, or succumbing to migraine, or seduction, so the word flourishes and the discrepancy between event and meaning widens.

It is the omniscient narrator who produces, by way of a conjuring trick, the book's one authentic (pure, complete) identity, that of the Reverend Shegog. When Shegog, a shabby, insignificant little man, rises to preach, he speaks at first "like a white man" (254). "I got the recollection and the blood of the Lamb!" (255) Gradually, however, his voice rises above the shabbiness and insignificance, until it provokes a response, "a woman's single soprano: 'Yes, Jesus!'" (255). The response transforms him. His "intonation" and "pronunciation" become "negroid," his words a glimpse of the power and the glory of God. He has been remade across and by means of the difference between man and woman, black and white. The narrative retranscribes his refrain: "I got de ricklickshun en de blood of de Lamb!" (256) Shegog's sermon, the most densely idiomatic passage in the book, is its narrative other (what "Penelope" is to *Ulysses*). The sermon's full black identity mirrors the full white identity of the impersonal narrator's omniscience. Both are conjuring tricks.

The fable of the emergence of white heterosexual identity, through Benjy's perpetual childhood and Quentin's protean adolescence to Jason's imitations of patriarchy, has been completed only by a supplement which reveals the lack at its center. For the discrepant exteriority of the omniscient narrative, far from gathering the pieces together and filling in gaps, as Faulkner himself suggested it did, merely reverses the discrepant interiority of Benjy's monologue. Both views are impossible: Benjy's words could not be his own; the omniscient narrator's words could go omnisciently on forever and still not touch Benjy's experience. Faulkner's fable about what is possible by way of identity (in Mississippi in 1928) shuttles fretfully backwards and forwards between those impossibilities.

Equivocations: Hemingway, Richardson

One might characterize Faulkner's subsequent career as a movement away from Joyce and Kafka back towards Conrad: *Light in August* (1932) has sometimes been compared to *Nostromo* (1904) in terms of its scope and to *Under Western Eyes* (1913) in terms of its treatment of salvation (or release) through suffering. The later sagas, which develop the fictional history of the American South inaugurated by *Flags in the Dust* (1928), extend and deepen his analysis of the construction of identity in or across racial and sexual difference. Joe Christmas, in *Light in August*, tries desperately to convert difference-within into the difference between himself and a series of lovers: he acts black when with white women, and white when with black women. But the only result of these encounters is to reopen the equivocation in himself, which he must then overcome through violence, and the identificatory retribution that violence brings down on him.

Ernest Hemingway, disciple of Gertrude Stein, started a lot closer to the center of Modernism than Faulkner, and moved away from it more rapidly. Hemingway became, after Joyce had conclusively demonstrated his ineradicable perversity in the later episodes of *Ulysses*, the poets' favorite prose writer. Ezra Pound approved. No prose writer stuck more closely to imagist principles: terseness, impersonality, attention to the world of objects. But objective correlatives were, for a brief period during the early 1920s, his theme rather than his method. When, in *In Our Time*, the dissatisfied wife in "Cat in the Rain" decides to feminize herself by letting her hair grow – "'I want to pull my hair back tight and smooth and make a big knot at the back that I can feel,' she said"[31] – the phantom knot is *her* objective correlative, not Hemingway's.

In *The Sun Also Rises* (1926), the bullfighter Pedro Montero, emblem of masculinity, wants Brett Ashley to let her hair grow – "He said it would make me more womanly" (181) – and then marry him: "After I'd gotten more womanly, of course" (182). Her refusal is a refusal of gendered identity, and it keeps her in the orbit of the narrator, Jake Barnes, whose war wound has destroyed his manhood. This relationship is of its essence mediated, equivocal, inauthentic. The novel's tripartite structure marks out the three stages of the rite of passage which might restore Jake to immediacy, and through immediacy to manhood: separation from the banal, purposeless, inauthentic Paris life described in book I; a liminal phase, described in book II, during which identity can be stripped down and rebuilt, in Spain, at the festival in Pamplona; and a return, transfigured, to ordinary existence, in book III. The map of Europe becomes a gigantic objective correlative. To cross the border between France and Spain is to move from a mundane into a sacred realm. But Jake disavows the *aficion*, the passion for the bullfight, which might have remasculinized him and rendered him whole again, when he introduces Brett to Pedro Montero; after that betrayal, the *aficionados* will not even speak to him. The sacredness of Spain, its restorative power, is compromised by the network of boundaries and checkpoints which divide one part of it from another: a *carabineer* asks for fishing permits; a customs officer in Pamplona searches baggage; a verger stops Brett from entering a church because she has no hat. An elsewhere thus divided from itself is no longer elsewhere, no longer the crucible of psychic restoration. Jake is always looking into things, into the cage where the bulls are penned, into the runway down which the bulls will chase the crowd. But, for him, unlike Gerald Crich or Gudrun Brangwen, to look into things is to look through them. It is after one of his inspections that Jake meets the *aficion*-free waiter who believes that bullfighting is bullshitting. On his way back into France, at the start of book III, he gets no further than Bayonne, before doubling back into Spain, and into Brett's doubling back from the arms of Montero.

Hemingway soon became, in his books, at any rate, the Hemingway of legend: the man who, enraged by Max Eastman's jibe about false chest hair, marched into the *New Republic* offices and bared all (or part). His fullest and least tragic exploration of androgyny, *The Garden of Eden*, was not published in his lifetime. During the 1920s and 1930s, androgyny – psychic, sexual and, so to speak, textual – was largely the province of women writers. Their explorations, for the most part published in their lifetimes, though frequently neglected by readers and reviewers, have over the last twenty years been richly and extensively reclaimed by feminism: reclaimed, more often than not, in the name of critical difference, of psychic and textual slipping around.

Female Modernism was an answer to the relentless conversion of difference-within into difference-between which had for so long sustained patriarchal ideology in general, and literary representations of women in particular. That is why Virginia Woolf insisted on the disabling exteriority of literary realism, in "Modern Fiction" (1919) and "Mr. Bennett and Mrs. Brown" (1924). In *Hilda Lessways* (1911), she complained, Arnold Bennett tries to make us believe in the reality of his heroine by describing the house she lives in, and the houses she can see from the house she lives in. "House property was the common ground from which the Edwardians found it easy to proceed to intimacy." Woolf thought that writers should proceed to intimacy from a different ground (the ground of difference-within itself): the "pattern" which each incident or impression "scores upon the con-

sciousness."[32] Identity was to be grasped by means of a poetic of awareness: the more aware a person is, the more representable he or she becomes;
and, by implication, the more representable, the more aware. Female
Modernism might thus be understood as a program for the conversion of
difference-between into difference-within.

The efficacy of this poetic of awareness was a matter of dispute from the
outset, even, or especially, among women writers. Dorothy Richardson
tested it to the limit in *Pilgrimage*, a sequence of thirteen novels (or
"chapters") beginning with *Pointed Roofs* (1915) and concluding with
March Moonlight, published posthumously in 1967. *Pilgrimage* describes
the experiences of Miriam Henderson, a woman forced out of the stifling
security of middle-class family life by her father's bankruptcy. In a 1918
essay on the first three volumes which Woolf read with approval, May
Sinclair, whose own *Mary Olivier: A Life* (1919) was distinctly Richardso-
nian, noted that Richardson had abandoned the objective method and
"taken Miriam's nature upon her."[33] As the distance between author and
protagonist collapsed, so did that between protagonist and world. This
much merging was not to everyone's taste. Katherine Mansfield, reviewing
Interim (1919), where the shocks of "inward recognition" are produced by
"such things as well-browned mutton, gas jets, varnished wallpapers,"
wondered whether the systematic dissolution of the differences between
self and world had not merely produced *in*difference. Miriam's closeness to
life, she concluded, "leaves us feeling, as before, that everything being of
equal importance to her, it is impossible that everything should not be of
equal unimportance."[34]

This is, I think, a significant disagreement, whose implications can be
grasped by comparing Mansfield's description of a sojourn in Germany in
In a German Pension (1913) with Richardson's in *Pointed Roofs* (1915).
Mansfield's cousin, Elizabeth von Arnim, had already made a successful
literary career out of witty assaults on German arrogance, philistinism,
boorishness, and misogyny. She herself chose the same targets, in stories
about appalling table manners (soup spilt on waistcoats, ears cleaned with
a napkin, and so on) and the unwelcome intimacies made possible by
umbrellas. The catalog of differences between England and Germany, men
and women, is a little too relentless, as she herself later recognized, but it
does sometimes produce a change of attitude: an encounter with a German
feminist, for example, forces the narrator to reconsider and reaffirm her
own, differently formulated convictions.

Germany proves less of an ordeal for Miriam Henderson, who has gone
there to teach English, than might have been expected, and certainly not
the land of soup-stained ties and umbrella harrassment depicted by Mans-

field. The success of her first class is said to be important not in itself but because it removes "an obstacle to gladness which was waiting to break forth."[35] Gladness breaking forth is very much the subject of the early volumes of *Pilgrimage*, and Germany counts only insofar as it hinders or encourages the breaking forth. Sitting in a *delikatessen*, surrounded by the girls from her school, she feels "securely adrift" (88). In Mansfield's stories, no one is ever *securely* adrift.

The mind grows rings: Joyce, Woolf, Ford

Deconstructive criticism has done greater justice to the aesthetic and political power of parody and self-parody, in *Ulysses*, than literary history ever did. But the preoccupation with textual and psychic splitting, like all preoccupations, has its limits. Critical difference becomes an absolute value, to be teased out from within the text, and then celebrated either as a pleasure or as an ideological unmasking. Attridge, for example, claims that his reading of "Sirens" does not so much explain the episode's "linguistic adventures" as participate in them, "enjoying and learning from them at the same time."[36] Joyce, however, reported that after completing "Sirens" he found it impossible to listen to music of any kind. There was a price to be paid for the pleasures of scorching.

Michael Levenson has most astutely assessed the cost of the book's commitment to parody and self-parody by associating it with the figure of Buck Mulligan, the mocking blasphemer whom Stephen names "Usurper." "The ear for verbal absurdity, the eye for moral weakness, the insatiable appetite for pun and paradox, the willingness to amuse until amusement irritates, the incessant unrepentant theatricality – these central features of Mulligan's sensibility become dominant features at the centre of *Ulysses*."[37] To the extent that the book endorses parody and self-parody, it endorses the actions of its two melodramatic villains, its two usurpers, Mulligan and Blazes Boylan: for it is Boylan's "erotic arousal" which the "linguistic adventures" of "Sirens" ensure, not Bloom's. Deconstruction cannot describe the moral and emotional cost of parody.

Modernist writers, on the other hand, could, and did. Thomas Mann's *Doctor Faustus* (1947) is both a novel and an essay on Modernism. It is the life of a brilliant young composer, Adrian Leverkuhn, as told, during the first years of the Second World War, by his older friend and critic, Zeitblom. As a student, Leverkuhn convinces himself that traditional forms have been exhausted. "Why does almost everything seem to me like its own parody? Why must I think that almost all, no, all the methods and conventions of art today *are good for parody only*?"[38] Leverkuhn's own music combines extreme formal austerity with the depiction of a universe in which humankind has been displaced by the elemental and the primal. Zeitblom, whose allegiance is to the "human and articulate," finds this combination "daemonic." Zeitblom's humanism is subjected to ironic treatment, but there can be no mistaking the pain which Leverkuhn's commitment to parody causes him. Similarly, there can be no mistaking the pain which Buck Mulligan's Faustian pact causes Stephen Dedalus, or the pain which Blazes Boylan's rather more visceral Faustian pact causes Leopold Bloom.

The last four episodes of *Ulysses* ("Circe," "Eumaeus," "Ithaca," "Penelope") exceed all others in length and range of reference. Rather than placing further stylistic screens around events, these episodes treat what has already happened during the day as a set of narrative elements to be endlessly combined and recombined. This final stage could be seen as a return from the fields burnt up by parody to the house of domestic fiction. With Stephen and Bloom united, then safely installed at 7 Eccles Street, while Molly sleeps upstairs, surely the book's "odyssey of style" is also complete?[39] Hugh Kenner has rightly drawn attention to "a governing rhythm of the book, whereby impression in the first half is modified by knowledge in the second."[40] "Penelope," an episode regarded as extramural by many, including Joyce himself, none the less provides more information about the Blooms than any other. But what prevents stylistic as well as thematic completion or return is a new emphasis, in the final episodes, on possibility rather than (usually the novel's sustaining convention) probability. In "Ithaca," when Bloom turns on the faucet, the question "Did it flow?" elicits a lengthy explanation of how and why the water flows (782–3). This explanation is a thought which could have occurred to Bloom as he turns on the faucet. Since we do not know whether it did or not, we are not much the wiser about his state of mind at that particular moment. But we have learned something about the kind of topic which would interest a person like him. This is virtual Bloom, if you like, rather than actual (novelistic) Bloom.

Virtual Bloom is actual Bloom's adjunct: neither conjoined, nor disjoined. Virtual Bloom has attracted relatively little attention, either from literary historians, who favour conjoining, or from deconstructionists, who favor disjoining. And yet he is surely amplified in our minds by the thoughts he may or may not have had. By dealing not in probability, but in possibility, Joyce renewed the genre of the novel. Seen from this point of view, his book's epic correspondences are another of its virtual realities (another way of conceiving virtual reality), rather than, as Eliot supposed, an ordering principle. In "Ithaca" and "Penelope," the question we ask of Leopold, Molly and Stephen is not "Who are they, finally?" but "What might they yet do for each other, in each other's lives?" The technique which supervenes on parody, in *Ulysses* and a number of other modernist novels, is a process of psychic and textual additiveness (a proliferation of virtual realities).

Virginia Woolf's notably disjunctive *The Waves* (1931) sets in parallel series the reflections of six characters, in such a way as to suggest the permeability or friability of selfhood. The elderly Bernard, whose Marlow- or Gerontion-like address to an unnamed dinner companion concludes the book, observes that it is not "one life" he looks back on: "I am not one person; I am many people; I do not altogether know who I am – Jinny, Susan, Neville, Rhoda, or Louis: or how to distinguish my life from theirs."[41] But it is striking that while he does speak of the dissipation or streaming away of identity, he also speaks of its accumulation, accretion, acceleration, augmentation and sedimentation. Jinny, Susan, and the rest are, among other things, his adjuncts, his virtual selves. "The mind grows rings; the identity becomes robust; pain is absorbed in growth" (198). Sometimes, as he is well aware, the growth is halted, the pain breaks through. But Bernard, simply by surviving, has won his glimpse of "eternal renewal." In that respect, he begins to seem less like Marlow or Gerontion, and more like a character in a novel by Arnold Bennett.

Many, if not most, plots, and certainly those favored by the great nineteenth-century realists, turn on moments of revelation, recognition scenes, when the illusions nurtured by timidity, prejudice, or habit fall away, and a naked self confronts a naked world. These are the moments when identity is begun, renewed, or completed. French Naturalism added a different plot, in which the revelation is gradual, and of something already known, but concealed: a moral or physical flaw, an organic "lesion." Both kinds of plot favor awareness. Illusions are there to be stripped away. There can be no personal freedom until they have been stripped away. Bennett was less interested in crises, and the comic or tragic awareness they bring, than in the illusions that remain. His protagonists are incapable of or do not want awareness. They advance their hollowness into a world which, as they age, becomes ever more crowded, ever more impenetrable. They feel the changes in pressure within them, but the shell of their nescience neither cracks nor fills with hard-earned wisdom, with love. Edwin Clayhanger, hero of the Clayhanger tetralogy (1910–18), is motivated in his youth by a fierce hatred of Methodism. But by the time he is asked, in middle age, to serve as District Treasurer of the Additional Chapels Fund, he does not even have enough animosity left for a contemptuous refusal. Ambition goes the same way: "his life has become a life of half-measures, a continual falling-short." Yet he is in his way fulfilled, even assertive. He has accumulated an identity. Bernard, in *The Waves*, knows something about epiphany, about rupture; but also something about the half-measures which may add up to eternal renewal. I do not mean to suggest that Woolf had abandoned her belief in moments of being, in not falling short: Miss La Trobe, the heroine of *Between the Acts* (1941), is about as un-Bennett-like a protagonist as one could possibly imagine. But I do think that she, like a number of other modernist writers, was more interested in cumulative models of selfhood than her most recent critics have supposed. "We all begin well, for in our youth there is nothing we are more intolerant of than our own sins writ large in others and we fight them fiercely in ourselves; but we grow old and we see that these our sins are of all sins the really harmless ones to own, nay that they give a charm to any character, and so our struggle with them dies away." That might quite plausibly have been an extract from a review of the Clayhanger novels. In fact, it is the fourth sentence of *The Making of Americans*.[42]

One writer whose reputation would probably be enhanced by a new interest in cumulative models of selfhood is Ford Madox Ford. Ford is known today primarily as the author of the elliptical *The Good Soldier*, as Modernism's most influential literary editor, at the *English Review* and the *Transatlantic Review*, and as one of its shrewdest theorists, whose contempt for arch medievalism is said to have saved Ezra Pound three years' work. His masterpiece, *Parade's End* (1924–8), although comparable to *Pilgrimage* or the earlier episodes of *Ulysses* in its rendering of interiority, has suffered a certain neglect: largely, I suspect, because the conception of identity it develops rests neither on difference-between nor on difference-within. The protagonist, Christopher Tietjens, statistician, soldier, and cuckold, is, above all, long-suffering: not for him the pain of abrupt recognition suffered by a Quentin Compson or a Nora Flood; not for him Miriam Henderson's long gladness.

The best way to demonstrate the idiosyncratic modernity of *Parade's End* is to compare it with Violet Hunt's *The Last Ditch* (1918), a novel from which, I believe, Ford learned a great deal. Hunt, Ford's quondam lover and companion, regarded herself as the model not only for Tietjens's sadistic wife, Sylvia, but for Valentine Wannop, the young suffragette he falls in love with in *Some Do Not* (1924) and settles down with in *The Last Post* (1928). She made her name as the author of ghost stories and somber studies of the New Woman. *The Last Ditch* has no pretensions to Modernism. Hunt's friend and best critic, May Sinclair, dismissed it out of hand, and it has since escaped critical comment altogether. The parallels with *Parade's End* suggest that it deserves better. Both novels are set immediately before and during the First World War, and are concerned with the destiny of a class (the landed gentry) to all appearances damaged beyond repair by slaughter in the trenches and democratization at home. This class finds itself, at parade's end, in the last ditch. And yet it endures and adapts.

The Last Ditch consists of letters written by a cultured aristocrat, the Lady Arles, and one of her daughters, Lady Venice St. Remy, later Lady Venice Bar, to another daughter, Mrs. Laura Quinney, who has married an American and now lives in Newport, Rhode Island. After a brief engagement to Percy Gregson, a Labour Member of Parliament and decent, God-fearing man of the "new order," Venice marries a very faintly indecent man of the old order, Sir Audely Bar, who has generally been regarded as her mother's property. Audely Bar is a model for Christopher Tietjens. He has Tietjens's impassive blondeness and cold blue stare. Like Tietjens, he is lazy and supine, but invariably competent when called upon to act, and possessing a wide range of knowledge. When Venice writes an article about "war babies" (she's in favor), Bar points out that there are no war babies to speak of; Tietjens disabuses Valentine's article-writing mother of the same notion. Both men are in their early forties; both volunteer for active service even though they are over age, and, when confined by injury or illness to administrative tasks, perform them with exemplary, fruitless dedication. Both end up with younger women.

The main difference between Bar and Tietjens is physical. Though lazy and supine, Bar is slim. His shapeliness makes him an English type, a regulation "good soldier." Tietjens, on the other hand, is decidedly stout, and his lack of shape is a continued affront to identities founded on social, moral, or sexual distinctions. When he and his brother Mark stand facing each other, Mark suggests carved wood, Christopher wheat sacks.[43] It is Mark who cracks up, while Christopher adapts. Christopher strikes Sylvia as physically and morally "lymphatic." "How, she said to herself, could she ever move, put emotion into, this lump!" (406) But the shapelessness is not a dispersal, a proliferation of differences-within. Tietjens does not slip around. He bulks and looms. He occupies space, and minds. He is described as "ballooning slowly" (261) from a doorway, or "lumping opposite" (294) a fellow officer at the mess room table, or "splurging heavily down" (342) on to his camp bed. Ford's book is more modern than Hunt's because it adapts ("ballooning," "lumping") or improvizes ("splurge") until it has found terms for an identity founded neither on difference-within nor on difference-between. So assertive is Tietjens's presence, so massively accumulated, so vivid in other people's minds, that he dominates the final volume of the sequence, *The Last Post*, without appearing in it at all. *The Last Post* introduces us to virtual Tietjens.

Both narratives subside rather than end. Audely will as usual will "fall soft," remarks Lady Arles, with his imminent marriage to Venice in mind; and he does. "It did not seem possible," Sylvia Tietjens reflects, "that Christopher should settle down into tranquil devotion to brother and mistress after the years of emotion she had given him." And *he* does, too. "It was as if a man should have jumped out of a frying pan into – a duckpond" (792). These soft landings, neither affirmation nor catastrophe, neither comedy nor tragedy, are something new in fiction.

Landings of any kind, soft or hard, presuppose a leap or a fall, such as the years of emotion Sylvia has given Tietjens: a discontinuity, a departure, a crisis. For a moment (a long moment, perhaps), everything is in the air. Hence, no doubt, the enduring symbolic potential of leaps and falls. But soft landings differ from hard in that they need not involve a change for the better or a change for the worse. They may leave things more or less as they were. Having dusted ourselves off, we go about our business. Soft landings partake neither of the meaningfulness we attribute to continuity nor of the meaningfulness we attribute to discontinuity. Tietjens's completeness emerges in that suspension at once of meaningful continuity and of meaningful discontinuity.

Soft landings are not a courtesy Conrad extends to Lord Jim, whose tumbles into water (from the bridge of the *Patna*) and mud (from Rajah Tunku Allang's compound) tend if anything to break him up. Jim violently resists such softness as there is in landings, and I would suggest, tentatively, that Conrad does a certain violence, by means of Marlow's fretting, to his representation of Jim's engulfment. "He reached and grabbed desperately with his hands, and only succeeded in gathering a horrible cold shiny heap of slime against his breast – up to his very chin. It seemed to him that he was burying himself alive, and then he struck out madly, scattering the mud with his fists."[44] Jim's gathering of slime is eerily enforced, or it may be eerily preempted, by Marlow's gathering of adjectives: not just horrible, not even just horrible and cold, but horrible, cold, and *shiny*. Marlow cannot allow the experience to be anything for Jim but a meaningful discontinuity, a death and resurrection. "It seemed to him that he was burying himself alive" (230). The madness would appear to be as much Marlow's as Jim's, as much Conrad's as Marlow's. Conrad, I think, a traditionalist at heart, found it hard to imagine a nonviolent rupture.

Ford is modern because he lets Tietjens land softly, rather than breaking him up. He was not alone in his forebearance. Nick Adams, pitched off the train on to the cinder track by a "lousy crut of a brakeman" (292) in "The Battler," halfway through *In Our Time*, manages to alight in a less bruising fashion in the concluding story, "Big Two-Hearted River" (340). Leopold

Bloom, about to enter his house via the area, allows his body to move freely in space by "separating himself from the railings and crouching in preparation for the impact of the fall." He, too, lands softly. Regaining "new stable equilibrium," he rises "uninjured though concussed by the impact" (799–80). Bernard's investment in the lives of his friends, Tietjens's presence even when absent, the thoughts Bloom might have had: these are as much the note of modernist fiction as Ursula Brangwen's rainbow and the equivocations of Miriam Henderson.

NOTES

1 Henry James, *Literary Criticism: Essays on Literature, American Writers, English Writers*, ed. Leon Edel and Mark Wilson (New York: Library of America, 1984), p. 101; Ford Madox Ford, *The English Novel from the Earliest Days to the Death of Joseph Conrad* (Manchester: Carcanet, 1983), p. 8.

2 T. S. Eliot, *Selected Prose*, ed. Frank Kermode (London: Faber and Faber, 1975), p. 177.

3 Ford Madox Ford, *Critical Writings*, ed. Frank MacShane (Lincoln: University of Nebraska Press, 1964), p. 41.

4 Ford Madox Ford, *The Good Soldier: A Tale of Passion* (Harmondsworth: Penguin, 1972), p. 20.

5 Michael Levenson, *Modernism and the Fate of Individuality: Character and Novelistic Form from Conrad to Woolf* (Cambridge: Cambridge University Press, 1991), pp. 111–12.

6 Philip Horne, "The Novel to 1914," in Martin Dodsworth, ed., *The Penguin History of Literature: The Twentieth Century* (Harmondsworth: Penguin, 1994), pp. 65–108, p. 72.

7 Peter Nicholls, *Modernisms: A Literary Guide* (London: Macmillan, 1995), pp. 172–3.

8 *Time and Western Man* (London: Chatto and Windus, 1927), pp. 52, 112–18.

9 Wyndham Lewis, *Tarr* (New York: Jubilee Books, 1973), pp. 37, 47.

10 Wyndham Lewis, *The Complete Wild Body*, ed. Bernard Lafourcade (Santa Barbara: Black Sparrow Press, 1982), p. 152.

11 Levenson, *Modernism*, p. 129.

12 Eliot, *Selected Prose*, p. 177.

13 Roger Fry, *Vision and Design*, revised edn (London: Chatto and Windus, 1927), p. 12.

14 James Joyce, *A Portrait of the Artist as a Young Man*, ed. Seamus Deane (Harmondsworth: Penguin, 1992), p. 226.

15 James Joyce, *Critical Writings*, ed. Ellsworth Mason and Richard Ellmann (London: Faber and Faber, 1959), p. 63.

16 D. H. Lawrence, *Selected Literary Criticism*, ed. Anthony Beal (London: Heinemann, 1956), p. 265.

17 D. H. Lawrence, *Letters*, ed. James T. Boulton *et al.*, 7 vols. (Cambridge: Cambridge University Press, 1979–93), vol. I, p. 526, and vol. II, pp. 182–3.

18 D. H. Lawrence, *The Rainbow*, ed. Mark Kinkead-Weekes (Cambridge: Cambridge University Press, 1989), p. 322.

19 Lawrence, *Letters*, vol. II, p. 431.

20 Frank Kermode, *The Sense of an Ending: Studies in the Theory of Fiction* (Oxford: Oxford University Press, 1966).

21 F. Scott Fitzgerald, *The Great Gatsby* (Harmondsworth: Penguin Books, 1950), p. 43.

22 Virginia Woolf, *To the Lighthouse*, ed. Margaret Drabble (Oxford: Oxford University Press, 1992), p. 18.

23 D. H. Lawrence, *Women in Love*, ed. David Farmer, Lindeth Vasey, and John Worthen (Cambridge: Cambridge University Press, 1987), p. 11.

24 David Bradshaw, "The Novel in the 1920s," in Dodsworth, ed., *Penguin History of Literature*, 195–224, p. 150.

25 Virginia Woolf, *Diaries*, ed. Anne Olivier Bell, 5 vols. (London: Hogarth Press, 1977–84), vol. III, p. 34.

26 James Joyce, *Ulysses* (London: Bodley Head, 1960), p. 65.

27 James Joyce, *Letters*, ed. Stuart Gilbert and Richard Ellmann, 3 vols. (London: Faber and Faber, 1957–66), vol. I, p. 129.

28 *Ibid.*

29 Eliot, *Selected Prose*, p. 48.

30 William Faulkner, *The Sound and the Fury* (London: Picador, 1989), p. 67.

31 *The Essential Hemingway* (London: Grafton Books, 1977), p. 316.

32 Virginia Woolf, *Essays*, ed. Andrew McNeillie, 4 vols. (London: Hogarth Press, 1986–94), vol. III, pp. 431, 33–4.

33 *The Gender of Modernism: A Critical Anthology*, ed. Bonnie Kime Scott (Bloomington: Indiana University Press, 1990), p. 443.

34 *Ibid.*, p. 310.

35 Dorothy Richardson, *Pilgrimage*, 4 vols. (London: Virago, 1979), vol. I, p. 56.

36 Derek Attridge, *Peculiar Language: Literature as Difference from the Renaissance to James Joyce* (London: Methuen, 1988), p. 172.

37 Levenson, *Modernism*, p. 181.

38 Thomas Mann, *Doctor Faustus*, trans. H. T. Lowe-Porter (London: Secker and Warburg, 1959), p. 134.

39 Karen Lawrence, *The Odyssey of Style in "Ulysses"* (Princeton: Princeton University Press, 1981).

40 Hugh Kenner, *Ulysses* (London: Allen and Unwin, 1980), p. 141.

41 Virginia Woolf, *The Waves*, ed. Kate Flint (Harmondsworth: Penguin, 1992), p. 212.

42 Gertrude Stein, *The Making of Americans* (New York: Something Else Press, 1966), p. 3.

43 Ford Madox Ford, *Parade's End* (Harmondsworth: Penguin, 1982), p. 199.

44 Joseph Conrad, *Lord Jim* (Harmondsworth: Penguin, 1989), p. 230.

4

JAMES LONGENBACH

Modern poetry

Not long ago, modern poetry – Yeats, Pound, Eliot, Stevens – seemed to occupy an enormous territory on the literary–historical map. But as the twentieth century comes to an end, the Modernism that once loomed so large now seems startlingly diminished. Beginning in the late 1950s, critics began to see through the smoke screen of New Critical antiromanticism, uncovering the important affiliations between romantic, Victorian, and modern poetics. Today, in the wake of pioneering work by Frank Kermode, Robert Langbaum, and especially Harold Bloom, Eliot not only seems indebted to Tennyson; his Modernism makes most sense when we understand it as part of a continuum beginning with the publication of the *Lyrical Ballads*.[1]

And if the historical integrity of Modernism has been encroached on by romanticism, an increasingly powerful postmodernism has exerted equal pressure from the opposite side. Certain modern poets – for Marjorie Perloff, Pound but not Stevens – are claimed as proto-postmodernists, leaving the impression that the remaining Modernists are a hapless, ineffectual lot.[2] And what makes this remapping of the moderns all the more complicated is that the various cartographers narrow the modernist field in different ways. For some, Stevens is in while Pound is out; for others, H.D. or Gwendolyn Brooks hold our attention at the expense of both Stevens and Pound.

What is most remarkable to me about Modernism's shrinking visibility, however, is that the historical record justifies it. In saying so, I do not mean to undermine the importance of modern poetry in the stories we tell about literary history. But in order to register that importance effectively, we need to recognize that as early as the 1930s, Modernism seemed to poets such as Randall Jarrell (born in 1914) to be a thing of the past – something to which they could respond but in which they could no longer participate. "Who could have believed that modernism would collapse so fast?" asked Jarrell in "The End of the Line" (1942), an essay that remains one of the subtlest accounts of Modernism we have. Even at this early date, modern poetry looked to Jarrell as it appears to us today – squeezed on the one side by its romantic precursors and on the other by its postmodern inheritors (Jarrell himself first used the word *postmodernist* in 1947). Flying in the face of his New Critical teachers (and foreshadowing the work of Bloom or Kermode), Jarrell insisted that modern poetry was nothing but what romantic poetry "wishes or finds it necessary" to become: "Romanticism holds in solution contradictory tendencies which, isolated and exaggerated in Modernism, look startlingly opposed both to each other and to the earlier stages of romanticism." Jarrell explained that any qualities associated with modern poetry – violence, disorganization, obscurity – are themselves romantic phenomena. And having uncovered this continuity, he wondered what modern poetry could possibly become in turn: "How can poems be written that are more violent, more disorganized, more obscure more – supply your own adjective – than those that have already been written?"[3]

Many other poets besides Jarrell were asking this question. Elizabeth Bishop was asking it in essays published around the same time; Robert Graves and Laura Riding's *Survey of Modernist Poetry* (1928) was written with a clear sense that Modernism could only be described retrospectively.[4] Edward Mendelson has recently characterized W. H. Auden as one of the first postmodern poets, and in saying so, he was preceded by Jarrell, who said as much in the early 1940s: "Auden at the beginning was oracular (obscure, original), bad at organization, neglectful of logic, full of astonishing or magical language, intent on his own world and his own forms; he has changed continuously toward organization, plainness, accessibility, objectivity, social responsibility."[5]

Jarrell was describing a transformation in Auden's career as it was happening. Having begun by taking Eliot and Yeats as his models, Auden turned in the late thirties to a poetry of more Augustan, civic virtues. A poet who began his career sounding like this

> Who stands, the crux left of the watershed,
> On the wet road between the chafing grass
> Below him sees dismantled washing-floors,
> Snatches of tramline running to a wood,
> An industry already comatose,
> Yet sparsely living.[6]

now wrote with a kind of talky, discursive ease that violated almost every modernist precept for good writing (as they were articulated, for example, in Ezra Pound's imagist "Don'ts": "Go in fear of abstractions" – "compose in the sequence of the musical phrase, not in sequence of a metronome").[7]

> We hoped; we waited for the day
> The State would wither clean away,
> Expecting the Millennium
> That theory promised us would come:
> It didn't. Specialists must try
> To detail all the reasons why;
> Meanwhile at least the layman knows
> That none are lost so soon as those
> Who overlook their crooked nose,
> That they grow small who imitate
> The mannerisms of the great,
> Afraid to be themselves, or ask
> What acts are proper to their task.   (175)

For Auden, this stylistic transformation was impelled by political as much as aesthetic considerations. The kind of poetry he wrote as a young man was inextricably linked with what came to seem to him the impossibly utopian political goals of the 1930s. At the end of the thirties, in the wake of the Nazi–Soviet pact, Auden could only conclude, as he put it in his elegy for Yeats, that "poetry makes nothing happen" (197). He meant, even more precisely, that the kind of poetry he himself had written made nothing happen – that poets had forgotten what acts are proper to their task. Auden realized that the modern poets, like Shelley before them, had thought of themselves as "unacknowledged legislators." And in the face of a world that had gone so tragically wrong, Auden could no longer sustain what now seemed to him such a romantic delusion. The result was a poetry of strategically circumscribed ambition; a poetry of civic rather than apocalyptic designs; a poetry that to Randall Jarrell seemed (at least for a moment – his opinion would change) to offer some hope for what poets might be able to do at the end of the line.

I have put the cart before the horse by discussing the first wave of postmodern reaction before discussing modern poetry itself. But it seems to me that the story of Jarrell's and Auden's negotiations with Modernism – their sense of its debt to romanticism, their sense of its quickly diminishing viability as the twentieth century wore on – highlights the very issues that ought to shape our reading of modern poetry today, more than half a century after Jarrell published "The End of the Line." In other words, Auden's and Jarrell's reaction to Modernism repeats a tension that was already embedded within modern poetry. The issue of poetic ambition – what the social effectiveness or responsibility of poetry might be – seems to me particularly crucial. In the story I tell, modern poetry grew from a sense (already highly developed by the Victorians) that the great claims made for poetry by the romantics were no longer viable. If Thomas Hardy, Marianne Moore, the imagist Pound, and the Yeats of *The Wind Among the Reeds* have anything in common, it is a desire to limit poetry's terrain. But few of the modern poets could remain content with this small world (Ezra Pound would go so far as to insist that poets ought to be considered *acknowledged legislators*). And by the time that Auden and Jarrell came of age, the great modern poems – *The Waste Land, The Tower, The Cantos* – seemed as ambitious, for better and for worse, as their romantic antecedents. Some modern poets (Hardy, Moore, Stevens) resisted the twentieth century's epic challenges, hanging on to a strategically circumscribed world, but all poets felt them.

These challenges are not particularly modernist, but they may be thought of as a distinguishing aspect of modernity, understood as a phenomenon beginning in the Enlightenment. Gazing upon this much larger field, a field of which modern literature is only a part, Jürgen Habermas has suggested that modernity is distinguished by the development of "autonomous spheres" of science, morality, and art. As art came to seem divorced from the culture at large, the work of the ivory tower rather than the community, artists paradoxically put greater pressure on art to perform substantive social work. This is the dilemma that the modern poets inherited – the dilemma that Pound tried to embrace and that Auden tried to reject. As Habermas points out, the dilemma often leads to a "false negation" of culture: everyday life "could hardly be saved from cultural impoverishment through breaking open a single cultural sphere – art."[8] (Or, as Kenneth Burke put it in 1931, speaking as someone who wanted to honor the social responsibilities of poetry, "one cannot advocate art as a cure for toothache without disclosing the superiority of dentistry."[9]) Growing out of romanticism, growing into postmodernism, this hope for the power of poetry was both the dream and the nightmare of the Modernist.

"If Galileo had said in verse that the world moved," said Hardy, "the Inquisition might have let him alone."[10] The novelist weathering the publication of *Jude the Obscure* turned to poetry precisely because nobody paid much attention to it, and far from lamenting poetry's marginal status, Hardy embraced it – harnessed it. As much as he admired Wordsworth and Shelley, Hardy felt that their ambitions for poetry were no longer plausible, given (among other things) the prominence of the novel. Hardy did not simply feel dwarfed by his romantic forebears; as James Richardson has suggested, he "felt even more strongly the necessity of his diminution, perceiving their styles, aspirations and modes of thought were, for him, not only impossible but also inappropriate."[11] The Pre-Raphaelite poet D. G.

Rossetti once complained about Shelley hatching "yearly universes," and, like Hardy, he embraced a "diminished" romanticism, focusing his poems on a tiny world of which he could be relatively certain. Spiritual consolation is hard to come by in such a world, and small objects, carefully detailed, become increasingly important. In the calculatedly antivisionary poem "The Woodspurge," Rossetti takes in the sublime grandeur of the natural world only to conclude one very particular thing: "The woodspurge has a cup of three."[12]

Similarly, in "Shelley's Skylark," Hardy explains that the bird that had flown "higher still and higher / From the earth" for Shelley had died for him:

> Maybe it rests in the loam I view,
> Maybe it throbs in a myrtle's green,
> Maybe it sleeps in the coming hue
> Of a grape on the slopes of yon island scene.[13]

Instead of rising to sing of a grander world, Hardy focuses on the concrete particulars of everyday life: the ground on which he walks, the myrtle's green, the ripening grapes. Spiritual presences have retreated from Hardy's landscape, and his world often seems ominously blank, untouched by divine or human agency: "a few leaves lay on the starving sod; / – They had fallen from an ash, and were gray" (1).

Yet Hardy was (to borrow the words of a late poem) someone who never expected much, and he consequently seems content with his diminished world. "The Darkling Thrush" recalls Keats's nightingale, but refuses any effort to merge the human soul with the bird's song: Hardy can imagine that "Some blessed Hope" *might* tremble through the bird's song, but he is in any case certain that it is something "whereof he knew / And I was unaware" (33). It is not pessimism but caution that makes contentment possible – just as it is for Robert Frost, the American poet who published his first important poems in England, sharing Hardy's fruitfully skeptical relationship to the romantic landscape. In "Come In," Frost stands at the edge of the woods (always a tempting threshold for him), and hears the thrush's song; but he refuses not only the invitation but the effort to hear the song as invitation: "I would not come in. / I meant not even if asked, / And I hadn't been."[14]

Frost's refusals of the pathetic fallacy are even craftier than Hardy's. In "The Need of Being Versed in Country Things" he plays on the word "verse" when he concludes that "One had to be versed in country things / Not to believe the phoebes wept" for human loss (242). Frost believed that we need to learn how to live in metaphor, and in poems like "Once by the Pacific" he tests our ability to do so: gazing at a frightening storm, Frost says that it looks *as if* the "shore was lucky in being backed by cliff" – *as if* "a night of dark intent / Was coming, and not only a night, an age" (250). An apocalyptic threat is not essential to the landscape but is imposed on it through metaphor. This skepticism is Frost's way of resisting easy pessimism. When he gazes into a well in "For Once, Then, Something," repositioning his head so that he sees neither the reflection of the clouds nor of his face, he cannot be certain of what he finally sees: "Truth? A pebble of quartz? For once, then, something" (225). That something – the one, particular thing he sees, however insignificant – is all the consolation he requires. The very title of this poem, says Richard Poirier in *Poetry and Pragmatism*, "indicates a willingness to celebrate not a gift of meaning but only an inconclusive promise of it."[15]

Rossetti's woodspurge, Hardy's grapes, Frost's something: in their different ways these poets focused on a world of little things, eschewing epic ambition and spiritual consolation. And in the relationship to their romantic forebears, these poets may be aligned with modern writers with whom they might otherwise seem to have little in common: the symbolist Yeats of *The Wind Among the Reeds* (1899), the imagist Pound of *Lustra* (1916), the war poetry of Wilfred Owen, and even the studiously modest poems of the Georgians (among whom Edward Thomas, close friend of Robert Frost, stands prominently). Early in his career, Yeats set out to write (as he put it in "The Autumn of the Body") "a poetry of essences, separated one from another in little and intense poems."[16] Yeats never forsook the ambition to plumb the world beyond (and neither did Pound), but he believed that the ambition had to be focused not in long poems but in self-contained, one-sentence poems like "The Fish."

> Although you hide in the ebb and flow
> Of the pale tide when the moon has set,
> The people of coming days will know
> About the casting out of my net,
> And how you have leaped times out of mind
> Over the little silver cords,
> And think that you were hard and unkind,
> And blame you with many bitter words.[17]

Yeats would remake his style over and over again throughout his career, but his pristine syntax, fulfilling the formal demands of the poem effortlessly, would remain constant. It has often been said that in the second decade of the twentieth century, Ezra Pound "modernized" Yeats's style, toughening his attitude and roughening his diction. (This story was determined at least in part by a New Critical prejudice against the nine-teenth century: having begun his career as an accomplished Victorian, Yeats supposedly needed to be rerouted into the modern world.) But it now seems clear that Yeats was far more influential in determining the direction of Pound's career. Pound began as a deep admirer of Browning and Yeats, and one way to understand his development of the imagist aesthetic is to see that he purged himself of Browning's gregariousness by embracing Yeats's purity of syntax and diction. In some ways, Pound's imagist program (the influential "Don'ts") seems poised against certain aspects of literary symbolism; but the two lines by Robert Burns that Yeats presents as "perfectly symbolical" in "The Symbolism of Poetry"

> The white moon is setting behind the white wave,
> And Time is setting with me, O![18]

employ a pristine diction that prefigures "In a Station of the Metro," the most famous of Pound's imagist poems.

> The apparition of these faces in the crowd;
> Petals on a wet, black bough.[19]

Neither do they seem unrelated to "Hermes of the Ways," the first poem to be published above the name *H.D., "Imagiste."*

> Hermes, Hermes,
> the great sea foamed,
> gnashed its teeth about me;
> but you have waited,
> where sea-grass tangles with
> shore-grass.[20]

Many other influences came together to produce Imagism, but whatever else they are, the poems are the work of diminished romantics – poets who needed to condense the universe of poetry into a space so small that it threatened to seem almost precious (as do many of the poems in *The Wind Among the Reeds*). But for H.D., that preciousness became a kind of weapon. "Large epic pictures bored her," she wrote in her novella *Paint It Today.* "She wanted the songs that cut like a swallow wing the high, untainted ether, not the tragic legions of set lines that fell like black armies with terrific force."[21] Erected during the First World War, when militarism and masculinity seemed to go hand in hand, H.D.'s lyric world was a strategic rejection of an epic imperative. Marianne Moore once admitted that H.D.'s work seemed "non-public and "feminine." But she went on to explain (in terms that elucidate her own work as well) that there is "a connection between weapons and beauty": "Cowardice and beauty are at swords' points and in H.D.'s work, . . . we have heroics which do not confuse transcendence with domination."[22]

The imagist Pound, in contrast, was surely the most self-consciously ambitious poet since Milton: he decided in his youth that he would write the epic of the West (as he once boasted) and, like Milton, he prepared himself assiduously for the task. The most influential aspect of Imagism was its scrupulous devotion to the craft of poetry; Pound never abandoned those values. But almost from the start, he was impatient with Imagism's studiously miniature world: "I am often asked whether there can be a long imagiste or vorticist poem," he wrote in 1914; at this time and Pound was already at work on *The Cantos*, the long poem that would preoccupy him nearly until his death in 1972.[23]

But how can a diminished aesthetic – one that eschews discursive breadth for obsessive precision, radical condensation, minute objects – produce a long poem? To approach an answer to this question, we should first notice that it is difficult to maintain a scrupulously diminished aesthetic. In some ways, Rossetti seems at the end of "The Woodspurge" to reject all visionary knowledge for the material world; yet the woodspurge's "cup of three" cannot help but evoke Christian iconography. Similarly, Hardy could never stop entertaining the possibility of a spiritually animated landscape, no matter how utterly he faced the earth's stark otherness. This tension produces the awkward final stanzas of "Shelley's Skylark," in which Hardy retreats from his catalog of the particular world, the skylark's resting place, commanding the "faeries" to "find / That tiny pinch of priceless dust, / And bring a casket silver-lined" to be its tomb (15). More often, however, this tension produces Hardy's greatest poems, poems in which we are assured that the landscape is devoid of spiritual presences at the same time that we are tempted, if only by metaphor, to search for those presences. In "The Voice," one of the "Poems of 1912–13" (a group of elegies for his first wife) Hardy cannot be sure if he hears a ghost's voice calling him or "only the breeze, in its listlessness / Travelling across the wet mead to me here, / You being ever dissolved to wan wistlessness." And the poem ends with the question undecided (and with Hardy's brilliantly irregular rhythms reinforcing the poem's sense of inconclusiveness).

> Thus I; faltering forward,
> Leaves around me falling,
> Wind oozing thin through the thorn from norward
> And the woman calling. (87)

But if it is relatively easy to see how spiritual presences reenter Hardy's diminished aesthetic, it is more crucial to see that those presences are always animating Pound's imagist poems. In his prose statements about Imagism (which have probably been more influential than the poems themselves), Pound usually makes the poetry sound stubbornly materialistic: "Direct treatment of the 'thing.'"[24] This was the kind of advice Pound wanted to give other writers, but as far as Pound himself was concerned, Imagism was an often visionary enterprise. In his less programmatic statements, such as the prose poem "Ikon" (published in 1914 in a spiritualist journal called the *Cerebralist*), Pound's justification of Imagism sounds much like the symbolist Yeats: "It is in art the highest business to create the beautiful image . . . . And if – as some say, the soul survives the body; if our consciousness is not an intermittent melody of strings that relapse between whiles into silence, then more than ever should we put forth the images of beauty" (251). After reading these sentences, one can not help but feel that "apparition" is the crucial word in "In a Station of the Metro." After reading H.D.'s "Notes on Thought and Vision" (1919), one can not help but feel that her invocations of the gods are something more than literary: "you will come, / you will answer our taut hearts, / you will break the lie of men's thoughts, / and cherish and shelter us."[25]

Even with this visionary undercurrent, however, Imagism quickly became a dead end for Pound. Describing Yeats's development, Paul de Man argues that *The Wind Among the Reeds* was a dead end because the book's language became completely self-referential; the words seemed only to invoke other words, other associations, having relinquished their referential power.[26] Yeats would go on, in the first decade of the twentieth century, to attempt to recapture that power: the line "Colder and dumber and deafer than a fish" (98) *seems* – a crucial word, since all poetic language is conventional, none of it closer to the heart or to the world than the other – to invoke the physical world more successfully than "The Fish." This is exactly what the imagist Pound needed to learn, for his imagist aesthetic would not allow him to speak meaningfully of contemporary culture.

> Over fair meadows,
> Over the cool face of that field,
> Unstill, ever moving,
> Hosts of an ancient people,
> The silent cortège. (110)

These are the final lines of "The Coming of War: Actaeon," the first poem that Pound published about the Great War (which began on 4 August 1914). To say that the poem is "about" the war hardly seems adequate, however, since imagist notions of poetic decorum seem to prevent Pound from making the kind of statement he wants to make. His prose of the period overflows with social commentary; Pound would subsequently credit the world war with instigating all of his later economic and political interests. But his poetry could not yet contain those interests. In "1915: February," a revealing poem that Pound himself never published, we can see Pound grappling with this dilemma. The poem builds to a violent rant against the war, suggesting that it has nothing to do with poets: "This war is not our war, / Neither side is on our side: / A vicious mediaevalism, / A belly-fat commerce." Yeats said basically the same thing – much more calmly – in "On Being Asked for a War Poem" (originally entitled "A Reason for Keeping Silent"), but Yeats was not struggling to develop an idiom capable of addressing public events. Pound's poem retreats completely from its own violent rhetoric, ending with a perfect imagist couplet – as if to suggest that he would continue writing in this way if only he could.

> We have about us only the unseen country road,
> The unseen twigs, breaking their tips with blossom.   (254)

These lines could only have been written by Pound, but Pound's wartime predicament is paradigmatic: a generation of studiously diminished lyric poets was confronted with an epic subject, one that seemed to cry out for the power and scope of the kind of poetry that Wordsworth wrote in the wake of the French Revolution. The results were *The Cantos*, *The Waste Land*, *Spring and All*, *Observations*, and *The Tower*: all the most ambitious work of the modern poets, coming in the twenties, was at least in part the result of the social and aesthetic challenge of the war. And as H.D.'s distaste for wartime "epic" suggests, the poets were all, to varying degrees, suspicious of their own achievement.

A comparison with Wordsworth is inevitable, for modern poetry's response to the First World War plays out a drama that was enacted by romantic poetry's response to the French Revolution. As the utopian dreams inspired by the Revolution were demolished by the Reign of Terror, Wordsworth (like many of his contemporaries) lost faith in the power of political action to effect social change; the result was (as M. H. Abrams and Jerome McGann have demonstrated in different ways) that poets looked to poetry to carry the burden of spiritual and cultural enlightenment.[27] As Habermas would say, art was called upon to perform work for which it is not particularly well-suited.

Since Wordsworth, major public events have provoked poetry's "internalization" of practical politics time and time again. We can see Melville, in the wake of the American Civil War, feeling that literature must perform what political culture as such could not. And we can see that after the death of Charles Stewart Parnell (the parliamentary leader who seemed nearly to make Irish home rule a reality), Yeats felt that poetry had no choice but to accomplish the work that liberal politics had failed to achieve: "The fall of Parnell had freed imagination from practical politics, from agrarian grievance and political enmity, and turned it to imaginative nationalism, to Gaelic, to the ancient stories, and at last to lyrical poetry and to drama."[28] In a sense, all Romantic poems are (to borrow the title of Yeats's 1913 pamphlet) poems written in discouragement.

I have suggested that *The Wind Among the Reeds* was an aesthetic dead end, but Yeats's style had to change (like Pound's) because he felt compelled to grapple more openly with contemporary events. As an Irish poet, Yeats felt this imperative well before his American and English contemporaries were jolted out of a diminished aesthetic by the war. The first decade of the twentieth century was a difficult period for Yeats. In 1903 Maud Gonne, his lifelong obsession, married John MacBride (whom Yeats would later call a "drunken, vainglorious lout" [181]). In 1904 Yeats founded the Abbey Theatre, and he would spend much of the following decade preoccupied with what he would later denounce as "Theatre business, management of men" (93). He worried that he had lost his "lyric faculty."[29] And when his *Collected Works* was published in 1908, the rumor was that Yeats was finished.

History conspired to keep Yeats going. When he reprinted his *Poems Written in Discouragement* in *Responsibilities* (1914), Yeats added a note explaining that three public controversies had stirred his imagination: the fall of Parnell, the riots over John Synge's *Playboy of the Western World*, and Dublin's refusal of Hugh Lane's gift of his important art collection. These events deepened Yeats's discouragement with "practical politics," but they provoked more ambitious poems, poems no longer content to traffic in discrete essences. In "To a Wealthy Man," Yeats spoke out sternly against the notion that Hugh Lane's paintings should not be supported unless the people wanted them: "What cared Duke Ercole, that bid / His mummers to the market-place, / What th' onion-sellers thought or did?" In "September 1913," surveying failed social policy and self-serving mercantilism, Yeats could only conclude that "Romantic Ireland's dead and gone." "You had enough of sorrow before death," he told the ghost of Parnell in "To a Shade," "Away, away! You are safer in the tomb" (107, 108, 110).

The more expansive and aggressive music of *Responsibilities* would become an important example to younger poets, who would soon grapple with the social discouragement that grew throughout World War I (both Pound and H.D. wrote stirring reviews of the volume).[30] Yeats himself was, at least at first, studiously tight-lipped about what seemed to him England's war, not Ireland's. But in the midst of the war, the Easter Rebellion of 1916 exploded every conclusion Yeats had come to about his fellow countrymen: romantic Ireland, in all its recklessness, seemed reborn – even in John MacBride (one of the organizers of the rebellion who was summarily executed).

> Was it needless death after all?
> For England may keep faith
> For all that is done and said.
> We know their dream; enough
> To know they dreamed and are dead;
> And what if excess of love
> Bewildered them till they died?
> I write it out in a verse –
> MacDonagh and MacBride
> And Connolly and Pearse
> Now and in time to be,
> Wherever green is worn,
> Are changed, changed utterly:
> A terrible beauty is born.   (181–2)

Having taken on this public voice, Yeats did not relinquish a more intimate lyric voice (the luminously quiet "Wild Swan's at Coole," with its "All's changed" [131], offers the private version of "Easter 1916"). And he would go on, in *The Wild Swans at Coole* (1919), *Michael Robartes and the Dancer* (1921), and *The Tower* (1928), to write poems of extraordinary power, both public and private. The impetus behind these poems was, in part, Yeats's marriage to Georgie Hyde-Lees and their subsequent communications (through automatic writing) with the spirit world. But the pressure of the worsening war, especially when it was reinforced by the Anglo-Irish war in 1919, was inescapable. Poems such as "The Second Coming" have seemed to several generations of readers to be completely idiosyncratic, bound up with Yeats's occult vision of the afterlife, and at the same time an expression of horror in which an entire culture could participate.

> The darkness drops again; but now I know
> That twenty centuries of stony sleep
> Were vexed to nightmare by a rocking cradle,
> And what rough beast, its hour come round at last,
> Slouches towards Bethlehem to be born?   (187)

To a reader versed in Robert Frost, however, these lines might also seem suspiciously uncritical of their own apocalyptic metaphors: has Yeats, following the pattern Wordsworth established, internalized public events so completely that he eschews any responsibility for them? Yeats himself wondered the same thing. "A Prayer for my Daughter" follows "The Second Coming" in *Michael Robartes and the Dancer*, and the apocalyptic cradle is suddenly domesticated: "Under this cradle-hood and coverlid / My child sleeps on." Yeats wonders here if his own fury has been determined less by unmanageable events than by "the great gloom that is in my mind" (188).

Yeats did write several poems more explicitly engaging the war after the son of his close friend Lady Gregory was killed in Italy. But Yeats himself was notoriously unsympathetic to the enormous amount of poetry that the war provoked; he defended his exclusion of Wilfred Owen's popular poems from *The Oxford Book of Modern Verse* by maintaining that "passive suffering is not a theme for poetry."[31] Another way to explain Yeats's lack of sympathy would be to say that the most successful war poetry (especially Owen's) continued to be written out of a studiously diminished aesthetic, while Yeats himself had been prodded on to much more aggressively ambitious poems, hatching universes as brilliantly as Shelley.

In his study of the modern elegy, Jahan Ramazani shows how Owen made the elegy "a more disconsolate and discordant genre – a genre less contaminated by its likeness to the compensatory discourse of patriotic propaganda."[32] Owen did this partly by following Hardy's example; and though Owen had no connection with the imagist movement, his poems reinforce T. E. Hulme's dictum that modern poetry "no longer deals with heroic action" but with "momentary phases in the poet's mind."[33] In "Dulce Et Decorum Est" Owen juxtaposes Horace's well-known wisdom ("it is sweet and fitting to die for the fatherland") with a horrifying account of a soldier being gassed: "Dim, through the misty panes and thick green light, / As under a green sea, I saw him drowning."[34] Heroism (or what Yeats might have called active suffering) can enter Owen's poems only through irony.

Owen's turn on Shelley's "Adonais" in "A Terre" is even more revealing of his "diminished" stance than his turn on Horace.

> "I shall be one with nature, herb, and stone,"
> Shelley would tell me. Shelley would be stunned:
> The dullest Tommy hugs that fancy now.
> "Pushing up daisies" is their creed, you know.   (65)

Considering the pantheistic consolation offered in "Adonais," Owen responds as Hardy did to Shelley's skylark, refusing to accept anything more than the vagaries of earthly experience. And in poems like "Anthem for a Doomed Youth," Owen's refusal to animate the natural world is as stern as Hardy's or Frost's: "What passing-bells for these who die as cattle? / Only the monstrous anger of the guns" (44). Refusing the consolations of the pathetic fallacy in the face of mass death, Owen reanimates the engines of destruction instead: guns are more human than nature.

Owen's are the poems of a combatant; he was killed in France in 1918. Wallace Stevens, who for most of his life worked as an insurance executive in Hartford, Connecticut, existed as far from action as could be; yet his first publications were war poems, and, as in Own's poems, nothing in the natural world commemorates the unprecedented slaughter of the war:

> Death is absolute and without memorial,
> As in a season of autumn,
> When the wind stops,
>
> When the wind stops and, over the heavens,
> The clouds go, nevertheless,
> In their direction.[35]

Harold Bloom sees in "The Death of a Soldier" (first published in 1918 as part of a sequence, inspired by the letters of a French soldier, called "Lettres d'un Soldat") the "emergence of the poet's most characteristic voice."[36] And it is true that, throughout his career, Stevens returns almost obsessively to a vision of the world that is untouched by human feeling, a world in which the otherness of the world grows not only stark but oddly compelling. In "The Snow Man" (collected along with "The Death of the Soldier" in *Harmonium*) Stevens emphasizes the difficulty of achieving this vision, insisting that one "must have a mind of winter" if one is

> not to think
> Of any misery in the sound of the wind,
> In the sound of a few leaves,
>
> Which is the sound of the land
> Full of the same wind
> That is blowing the same bare place
>
> For the listener, who listens in the snow,
> And, nothing himself, beholds
> Nothing that is not there and the nothing that is.   (10)

Stevens is surely relying on a literary topos here; Robert Frost reveals a similar interest in the wintery blankness of the natural world in poems like "Desert Places": "The woods around it have it – it is theirs. / All animals are smothered in their lairs. / I am too absent-spirited to count; / The loneliness includes me unawares" (296). But it is important to register the fact that Stevens's "most characteristic voice" first came to him when he attempted, like Owen, to account for a kind of death which made any elegiac consolation seem thin. Stevens is well known as a poet who built an entire world from words, and he partly is such a poet: his poems often seem to weave one giant "endlessly elaborating poem" (as he put it in "An Ordinary Evening in New Haven" [486]). But Stevens is also a poet who, like his contemporaries, was pushed into song in the aftermath of the social debacles of his time. It is especially revealing that, after publishing *Harmonium* in 1923, Stevens did not write poems again until a decade later, when the Great Depression prodded him to write some of the most intelligent poems we have about the strengths and limitations of poetry in a time of social strife.

"The Snow Man," characteristic as it is, reveals only half of Stevens's sensibility. For as often as Stevens wrote about the pressure of reality on the vacant mind, he wrote about imagination exerting an equal pressure on the recalcitrant world. He thought of "Tea at the Palaz of Hoon" as a companion to "The Snow Man":

> I was the world in which I walked, and what I saw
> Or heard or felt came not but from myself;
> And there I found myself more truly and more strange.   (65)

Between these two extremes (he often spoke of them, somewhat blandly, as reality and imagination) Stevens wove his endless elaborations, first emphasizing the mind's ability to fabricate metaphors or structures of belief and then cautioning us to remember that those structures will always inevitably collapse in the face of events that even our most cherished beliefs cannot encompass. Stasis and enclosure are what Stevens fears most; change and uncertainty are his highest values.

In "Esthétique du Mal" (1944) Stevens confessed that the "death of Satan was a tragedy / For the imagination." This is the diminished poet's lament: there are no more universes to be hatched. But Stevens was also adamant that this tragedy was also "the imagination's new beginning": we require "another chant" to replace the outmoded fictions in which we no longer believe (319–20). In many ways the title of the long poem *Notes toward a Supreme Fiction* (1942) may stand for Stevens's poetry at large: throughout his career (though less systematically at the beginning of it) he was attempting to satisfy the will-to-believe in the midst of a skeptical age. The supreme fiction was, for Stevens, something to which we assent while knowing it to be untrue; like William James, the American pragmatist philosopher, Stevens was interested in the usefulness of the stories we tell ourselves rather than their singular truth. Various poems, from the early "Sunday Morning" to the late "To an Old Philosopher in Rome," seem to offer a fiction in which we might believe. But the only thing of which we can be certain in Stevens is that the fiction must change – the palaz of Hoon giving way to the snowman – since the world for which the fiction accounts is changing too. "It can never be satisfied, the mind, never," insisted Stevens (247), because he was scrupulously aware of the imperatives of an historical world that will not allow us to languish in satisfaction.

It was Stevens's cautiousness, his inability to believe anything for certain or for long, that made him seem evasive to certain readers. Taken out of context, his response to a 1939 *Partisan Review* questionnaire ("A war is a military state of affairs, not a literary one") might suggest that Stevens was not interested in military affairs.[37] On the contrary, it was precisely Stevens's interest in such affairs that made him uneasy with assertions of poetry's social clout. Although Stevens eventually wrote some of the most ambitious poems of the century, he rarely surrendered the diminished poet's carefully circumscribed sense of his own knowledge and power. Neither did Marianne Moore, who (like Stevens) was for a long time considered a lesser poet than Pound, Eliot, or Yeats because her poems did not seem to engage the crises of the modern world. But what may first appear to be a refusal to engage is really something far more intelligent, far more cognizant of the difficulties that poets since Wordsworth have faced whenever they have asserted poetry's power.

Stevens was well aware, embracing a diminished aesthetic during the First World War, that he was also embracing an aesthetic that his literary culture thought of as feminine; Virginia Woolf once explained that the feminine sensibility, as it is commonly conceived, "ranged among almost unknown or unrecorded things; it lighted on small things and showed that perhaps they were not small after all."[38] Stevens was often threatened by the gendered implications of diminishment, especially at a time when even his own sister was working for the Red Cross in the battlefields of France. Writing as a woman, Marianne Moore had an even more overdetermined relationship to an aesthetic that valued little things over epic ambitions. Sandra Gilbert has argued (much as Moore herself said of H.D.) that Moore became a "female female impersonator": by translating "the 'handicap' of 'femininity' into an aesthetic advantage," she deployed femininity "as both defense and offense – defense against trivialization, offense against masculinism."[39] And throughout Moore's early poems, as in H.D.'s, masculinism is often linked with wartime aggression and epic ambition.

The vestibule to experience is not to
    be exalted into epic grandeur. These men are going
To their work with this idea, advancing like a school of fish through

still water – waiting to change the course or dismiss
    the idea of movement, till forced to. The words of the Greeks
ring in our ears, but they are vain in comparison with a sight like this.[40]

Throughout this poem – "Reinforcements" – Moore plays with the implications of her title, suggesting that the language of an eagerly ambitious poetry might, like additional troops, become a "reinforcement" of war. The words of Homer ring in our ears; we see a vast war and feel that poets ought to exalt it with epic grandeur – offer major statements about it. Speaking as a self-consciously marginal poet in "Phases," his 1914 sequence of war poems, Stevens made a similar point: "The crisp, sonorous epics / Mongered after every scene."[41] But Moore harnessed the power of her feminized position. Her response to the war was to write self-consciously little poems rather than ambitious (and, for Moore, masculine) poems that answer an epic challenge.

Throughout her long career, Moore would continue to embrace humility and understatement as her highest values, transforming them into weapons more potent than aggression. But Moore was a notorious reviser and winnower of her own work, and in her early poems, collected in *Poems* (1921) and *Observations* (1924), the ironic edge of her position seems more pronounced. This change in her work was partly temperamental, but it was also due to the fact that these early poems were written during a time when the First World War gave a great deal of cultural weight to Moore's analysis of masculine aggression. In "Sojourn in the Whale" (published soon after the Easter Rebellion) Moore presents Ireland as an example of the "feminine temperament" that, underestimated by men, merely "seeks its own level." Moore's rejoinder is stern: "'Water is motion is far / from level.' You have seen it, when obstacles happened to bar / the path, rise automatically."[42] Moore seems to be describing herself when she praises "feigned inconsequence" at the end of "In This Age of Hard Trying": in contrast to those who do "not venture the / profession of humility," who speak the "uncompanionable drawl / of certitude," there is one whose

                    by-
        play was more terrible in its effectiveness
            than the fiercest frontal attack.
            The staff, the bag, the feigned inconsequence
        of manner, best bespeak that weapon, self-protectiveness.   (34)

Moore feigned inconsequence for strategic purposes, much as Hardy embraced inconsequence in poetry in order to express more freely the sentiments for which, as a novelist, he was condemned. But Moore's purposes were of course different from Hardy's, as H.D. recognized in her essay of 1916 on Moore's poems: however "frail" they might appear, the poems are intended to "endure longer, far longer than . . . the world of shrapnel and machine-guns in which we live."[43]

Moore's formally distinctive poems (which, depending on one's point of view, can seem either archly fastidious or recklessly arbitrary) are often organized syllabically; they frequently incorporate quotations from a wide variety of sources, challenging the usual decorum of poetic language ("nor is it valid / to discriminate against 'business documents and / school-books,'" she says in "Poetry" [267]). Inclusiveness, or what Moore calls, quoting Henry James, "accessibility to experience" (54) is the hallmark of her poetry, both formally and thematically. Moore would never write the kind of inclusive long poem that her male contemporaries all published in the 1920s. But her *Observations* ought to stand beside *Hugh Selwyn Mauberley, The Waste Land, Harmonium, Spring and All,* and *The Tower* as a postwar book that ventures a major statement and simultaneously questions the ways in which major statements are made. "She is not, she seems to suggest, writing anything so grand as a poem," says Bonnie Costello of Moore.[44] *Observations* is a collection of short poems ("The Octopus" and the astonishing "Marriage" are the longest) that seems to diffuse any sense of a culminating achievement; yet Moore indexed the volume, suggesting that a different kind of coherence, more metonymic, more tenuous, underlies its strategically circumscribed ambitions.

Pound's *Hugh Selwyn Mauberley* (1920), a long poem made by juxtaposing shorter poems and fragments, certainly challenges conventional notions of poetic wholeness and closure. But inasmuch as Pound's effort to write a long poem was coterminous with his effort to write a poem addressing the social catastrophe of the war, *Mauberley* adopts the kind of rhetoric Moore wanted to avoid in "Reinforcements":

> There died a myriad,
> And of the best, among them,
> For an old bitch gone in the teeth,
> For a botched civilization. (188)

Hugh Selwyn Mauberley is at times a moving elegy for the world of artistic and social possibility that the war seemed to obliterate; Pound looks back with a delicate combination of affection and irony at earlier vanguard movements in the arts (especially the Pre-Raphaelites and the Rhymers'

Club, with which Yeats was associated in the 1890s), noting their inadequacies but excoriating the culture that rejected their energies. But *Mauberley* also offers glimpses of the obsessions with crack-pot economics and Jewish financiers that would more often mar Pound's later work: "usury age-old and age-thick / and liars in public places" (188).

Devoting the rest of his life to *The Cantos*, Pound became the most exaggeratedly romantic poet of his generation. *The Cantos* is a poem written out of an aesthetic that stresses condensation, concrete expression, and lyric intensity but which attempts simultaneously to forge a mythopoeic "multiverse" as expansive and idiosyncratic as Blake's. Added to this irreconcilable pair of ambitions is Pound's desire to be the acknowledged legislator of the world. "All values ultimately come from our judicial sentences," he said in 1922. "This arrogance is not mine but Shelley's, and it is absolutely true."[45] But while Shelley thought of the poet as the servant of humanity, Pound thought of himself as an inflated version of the Confucius to whom princes came for schooling or the Flaubert who said that his *Education Sentimentale* would have prevented the Franco-Prussian War. Unlike Moore or Stevens, who in different ways stressed the limitations of the poet's social function, Pound saw few limits to his responsibilities. And with this kind of pressure on every line, *The Cantos* was probably doomed to rhetorical excess and increasing fragmentation: "Usura slayeth the child in the womb / It stayeth the young man's courting." Paradoxically, yet understandably, the most persuasive moments in the poem occur at those points (such as the *Pisan Cantos*, written while Pound was incarcerated at the end of World War II, waiting to be charged with treason) when Pound accepts his diminished possibilities and remembers his place in a very small world.

> When the mind swings by a grass-blade
> an ant's forefoot shall save you.
> the clover leaf smells and tastes as its flower.[46]

In retrospect, *Hugh Selwyn Mauberley* seems like a watershed not only in Pound's career but in modern poetry at large. Pound solved the problem of writing a long poem for himself, and, more importantly, he provided an example for his contemporaries. *The Waste Land* would have been inconceivable without the precedent of *Mauberley*, and the long poems of Williams and Stevens (with the exception of "The Comedian as the Letter C") would also be constructed through the juxtaposition of discrete poetic moments. Of course Tennyson did much the same thing in *In Memoriam*; but the technique needed to be reinvented for the world after World War I.

Mauberley was itself the product of a moment of particularly close collaboration between Pound and Eliot. Like most of the poems in Eliot's *Ara Vos Prec* (1920), *Mauberley* was written in crisply rhymed quatrains: working side by side, Pound and Eliot decided that the imagist movement had gone too far and that a "counter-current" to free verse needed to be established.[47] This decision was provoked in part by aesthetic concerns, but it was also determined by Pound's inability to remain content with Imagism's implicitly feminized aesthetic – especially after Amy Lowell took a more active role in the movement. At the particular time at which *Mauberley* was written, Pound could offer a major (which is to say, in some sense, manly) statement in poetry only by adopting a poetic decorum resolutely at odds with Imagism.

While Eliot was writing his poems in quatrains, he was also writing the essays that would be collected in *The Sacred Wood* (1920), perhaps the most influential volume of literary criticism published in the century. In "Tradition and the Individual Talent," Eliot advocated a poetry that was "impersonal" and profoundly historical, written out of a self-conscious awareness of "the whole of the literature of Europe from Homer."[48] Poems such as "Whispers of Immortality" were the result of such thinking.

> Donne, I suppose, was such another,
> Who found no substitute for sense,
> To seize and clutch and penetrate;
> Expert beyond experience,
>
> He knew the anguish of the marrow
> The ague of the skeleton;
> No contact possible to flesh
> Allayed the fever of the bone.[49]

Honoring John Donne and implicitly depreciating Wordsworth (by recalling "Intimations of Immortality"), these lines seem designed both to discuss and embody Eliot's notion of the "dissociation of sensibility," which he described in his 1921 essay on metaphysical poetry: "When a poet's mind is perfectly equipped for its work, it is constantly amalgamating disparate experience; the ordinary man's experience is chaotic, irregular, fragmentary." This sentence makes the dissociation of intellect and emotion seem like a problem that could arise at any moment, but Eliot also maintained that the dissociation was a specifically historical phenomenon – "something which happened to the mind of England between the time of Donne" and the time of Tennyson.[50]

Eliot's early criticism is interestingly (perhaps even productively) paradoxical, since on the one hand he insists on a kind of scrupulous formalism, criticizing Matthew Arnold for his social concerns; but on the other hand, Eliot's critical formulations are predicated on historical and political agendas, however implicitly. It is as if Eliot wants simultaneously to say that his concern is *only* with poetry but not *merely* with poetry: discussing Donne, he is discussing the fate of Western culture. This is another version of the diminished poet's dilemma: Eliot wants to assert the kind of powers Shelley claimed for poetry without sounding like Shelley. And this dilemma would ultimately help to determine the shape of *The Waste Land*, a poem that has never been read comfortably as *both* a lyric poet's personal lament *and* a sage's pronouncement on the fate of post-war Europe.

When Pound met Eliot in 1914, one month after the war began, he exclaimed that Eliot had actually "modernized himself *on his own*."[51] Pound was talking about the diction, structure, and sensibility of "The Love Song of J. Alfred Prufrock"

> Let us go then, you and I,
> When the evening is spread out against the sky
> Like a patient etherised upon a table   (3)

but Eliot's modernity was nurtured not in prewar London but at Harvard University, where (like Stevens and Frost) Eliot studied in the philosophy department of William James and Josiah Royce. Like Stevens and Frost, Eliot absorbed from his teachers a stringent sense of the contingency of human values: we must think of the world not as "ready made," insists Eliot in his Ph.D. dissertation (written several years after "Prufrock"), but "as constructed, or constructing itself."[52] And when Eliot says in "The Metaphysical Poets" that the poet's mind is "always forming new wholes," he is aware that the mind has no choice but to do so; wholeness and order are not inherent in the world we experience – and certainly not in the world Prufrock experiences. But Eliot was never as comfortable with such a world as Stevens, Frost, or Moore were: what seems like business as usual to them (the making of fictions or metaphors) more often seems to Eliot like a problem that must be solved. As Michael North suggests, Prufrock "recoils equally from fragment and whole," unable to "find a mediation between them."[53] The same could be said about Eliot, who feared the democratizing force of totality as much as he feared chaos.

Reading *The Waste Land*, Michael Levenson has drawn attention to Eliot's comment that "the problem of the unification of the world and the problem of the unification of the individual, are in the end one and the same problem."[54] *The Waste Land* may be understood as a sequence of attempts to unify the world through the unifications of individuals, as Eliot suggests in his note on Tiresias: he is "the most important personage in the poem, uniting all the rest. Just as the one-eyed merchant, seller of currants, melts into the Phoenician Sailor, and the latter is not wholly distinct from Ferdinand, Prince of Naples, so all the women are one woman, and the two sexes meet in Tiresias" (52). This sentence offers a highly idealized and overly schematic account of the poem, but it nudges readers in the right direction: to borrow the language of "The Metaphysical Poets," Eliot is attempting (especially through his highly developed use of allusion) to "form new wholes" throughout the poem, merging not only individuals but different cultures and different moments in history. Still, however success-fully the poem constructs a provisional sense of wholeness, its thematic content remains at odds with its structural goal: that is, no matter how convinced we become that Tiresias does come to embody the unification of the world, Tiresias sees only the failure of individuals to achieve any sense of unity. Throughout *The Waste Land*, social fragmentation is suggested most powerfully by the fact that (whatever the note on Tiresias says) the sexes never truly meet:

> The time is now propitious, as he guesses,
> The meal is ended, she is bored and tired,
> Endeavours to engage her in caresses
> Which still are unreproved, if undesired.
> Flushed and decided, he assaults at once;
> Exploring hands encounter no defence;
> His vanity requires no response,
> And makes a welcome of indifference.
> (And I Tiresias have foresuffered all
> Enacted on this same divan or bed;
> I who have sat by Thebes below the wall
> And walked among the lowest of the dead.)
> Bestows one final patronizing kiss,
> And gropes his way, finding the stairs unlit . . .   (44)

Pound persuaded Eliot to cut the concluding lines to this passage ("And at the corner where the stable is, / Delays only to urinate, and spit"), commenting that they were "probably over the mark."[55] Just how far over the mark they are suggests how difficult it was for Eliot to believe in his effort to construct a whole world from the stuff of mere human beings.

Eliot could never insure that the problem of the unification of the world and the problem of the unification of individuals would remain the same problem, no matter how hard he worked to find the solution to social problems in lyric poetry without necessarily talking about society as such. This is why it was inevitable that, after he declared himself "classicist in literature, royalist in politics, and anglo-catholic in religion" in 1928, Eliot would insist that literary criticism could no longer be exclusively literary.[56] In his later career, Eliot was more apt to confuse tradition (a process of becoming) with authority (a steady state). And he consequently attempted – almost as soon as the poem was published – to give *The Waste Land* a much clearer sense of order and wholeness than it really had. Early in 1922, Eliot handed over a sheaf of poetic fragments (which he had provisionally entitled *He Do the Police in Different Voices*) to Pound, who, fresh from the experience of writing *Mauberley*, gave *The Waste Land* its final shape, excising narrative and emphasizing discrete moments of intensity. The myth of the Holy Grail, invoked by the poem's final title, had almost nothing to do with the poem's composition. But Eliot would imply in "*Ulysses*, Order, and Myth" that he had written *The Waste Land* according to a "mythical method," something that would give "a shape and a significance to the immense panorama of futility and anarchy which is contemporary history."[57] Surrounded by critical comments like these, *The Waste Land* was inevitably read as a pronouncement on the problem of cultural unity – not the evidence of the state of one poet's mind.

But like any other postromantic poet, Eliot was made nervous by large claims for poetry, even when he provided the terms with which those claims were made. Consequently, he also felt the need to diminish the scope and design of *The Waste Land* severely, dismissing it (much like Yeats looking back at "The Second Coming" in "A Prayer for my Daughter") as the result of a bad mood, "a personal and wholly insignificant grouse against life; it is just a piece of rhythmical grumbling."[58] As more information about Eliot's sordid personal life has become available (along with his uncollected critical writings), readers of *The Waste Land* have tended to agree with this assessment. But readings of the poem tend to repeat the struggle of the poem itself: a sense of the poem as a diminished account of one poet's sensibility is often bought at the expense of any sense in which the poem remains one of the most ambitious assessments of culture in poetry since Wordsworth or Tennyson.

Having so quickly distanced himself from *The Waste Land* and *The Sacred Wood*, Eliot became a far more explicitly social critic (sometimes an intolerant one) in *After Strange Gods* (1934) and a far more explicitly Christian poet in *Ash Wednesday* (1930). His *Four Quartets*, published between 1936 and 1942, are at least as important an achievement as *The Waste Land*, but however much Eliot's work changed in his later career, the poet-critic of the years 1918–22 continued to cast the longest shadow over his contemporaries. And since *The Waste Land* was read so quickly and powerfully as a work of social criticism, poets writing in its wake needed to diminish the achievement. Stevens did so in much the same way that Eliot himself later would: "If it is the supreme cry of despair it is Eliot's and not his generation's."[59] Decades before it became fashionable to do so, Elizabeth Bishop would argue that Eliot's poem is "'about impotence.' Not symbolic impotence – it's about the thing."[60]

In contrast, Hart Crane and William Carlos Williams, who conceived their long poems *The Bridge* (1930) and *Spring and All* (1923) at least in part as responses to Eliot, tended to accept and even to strengthen the typical reading of *The Waste Land* in order to distinguish their own efforts. Williams said in his autobiography that *The Waste Land* "wiped out our world as if an atom bomb had been dropped upon it," and he set out in *Spring and All*, a book-length poem built from both poetry and prose, to prove that April is not the cruelest month.[61]

> They enter the new world naked,
> cold, uncertain of all
> save that they enter. All about them
> the cold, familiar wind –
>
> Now the grass, tomorrow
> the stiff curl of wildcarrot leaf
>
> One by one objects are defined –
> It quickens: clarity, outline of leaf.[62]

The poems of *Spring and All* are focused intently on American localities ("rooted they / grip down and begin to awaken" [183]); yet the work feels far more French, far more infused with the playful, dadaist spirit of Marcel Duchamp (with whom Williams was in contact during the war years), than anything Eliot or Pound ever wrote. In the 1918 preface to *Kora in Hell*, a book of prose improvizations, Williams censured Eliot for betraying American poetry. Responding to Williams (who was after all a first-generation American), Pound said this: "you haven't a drop of the cursed [American] blood in you, and you don't need to fight the disease day and night; you never had to. Eliot has it perhaps worse than I have – poor devil."[63]

Williams would come to agree with this assessment ("The pure products of America / go crazy," begins one of the great poems in *Spring and All* [217]), but his early dialogue with Eliot and Pound suggests how difficult it is – even today – to write a clearly oppositional story about moving beyond *The Waste Land* (or beyond Modernism at large). If we accept too unequivocally the idea of Eliot encouraged by Eliot's more programmatic critical statements, it paradoxically becomes easier to provide evidence showing that Eliot's poetry is in fact (to focus on values important to

Williams and Crane) personal, American, optimistic, or democratic. And whatever Crane's more programmatic statements might have implied, Crane himself knew this was true. One of his favorite passages in Eliot's criticism came from "Reflections on Contemporary Poetry" (1919), an uncollected essay that offers metaphors for the "historical sense" that are wildly at odds with those of "Tradition and the Individual Talent":

> This relation is a feeling of profound kinship, or rather of a peculiar personal intimacy, with another, probably a dead author . . . We may not be great lovers; but if we had a genuine affair with a real poet of any degree we have acquired a monitor to avert us when we are not in love . . . We do not imitate, we are changed; and our work is the work of the changed man; we have not borrowed, we have been quickened, and we become bearers of a tradition.[64]

In the last two decades, these sentences have become as central to discussions of Eliot as chatter about impersonality and the mythical method once was. Hart Crane, who like Auden may be thought of as one of the earliest postmodern poets – a poet who came of age with a strong sense that Modernism was behind him – was aware of this hidden aspect of Eliot all along.

We do not necessarily need to uncover Eliot's uncollected prose to be reminded of the vast multiplicity of aesthetic and ideological positions that coexist in modern poetry: simply returning to Yeats, after reading Williams, will do the job. It is chastening to remember that the modern poets are a wildly various lot, and I have told a coherent story about them at my own risk.

Yet it is instructive to remember that Ezra Pound could as easily befriend and support Yeats as he could Williams. And like so many of his contemporaries, like so many of his forebears, Yeats was still grappling with the contradictions of a diminished romanticism up until his death in 1939. His posthumously published *Last Poems* ended with "Under Ben Bulben," in which Yeats assumes an aristocratically prophetic voice, chanting of personal and political destiny. But a more recently discovered table of contents reveals that Yeats intended the volume to begin with "Under Ben Bulben" and to end with these lines from a little poem called "Politics."

> And maybe what they say is true
> Of war and war's alarms,
> But O that I were young again
> And held her in my arms.   (348)

Yeats wanted our vision of his career to conclude with this severely, touchingly diminished sense of a poet's vocation. But the fact that these lines allude to "Westron Wind," probably the oldest lyric poem in the English language, suggests that Yeats also wanted to claim the grandest possible heritage for a thing so small.

"Politics" does not negate the distasteful bombast of "Under Ben Bulben" ("'Send war in our time, O Lord!'" [326]), but each poem qualifies the other. Marianne Moore, who was nobody's fool, once said that if one is "tempted to think harshly of [Yeats] in his tower, one may well recall what he says about the death of Henley's daughter; or read those retrospective words in which, having been a trouble to parents, grandparents, and himself, he wonders if he is to make a success of his life."[65] Moore is reminding us that Yeats's finest quality is his capacity for self-criticism, his willingness to entertain divergent points of view. I would add that this is the finest quality of modern poetry at large: reading the moderns, we need to remain open to their variousness, their duplicities, their contradictions. I find it harder to achieve this openness when reading Eliot or Pound, easier when reading Hardy or Stevens, but I nonetheless believe that it is crucial, given that Modernism passed into literary history so long ago, that we guard against a strategically limited reading of modern poetry – a reading that emphasizes certain qualities at the expense of others, forcing us to choose between the poets, rather than from among them.

Consider again Randall Jarrell's response to the New Critics' strategically limited reading of romanticism: "Romanticism holds in solution contradictory tendencies which, isolated and exaggerated in Modernism, look startlingly opposed both to each other and to the earlier stages of romanticism." The relationship of Modernism and postmodernism must be seen in a similarly dialectical way. So if it seems that Auden was turning against Yeats, turning against a modernist hope for literature's intervention in society, by saying that "poetry makes nothing happen," it is important to remember that Yeats, at least in some moods, said pretty much the same thing. It would be an oversimplification (but a telling one) to say that Auden's career transforms a tension within Modernism into a linear trajectory. One could say the same thing about Robert Lowell – the poet about whose poetry Randall Jarrell first used the word *postmodernist* in 1947: Lowell's career is often presented as a movement from a closed, modern sensibility to an open, postmodern sensibility. But such enticingly linear narratives (more attractive to those of us who tell the stories of literary history than those of us who live them) always depend on an artificial segregation of aesthetic and ideological principles. Fifty years from now, whatever postmodern poetry will appear to have been, it will not have been other than what modern poetry wished or found it necessary to become.

NOTES

1 See Frank Kermode, *Romantic Image* (New York: Macmillan, 1957); Robert Langbaum, *The Poetry of Experience* (New York: Norton, 1957); and among Harold Bloom's many writings, see "Reflections on T. S. Eliot," *Raritan*, 8 (Fall 1988): 70–87.

2 See Marjorie Perloff, "Pound/Stevens: Whose Era?" and "Postmodernism and the Impasse of Lyric" in *The Dance of the Intellect: Studies in the Poetry of the Pound Tradition* (Cambridge: Cambridge University Press, 1985), pp. 1–32, 172–200.

3 Randall Jarrell, *Kipling, Auden & Co.* (New York: Farrar, Straus and Giroux, 1980), pp. 81, 78, 81. Jarrell's opinion on Auden's later work would change; see the essays on Auden collected in *The Third Book of Criticism* (New York: Farrar, Straus and Giroux, 1965). For Jarrell's first use of the word *postmodernist* see *Poetry and the Age* (New York: Knopf, 1953), p. 195.

4 See Elizabeth Bishop, "Dimensions for a Novel," *Vassar Journal of Undergraduate Studies*, 8 (May 1934): 95–103, and Laura Riding and Robert Graves, *A Survey of Modernist Poetry* (New York: Doubleday, 1928). See also James Longenbach, "Elizabeth Bishop and the Story of Postmodernism," *Southern Review*, 28 (1992): 469–84.

5 Jarrell, *Kipling, Auden & Co.*, p. 36. Mendelson says in his introduction to Auden's *Selected Poems* (New York: Vintage, 1979) that except in Auden's earliest poems, "there is virtually nothing modernist about him" (p. xi). Mendelson offers a richer version of this argument in *Early Auden* (New York: Viking Press, 1981).

6 W. H. Auden, *Collected Poems*, ed. Edward Mendelson (New York: Random House, 1976), p. 41. Further page references will be given in the text.

7 Ezra Pound, *Literary Essays*, ed. T. S. Eliot (New York: New Directions, 1968), pp. 5, 3.

8 Jürgen Habermas, "Modernity – An Incomplete Project" in *The Anti-Aesthetic: Essays on Postmodern Culture*, ed. Hal Foster (Port Townsend: Bay Press, 1983), p. 11.

9 Kenneth Burke, *Counter-Statement* (Berkeley: University of California Press, 1968), p. 90.

10 Florence Emily Hardy, *The Later Years of Thomas Hardy* (London: Macmillan, 1930), p. 58.

11 James Richardson, *Thomas Hardy: The Poetry of Necessity* (Chicago: University Of Chicago Press, 1977), p. 2.

12 See David Riede, *Dante Gabriel Rossetti and the Limits of Victorian Vision* (Ithaca, NY: Cornell University Press, 1983), pp. 113, 57–8.

13 *Thomas Hardy: A Selection of his Finest Poems*, ed. Samuel Hynes (New York: Oxford University Press, 1994), p. 15. Further page references will be given in the text.

14 *The Poetry of Robert Frost*, ed. Edward Lathem (New York: Holt, 1967), p. 334. Further page references will be given in the text.

15 Richard Poirier, *Poetry and Pragmatism* (Cambridge, MA: Harvard University Press, 1992), p. 145.

16 W. B. Yeats, *Essays and Introductions* (New York: Macmillan, 1961), pp. 193–4.

17 W. B. Yeats, *The Poems*, ed. Richard Finneran (New York: Macmillan, 1989), p. 58. Further page references will be given in the text.

18 Yeats, *Essays and Introductions*, p. 155.

19 Ezra Pound, *Personae*, ed. Lea Baechler and A. Walton Litz (New York: New Directions, 1990), p. 111. Further page references will be given in the text.

20 H.D., *Collected Poems*, ed. Louis Martz (New York: New Directions, 1983), p. 39.

21 H.D., *Paint It Today*, ed. Cassandra Laity (New York: New York University Press, 1992), p. 11. See also Rachel Blau DuPlessis, *H.D.: The Career of that Struggle* (Bloomington: Indiana University Press, 1986), pp. 19–20.

22 Marianne Moore, *Complete Prose*, ed. Patricia Willis (New York: Viking Press, 1986), p. 82.

23 Ezra Pound, *Gaudier-Brzeska* (New York: New Directions, 1970), p. 94.

24 Pound, *Literary Essays*, p. 3.

25 H.D., *Collected Poems*, p. 31. See also *Notes on Thought and Vision* (San Francisco: City Lights, 1982).

26 See Paul de Man, *The Rhetoric of Romanticism* (New York: Columbia University Press, 1984), pp. 162–72.

27 See M. H. Abrams, "English Romanticism: The Spirit of the Age" in *Romanticism and Consciousness*, ed. Harold Bloom (New York: Norton, 1970), pp. 90–118, and Jerome McGann, *The Romantic Ideology* (Chicago: University of Chicago Press, 1983). McGann is more critical of this aspect of Romantic poetry than Abrams.

28 W. B. Yeats, *Explorations* (New York: Macmillan, 1962), p. 343.

29 W. B. Yeats, *Memoirs*, ed. Denis Donoghue (New York: Macmillan, 1972), p. 172.

30 See Pound, *Literary Essays*, pp. 378–81. H.D.'s previously unpublished review appeared in *Agenda*, 25 (Autumn/Winter 1988): 51–3.

31 W. B. Yeats, "Introduction" in *The Oxford Book of Modern Verse* (Oxford: Clarendon Press, 1936), p. xxxiv.

32 Rahan Ramazani, *Poetry of Mourning: The Modern Elegy from Hardy to Heaney* (Chicago: University of Chicago Press, 1994), p. 71. On Hardy's crucial influence on war literature generally see Paul Fussell, *The Great War and Modern Memory* (New York and London: Oxford University Press, 1975), pp. 3–7.

33 T. E. Hulme, *Further Speculations*, ed. Sam Hynes (Minneapolis: University of Minnesota Press, 1955), p. 72.

34 Wilfred Owen, *Collected Poems*, ed. C. Day Lewis (New York: New Directions, 1965), p. 55. Further page references will be given in the text.

35 Wallace Stevens, *Collected Poems* (New York: Knopf, 1954), p. 97. Further page references will be given in the text.

36 Harold Bloom, *Wallace Stevens: The Poems of Our Climate* (Ithaca, NY: Cornell University Press, 1977), p. 48.

37 Wallace Stevens, *Opus Posthumous*, ed. Milton Bates (New York: Knopf, 1989), p. 310.

38 Virginia Woolf, *A Room of One's Own* (New York: Harcourt Brace Jovanovich, 1929), p. 96.

39 Sandra Gilbert, "Marianne Moore as Female Female Impersonator" in *Marianne Moore: The Art of a Modernist*, ed. Joseph Parisi (Ann Arbor: University of Michigan Research Press, 1990), pp. 31, 43.

40 Marianne Moore, *Poems* (London: Egoist Press, 1921), p. 13.

41 Stevens, *Opus Posthumous*, p. 11.

42 Marianne Moore, *Complete Poems* (New York: Viking Press, 1981), p. 90. Further page references will be given in the text.

43 H.D., "Marianne Moore," *Egoist*, 3 (1916): 118.

44 Bonnie Costello, "The Feminine Language of Marianne Moore," in *Women and Language in Literature and Society*, ed. Sally McConnell-Ginet, Ruth Barker, and Nelly Furman (New York: Praeger, 1980), p. 225.

45 Ezra Pound, *Selected Letters of Ezra Pound, 1907–1941*, ed. D. D. Paige (New York: New Directions, 1950), p. 181.

46 Ezra Pound, *The Cantos* (New York: New Directions, 1975), pp. 230, 533.

47 Pound described this moment in "Harold Monro," *Criterion*, 11 (July 1932): 590.

48 T. S. Eliot, *The Sacred Wood* (New York: Methuen, 1972), p. 49.

49 T. S. Eliot, *the Complete Poems and Plays* (New York: Harcourt Brace and World, 1971), pp. 32–3. Further page references will be given in the text.

50 T. S. Eliot, *Selected Essays* (New York: Harcourt Brace Jovanovich, 1964), p. 247.

51 Pound, *Selected Letters*, p. 40.

52 T. S. Eliot, *Knowledge and Experience in the Philosophy of F. H. Bradley* (New York: Farrar, Straus and Giroux, 1964), p. 136.

53 Michael North, *The Political Aesthetic of Yeats, Eliot, and Pound* (Cambridge and New York: Cambridge University Press, 1992), p. 76.

54 T. S. Eliot, "Religion Without Humanism," in Norman Forester, ed. *Humanism and America* (New York: Farrar and Rinehart, 1930), p. 112. See Michael Levenson, *A Genealogy of Modernism: A Study of English Literary Doctrine, 1908–1922* (Cambridge and New York: Cambridge University Press, 1988), p. 197.

55 *"The Waste Land": A Facsimile and Transcript of the Original Drafts*, ed. Valerie Eliot (New York: Harcourt Brace Jovanovich, 1971), p. 47.

56 See the preface to *For Lancelot Andrewes* (London: Faber and Faber, 1928), p. ix.

57 T. S. Eliot, *Selected Prose*, ed. Frank Kermode (London: Faber and Faber, 1975), p. 177.

58 See *"The Waste Land": A Facsimile*, p. 1. Critical studies that have made this remark meaningful include Lyndall Gordon, *Eliot's Early Years* (Oxford and New York: Oxford University Press, 1977) and Ronald Bush, *T. S. Eliot: A Study in Character and Style* (Oxford and New York: Oxford University Press, 1984).

59 Alan Filreis, ed., "Voicing the Desert of Silence: Stevens' letters to Alice Corbin Henderson," *Wallace Stevens Journal*, 12 (Spring 1988): 19.

60 See Gary Fountain and Peter Brazeau, *Remembering Elizabeth Bishop: An Oral Biography* (Amherst: University of Massachusetts Press, 1994), p. 153.

61 William Carlos Williams, *Autobiography* (New York: Random House, 1951), p. 174.
62 William Carlos Williams, *Collected Poems*, vol. I, ed. A. Walton Litz and Christopher MacGowan (New York: New Directions, 1986), p. 183. Further page references will be given in the text.
63 Pound, *Selected Letters*, p. 158. See also A. Walton Litz, "Williams and Stevens: The Quest for a Native American Modernism" in *The Literature of Region and Nation*, ed. R. P. Draper (London: Macmillan, 1989), pp. 180–93.
64 T. S. Eliot, "Reflections on Contemporary Poetry [IV]," *Egoist*, 6 (July 1919): 39. See also Langdon Hammer, *Hart Crane and Allen Tate: Janus-Faced Modernism* (Princeton: Princeton University Press, 1993), pp. 117–44.
65 Moore, *Complete Prose*, p. 296.

5

CHRISTOPHER INNES

Modernism in drama

At first sight it might seem contradictory to include drama in a discussion of Modernism. As a movement, "Modernism" has been defined in artistic terms through the sculptures of Jacob Epstein or Henri Gaudier-Brzeska and the paintings of Wassily Kandinsky or Wyndham Lewis, while in literary terms its usage has been restricted to the work of poets and novelists: preeminently T. S. Eliot, Ezra Pound, James Joyce, D. H. Lawrence, and Virginia Woolf. Indeed, in the various critical studies of the movement published over the last half-century, drama has been conspicuous by its absence; and where mentioned at all, it is generally dismissed as following a different – even anti-modernist – agenda.[1] This may be partly due to the specifically English and American focus of studies that site the defining moment of literary Modernism in the Pound–Eliot nexus. By contrast, drama in the twentieth century has been highly international, with English-speaking playwrights and directors responding to innovations from Europe, and having their experiments picked up in turn. It is also true that theatrical developments over the century do not fit the same chronological frame as that for poetry or the novel, where the two decades from 1910 to 1930 are generally held to mark the boundaries of the movement. By comparison, drama had already staked out a distinctively modernist territory by the turn of the century with a work like August Strindberg's *A Dream Play* (1902). But perhaps the main explanation for the omission of drama from the history of Modernism up to this point is that, for various reasons connected with the nature of theatre itself, on the stage the movement has produced extremely diverse work. Directors and dramatists, several of whom were primarily poets and made significant contributions to Modernism in their poetry, may have had the same artistic aims and been responding to the same perception of twentieth-century realities. But their plays and productions use a wide range of stylistic solutions to express this. So any discussion of dramatic Modernism must take a wide focus in following a multifaceted development.

Certainly the theatre is an institution in a way that publishing houses are not; and writing for performance is very different to writing for a literary magazine, or creating art in a studio. Any stage has a pre-set architectural frame, which conditions the dramatic material and is inherently resistant to change. Even an alternative space outside the format of mainstream theatre establishes specific actor–audience relationships that automatically become interpreted in conventional terms, as the example of the Dadaists indicates. Nothing could have been more iconoclastic than their Zurich performances during the First World War, which assaulted bourgeois sensibilities through sound poetry and nonsense dialogue, musical cacophony, and deliberately tawdry nonrepresentational costuming in minidramas that parodied any aesthetic expectations. Yet even these aggressive, anti-art presentations became codified in the cabaret form.

As a public event, performances are not only more open to censorship, but subject to normative pressures from the spectators as a group. There are also other basic elements of theatre that compromise innovation. By contrast with other forms of authorship, playwrights cannot communicate directly with those being addressed, and so retain only a limited control over their creation. Their work becomes literally interpreted by actors whose techniques are normally already established, and therefore liable to mould the final product in traditional ways. Indeed, this problem was recognized as so crucial that several of the leading modernist theatre-artists either trained actors in their own theatre companies, like Artaud and Brecht, or used untrained amateurs, like Gordon Craig who ended up by rejecting actors altogether.

Although such generalizations may seem obvious, they need to be taken into account since all these factors inhibited the experimental freedom that characterizes the modernist movement in other artistic fields. In addition, the nature of theatre as both a group activity and to some degree a mass medium contradicts such significant facets of Modernism as its stress on the individual egoism of the artist and its elitism.

At the same time, the theatre's intrinsic connection to physical reality and social existence (communicated at a minimum through the bodies of the actors and their relationship to each other) make some of the key modernist principles inapplicable. On the stage, art could neither assert itself as an autonomous activity, independent of external experience, nor aspire to pure form. In sharp contrast to the modernist drive in poetry or painting, imitation was always present, being the essential basis of acting. Simply presenting a sequence of actions in a temporal and spatial frame evoked the "narrative method" that Eliot rejected, along with Kandinsky, whose declaration that "the literary element, 'storytelling' or 'anecdote' must be abandoned" was picked up by Pound and the Vorticists.[2] Abstraction too proved possible to only a very limited degree. Both the Dadaists and the Futurists attempted to distort or disguise the human element by using sharply focused lighting to fragment the performer's figure and geometrical costumes to reduce bodily shapes to cones, globes, cylinders, or straight lines. The Dada cabaret tended to grotesque deformation, while Marinetti called for "The Anti-Psychological Abstract Theatre of Pure Forms and Tactilism" (the title of a futurist manifesto of 1924). Corresponding to Gaudier-Brzeska's antirepresentational concept of modernist art – summed up as "the appreciation of masses in relation . . . the defining of these masses by plane" – this abstract tendency was taken to its purest extreme in the *Triadic Ballet* of the German Bauhaus (1922): a "clinically isolated concentration of action on the stage," explicitly "without purpose" or even dramatic situation, let alone story line, designed to investigate the phenomena of form and space, as well as the process of human perception. But the effect of these experiments was either (unintentional) self-parody or restricted movement so much that the performance became static. Even at its most abstract and mechanistic, theatre was incapable of responding to a call like that of Pound's early collaborator, Wyndham Lewis, for "Dehumanization" as "the chief diagnostic of the Modern World."[3]

Despite this, several of the leading modernist poets – in particular W. B. Yeats and T. S. Eliot – turned to the theatre, as did the novelist D. H. Lawrence. Even the painter Wyndham Lewis wrote plays, as did the Austrian painter Oskar Kokoschka. And, with the possible exception of Lewis's *The Enemy of the Stars*, all their dramatic scripts were specifically written for performance. One of the defining characteristics of the movement is an explicit attempt to formulate a unified theory of modernity. To be complete this would have to include drama, although taking into account the nature of the theatre as an artistic instrument and as a social institution, the qualities displayed are rather different than in poetry or painting, even though theatrical performance includes both forms. What in those types of art might count as traditionalist, even a reaction against Modernism, may be an expression of the modernist spirit in the theatre.

As a close associate of Joyce, Eliot and above all Ezra Pound – whom he extolled as "a born revolutionary, a Trotsky of the written word and the painted shape" – Wyndham Lewis was at the forefront of the modernist movement in England. It is therefore significant that he chose a dramatic form to experiment with in translating the qualities of his vorticist painting into words, and equally significant that this was among his very first literary attempts. Published as an artistic manifesto in the first issue of the vorticist journal *Blast*, *The Enemy of the Stars* is a composite of fragmented cubist "visions from within." The text is a treatise on the egoistic philosophy of Modernism. Stirner appears, together with his book *The Ego and Its Own* which Pound had adopted as a key text of the movement, and the action illustrates that "Self, sacred act of violence, is like murder on my face and hands. The stain won't come out. It is the one piece of property all communities have agreed it is illegal to possess." The titanic and perpetual conflict of the twin characters, Arghol and Hanp (representing mind and body: "humility and perverse asceticism opposed to vigorous animal glorification of self"), ends with one murdering his *alter ego* then leaping off a bridge to drown himself, "his heart a sagging weight of stagnant hatred." These inseparable, antagonistic figures are progenitors of Joyce's Dedalus–Bloom duo in *Ulysses*, and – being presented as circus clowns, one of whom is attacked by anonymous booted figures every night – even more clearly foreshadow Samuel Beckett's double pairings of Didi and Gogo (clowns), Pozzo and Lucky (physical versus intellectual existence) in *Waiting for Godot*. At the same time, Lewis's play is hardly conceivable in terms of the stage, being not only a "dream of action," but indeed a dream specifically within a dream, within a circus performance where the spectators are "POSTERITY . . . SILENT, LIKE THE DEAD, AND MORE PATHETIC." The perspective is deliberately impossible: "AUDIENCE LOOKS DOWN INTO SCENE, AS THOUGH IT WERE A HUT ROLLED HALF ON ITS BACK, DOOR UPWARDS, CHARACTERS MOUNTING GIDDILY IN ITS OPENING." The scale is super-human and the script, almost without dialogue, calls for effects quite beyond the range of theatre.

> The night plunged gleaming nervous arms down into the wood, to wrench it up by the roots. Restless and rhythmical, beyond the staring red-rimmed doorway, giddy and expanding in drunken walls, its heavy drastic lights shifted.
> Arghol could see only ponderous arabesques of red cloud, whose lines did not stop at door's frame, but pressed on into shadows within the hut . . .[4]

Violent, subliminal, this drama of the mind might stand as the epitome of Modernism, with human figures expanded to puppet-like monsters in a technologically conceived universe where the stars are "machines of prey" and the imagination determines reality. Needless to say, it has never been produced.

However, Lewis's experiences as an artillery officer in the First World War led him to explicitly repudiate the revolutionary artistic violence of *The Enemy of the Stars* in his next play, *The Ideal Giant*. Written in 1918, this short piece is set in 1914 – significantly the year when Vorticism had first been proclaimed in *Blast* and just after the publication of *The Enemy of the Stars* – and it focuses on the issue of art-versus-action in the context of the Great War. Its protagonist is an avant-garde writer, who mouths the principles that Lewis and Pound had been proclaiming at the time: "*Reality* is the 'thing which is not,' for the creative artist. An artist would have precisely that feeling of 'malaise' and disgust if he had put into another man's head . . . the actual biological appearance of nature" – "Art is much the purer and stronger [than war], and against its truths and impositions we must revolt" – "'Revolution is the normal state of things." But what happens in the play demolishes the concept of the avant-garde artist as "ideal giant": all that his slogans have led to is his female disciple's murder of her banker-father. The almost completely naturalistic discussion-play format of *The Ideal Giant* is a denial of the whole Vorticist approach; and when the woman is arrested by the police, the artist is left sitting "*with his white profile, and large eye distorted with shame and perplexity.*" In contrast to his earlier futuristic praise of "RESTLESS MACHINES . . . heavy insect dredgers / monotonous cranes . . . steep walls of factories," after his exposure to the mechanistic slaughter of the First World War Lewis denounced modern technology and its reflection in modernist art as a tool of oppression.[5] Anticipating his close associate, T. S. Eliot, Lewis turned to classicism.

A quite different application of modernist principles to the stage can be seen in the dramatic work of W. B. Yeats and Gordon Craig respectively. Yeats, of course, was preeminently a poet; but he experimented with drama as an organic development of his verse through most of his literary career, writing one series of plays between 1902 and 1908, and another between 1930 and 1938. The elements developed in the first grouping were given their clearest expression eight years later in *At the Hawk's Well* (1916); the second culminated in his last play, *The Death of Cuchulain*. His earliest play, *The Shadowy Waters* (written in 1895) echoed Villiers de l'Isle-Adam's *Axel* from a year earlier. However, once Yeats turned to specifically Irish themes, his drama shifted from nineteenth-century symbolism. Even though the Salome image – the emblem of *fin de siècle* romanticism – recurs in two of his later pieces, in articulating a Celtic mythology for the nationalist movement he moved increasingly to artistic autonomy and abstraction. Discarding his early technique of depicting superficially or-dinary characters whose reality lies on a mythic plane (for instance, an old woman representing the spirit of Ireland in *Cathleen ni Houlihan*), Yeats's figures become pure images, divorced from social context and ultimately even human form. He also adopted the least representational mode of performance, the dance. These "plays for dancers" are subjective. The author identifies with his mythological hero, Cuchulain, and the underlying subject of the plays is art: the myths are recreated to illustrate the process of mythmaking. At first glance, the consciously archaic style derived from Japanese Noh drama is anything but modernist. Even so, borrowing from Oriental models in fact becomes a standard characteristic for the dramatic side of the movement. Craig and (more indirectly) Brecht draw on Chinese theatre; Artaud took Balinese trance drama as his ideal; and, like Yeats, Stravinsky's *Les Noces* copies the Japanese Noh model.

However traditional in their context, when transposed to the European stage the effect is a radical break with tradition; and as Yeats emphasized, the value of Noh stylization was its "strangeness." Unconsciously based on the colonialist view of the East as "other", oriental models assert opposition to Western culture. This may be less explicit in Yeats, since *Japonisme* had become a popular cult with the turn of the century theatrical tours of the Geisha dancer Sada Yakko, followed by Michio Ito, who danced as the bird spirit in *At the Hawk's Well*. Yet it was Ezra Pound who introduced Yeats to Noh drama, which from a European perspective incorporated key modernist qualities of internal unity and antirealism. As Fenellosa, the first translator of Noh plays, described the form, "All elements – costume, motion, verse and music – unite to produce a single clarified impression . . . elevated to the plane of universality by the intensity and purity of treatment." And, in the Noh Yeats found his model for a style of theatre "close to pure music . . . that would free [the stage] from imitation, and ally [dramatic] art to decoration and the dance."[6]

Yeats's aim was to create a form of drama in which the dancer would be inseparable from the dance, in a total unity of theme and expression. The characters of *At the Hawk's Well* mirror each other – the Old Man, who competes for the waters of eternal life with Cuchulain, being a projection of what the Hero might become. The hawk-girl guardian is not only the impersonal force of fate, but the immortal muse of poetry. The well is both the object of the heroic quest and the source of poetic creation. This internalization goes along with a simplification and deliberate restriction of the dramatic means. The original epic material is reduced in each of the "dance plays" to a single event, framed by the ritual unfolding of a cloth with an invocation "to the eye of the mind" and culminating in a formal dance diametrically opposed to "the disordered passion of nature."[7] Scenery is pared down to a single blank screen at the back of the acting area, a square of blue fabric on the floor for the well; and in *The Death of Cuchulain*, the central action itself – the beheading of the Hero – takes place behind the screen, while his severed head is abstracted to a black parallelogram. This is drama at its most minimal, and in the last play the presenter, who is both the Old Man from *The Hawk's Well* and Yeats's *alter ego*, acknowledges that such plays have not only become distanced from the modern experience ("this vile age" that overwhelms the mythic ideal) but also represent a withdrawal from theatre: something implicitly recognized in the gap between the writing of *The Death of Cuchulain* and its first performance in 1949, over a decade after Yeats's death.

Yeats hailed Craig's first productions as "not drama but the ritual of a lost faith," and together with Ezra Pound in 1912 joined a committee "to promote the Art of the Theatre as interpreted by Gordon Craig."[8] A year before that, Yeats had staged three of his own plays at the Abbey using a scenic system of moveable ivory-colored screens designed by Craig. Indeed he even completely rewrote one of the pieces (*Deirdre*, first performed in 1906) to take full advantage of the abstract-impressionist effects that could be achieved through Craig's screens.

Craig's real strength was as a painter and designer, though in the 1890s he had won recognition as one of the leading young actors in England, and the series of Purcell and Handel operas that he directed between 1900 and 1902 were poetically simplified. In each, the action was structured into a unified emotional progression; scenes were orchestrated around a single emblematic stage-property; sweeping movement and groupings were geometrically patterned; imaginative and evocative lighting (the first coherent use of electric illumination on the European stage) synthesized all the elements of the performance. Visual effects were created with the most economical means, all realistic detail being avoided. The suggestiveness and harmony – as Yeats wrote – "'created an ideal country where everything was possible, even speaking in verse or in music, or the expression of the whole of life in a dance." Two effects from *Acis and Galatea* illustrate Craig's new Art Theatre. The monster Polyphemus appeared only as an enormous shadow projected on to the backcloth, coalescing out of a deep indigo sky to tower menacingly over the "wretched lovers"; and as the light grew a single fold of purple mantle, sweeping down from the flies, was enough – as one enthusiastic reviewer announced – to evoke the brooding form of "the only real and impressive giant ever seen on any stage." In striking contrast, the next scene replaced the romantic Arcadian landscape of Handel's libretto with the bare suggestion of a tent, formed out of long white strips of cloth, draped from behind the proscenium to hang at the rear, through which a hot light filtered and illuminated a skyscape painted on the backcloth behind. Designed "to wave now and then as if in the mind," these strips gave an impression of transparency, swaying and opening as the performers moved about by them, and were echoed in the performers' costumes, made of inch-wide tape hanging from the shoulder – cream outside and colored on the reverse – which made all movement rhythmic and shimmering.[9] A physical realization of the Pateresque assertion that "All art constantly aspires to the condition of music," the whole was designed to create the floating evanescence of a dream.

After these productions, Craig progressively withdrew from the stage in search of pure form, anticipating Pound's commitment to "form, not the *form of anything*." His last major production, for Stanislavski and the Moscow Art Theatre in 1912, was an interiorized interpretation of *Hamlet*, conceived as a conflict between Hamlet-as-spirit versus Claudius and all that surrounds him as material existence, which used Craig's system of screens. Designed as a universal, unitary setting specifically for poetic drama, the self-standing screens could be moved during a performance and by combining them in different perspectives "1,000 shapes" could be created. Their significance lay in "suggestion, not representation," with the play of light over their neutral surfaces being the operative factor.[10] Experimenting with the screens on a model stage, Craig developed "black figures" to substitute for actors – scaled-down hieratic human shapes – and it was a short step from this to his ideal of an "Übermarionette." Based on the idea of a semi-divine puppet that Craig traced to ancient Oriental performance, these figures would replace human actors, whose display of personality and lack of physical precision Craig had come to see as irreconcilable with art. Craig devoted his time increasingly to theory after founding his own journal (the *Mask*) in 1908 and publishing his influential book *On the Art of the Theatre* in 1911, while experimenting with what he came to call "Scene." This could be considered the reflection of modern conditions as a purely mechanical and architecturally abstract concept: a multiplicity of columns in various dimensions, rising out of the stage floor or descending from the flies in continual progression and variety, in conjunction with everchanging flows of light. It marked a decisive move from impressionism to abstraction. Drawing an analogy to Bach's oratorios – which he saw as relying "on compact and simple *form* to move us" – Craig's vision was of an artist orchestrating all these elements in symphonic movement that would communicate a series of "moods," the aim being "*to represent the idea* . . . to endow with soul lifeless material."[11]

If Yeats and Craig represent the imagist line of Modernism, it might be logical to conclude that the movement was incompatible with theatre, since their artistic principles drove them to withdraw from the stage. Each in their own way are infected by the elitism inherent in much modernist art – which in the form of a pseudo-aristocratic concept of passionless remoteness is the weakest aspect of Yeats's poetry as well as of his plays – and this inevitably conflicts with the populist quality of stage performance. Yeats expressed the wish to rehearse his actors in barrels, ruling out gesture to restore the sovereignty of words. Despite his central role in founding the Abbey Theatre and in promoting the plays of Synge and other Irish Naturalists, Yeats turned his back on the public stage (preferring private performances in the houses of the elite) "to create for myself an unpopular theatre and an audience like a secret society." Craig cut out the actor completely, together with the spoken word, and effectively ceased performances for spectators at all. Both progressively discarded standard elements of theatrical communication to evolve their own types of minimalist drama. This has in fact proved the most valuable part of their art (being picked up respectively by postmodern artists like Samuel Beckett or Robert Wilson), yet what each was actually working towards has to be seen as a quite different nondramatic mode of expression: an artistic form with as little relation to theatre as Wyndham Lewis's *The Enemy of the Stars*. Indeed, Craig was quite explicit about this: "*If you can find in nature a new material, one which has never yet been used by man to give form to his thoughts, then you can say you are on the high road towards creating a new art.*"[12]

However, the principles of Modernism were adopted by a wide range of other playwrights and directors, who explored alternative ways of expressing the modernist vision. Craig and Yeats might be said to have attempted too direct a translation from poetry and painting to drama. So it is only to be expected that modernist qualities would undergo changes if they were to be successfully applied in stage terms. Even where there are clear parallels – say with the novel, which is perhaps the most similar in using characterization and narrative techniques – the theatrical forms of Modernism are distinct. For instance, from Proust through James Joyce and Virginia Woolf one major modernist concern was the depiction of interior experience, where reality is the subjective apprehension of the world, and art is an "*im*pressionist" record of "stream of consciousness." In drama the equivalent is *ex*pressionism, which seeks to represent (and appeal directly to) the *sub*conscious. While their plays tended to be equally autobiographical, the Expressionists' focus on archetypes intrinsically denies the validity of both the individual ego and intellectual awareness. Thus the aim of the expressionist actor was to "completely forget himself in his soul . . . going onto the stage as someone sleepwalking" and the ideal form of communication was "a scarcely verbalized cry," signifying "the excess of a sensation – full of pathos because arising out of passion – solely with the aim of generating passion."[13] A representative title for the modernist novel might be Woolf's

A Room of One's Own, which carries contrasting premises to classic expressionist play titles such as Strindberg's *A Dream Play*, or Walter Hasenclever's *Humanity*.

As Strindberg stated in his programmatic author's note, the structure of *A Dream Play* transcribes "the inconsequent yet transparently logical shape of a dream. Everything can happen, everything is possible and probable. Time and space do not exist; on an insignificant basis of reality the imagination spins, weaving new patterns . . . The characters split, double, multiply, evaporate, condense, disperse, assemble. But a single consciousness holds sway over them all – that of the dreamer." The recurring phrase "Alas for mankind . . ." becomes a controlling motif in the dialogue. Objects – a door, said to conceal the secret of life, which turns out to have nothing behind it; the doorkeeper's shawl that becomes laden with glistening tears – are reused from scene to scene, taking on continually new symbolic connotations. The husband of the central female soul-figure (with a characteristically universal name: the Daughter) switches between an Army Officer, a Lawyer and a Poet. The whole dramatic action, extended on one temporal plane, lasts scarcely an eyeblink in the time frame of the opening and closing scenes. Catching sight of a chrysanthemum bud crowning the gilded roof of a growing castle that rises above a wall of gigantic hollyhocks, the Daughter asks, "Won't it flower soon? We're past midsummer" – to which the Daughter receives the reply "Don't you see the flower up there?"[14] Already unfolding as she first opens her eyes, the final tableau of the play – where the flower bursts into full bloom – follows straight on these opening lines, yet our perception is assumed to have been changed by the intervening experience. As the castle flares up in an image of spiritual transcendence, the light of its flames transforms the hollyhocks into a wall of agonized human faces. The Poet/author figure in the play may be able to see reality, since (as the Daughter tells him) poetry, dreaming, and reality are all synonymous. Yet the Poet is not the dreamer; and the religious imagery that imbues *A Dream Play*, which is typical of expressionist drama, points to its underlying mythological theme. Prefiguring Joyce and Eliot, Strindberg is using myth as a controlling pattern that makes the apparent chaos and futility of the modern experience meaningful. But unlike Eliot, he was consciously borrowing from Eastern mysticism, in which life itself is seen as the dream of a god trapped in material existence by desire. The psyches of human individuals are illusory projections of fragmentary impulses from this divinity, who can only regain full consciousness through the eventual destruction of the world, the catalyst for which is suffering that makes people's daily lives unendurable and so liberates the god from his love of physical being.

The rejection of Victorian orthodoxies, along with the logical and chronological structures of traditional narrative, may be standard for modernist poets. The theatre took this to an extreme, following Strindberg in denying the whole of Western civilization, with its emphasis on rationalism and its materialism. The Expressionists reflected the same sense of a disintegrating culture, dissociated personalities and fragmented consciousness, but went further in working for spiritual transcendence. Their themes also tended to be more extreme, intensified by the physicality of performance.

A good example of this is Kokoschka's *Murder Hope of Women*. The play depicts "the fatal confrontation" between the opposing poles of existence that Kokoschka saw as "the basis of our dreams, Eros and Thanatos," through a sexual war-to-the-death between "the female principle" (identified with the moon) and the archetypal warrior male.[15] The dynamic rhythms of curvilinear shapes and symbolic use of color that characterize Kokoschka's paintings were transposed into swirling, ritualistic choreography and emotive, imagistic phrases. The network of lines that dissolve the features in his portraits, when painted on the bodies of his almost nude actors appeared as nerves and tendons, making it seem that surface individuality had been flayed away to primal (and physical) essence. Avoiding narrative progression, the action is composed of mythic elements linked by an erotic pattern of violence. Inverted Christian images – a cock crowing three times to announce a massacre, a woman's body spread into a white cross to be strangled by her rapist – form an extended orgasm with crucifixion as the sexual climax. Brutal and primitivistic, *Murder Hope of Women* caused a riot when first performed at Vienna in 1909, but achieved the status of a modernist classic, with five reprintings of the text between 1910 and 1920. It featured in the repertoire of Max Reinhardt (Germany's leading director and impresario) between 1918 and 1921, and was performed throughout the 1920s as an opera, with a musical score by Hindemith.

This primitivism is one of the characteristic lines in theatrical Modernism, stretching from Wyndham Lewis, through Antonin Artaud in the 1930s, to the Living Theatre and the American avant-garde in the late 1960s. It was perhaps most fully realized in modern ballet, where the evocative qualities of music and the symbolic abstraction of dance could create powerful emotional effects through rhythm, as exemplified in Stravinsky's *Rite of Spring*. The physical energy of barbaric dancing, together with the polytonal dissonances, melodic repetitions and driving beat of Stravinsky's score configure the pagan fertility ritual of prehistoric human sacrifice, connecting with sexual urges to produce an overwhelming sense of atavism. First performed in 1913, *Le Sacre du Printemps* was immensely influential, and became part of the repertoire of dance groups throughout the 1920s. Perhaps the leading exponent of this primitivistic Modernism was Mary Wigman, whose dance-dramas gained a cult status in Germany – but the influence of Stravinsky's primitivism can also be traced in literary theatre.

Some of the same qualities carry over into the early plays of Eugene O'Neill, when he was setting out to create a modernist theatre for America. Explicitly influenced by Strindberg, *The Emperor Jones* (1920) depicts a journey into the subconscious during which the black protagonist is stripped of his individuality in a journey back through racial history to an elemental unity with death, while *The Hairy Ape* (1921) extends the same theme into a condemnation of urban industrial civilization as a cage that deforms and destroys humanity. O'Neill – like the majority of modernist playwrights – retains chronological narrative structures, although the time sequence is reversed in one play and the scenes of both have the brevity of snapshots. But he also exalts primitivism in Jones's atavistic reversion to savagery, as well as in his use of drumbeats running through the whole performance in increasing tempo to regulate the pulse rate of the audience and involve them emotionally in the visionary dreamworld of the protagonist's consciousness. Though in O'Neill's subsequent plays such expressionist elements became increasingly disguised beneath a naturalistic surface, the universalized characters he introduced and the distorted world reflecting their perception, the depiction of dreams and the symbolic representation of reality continued to appear on the American stage up to the end of the thirties in the plays of Elmer Rice or Thornton Wilder. Indeed, they carry over into the work of Arthur Miller and Tennessee Williams, particularly in their autobiographical plays such as *After the Fall* (1964) or *The Glass Menagerie* (1945). By the end of the twenties, Expressionism had also transferred to England and Ireland, appearing in Sean O'Casey's First World War play, *The Silver Tassie*, and conditioning the political verse dramas of Auden and Isherwood in the mid-1930s.

It was a short step from the expressionist realm of the collective unconscious to the Surrealists, whose belief that the free flow of imagination would liberate the deepest levels of the psyche led to experiments with automatic writing. André Breton's concept of "psychic automatism" was related to both the psychotherapist's tool of spontaneous speech and to the spiritualist seance: "A dictation of thought without any control of reason, outside all aesthetic or moral preoccupation."[16] However, in practice – as with *If You Please* by Breton and Phillipe Soupault (1920), or Louis

Aragon's play *The Mirror-Wardrobe One Fine Evening* (1923) – this tended to the reproduction of cultural clichés. Despite irrational structures and verbal inventiveness, the attempt to reach fundamental experience reduced their dramatic situations to the banal. *If You Please* is a compendium of outworn extramarital relationships: adultery with the husband's willing connivance, the murder of a mistress, a man picking up a prostitute in a bar. In *The Mirror-Wardrobe One Fine Evening* a husband returns home hoping to catch his wife with her lover, whom he suspects is hiding in the bedroom. Even so, surrealist drama was capable of rising to delicate and evocative poetic fantasy, as in *La Place de l'Etoile* by Robert Desnos. While produced by his "dream-dictation" technique, this can hardly be classed as spontaneous writing, having been begun in 1927 but only completed in 1944. The permutations of sexual desire, so characteristic of surrealist plays because of the possibilities for emotional intensity, are here treated lyrically and grounded in inconsequential bar-room conversation, where there are no boundaries between reality and illusion, consciousness and sleep, or even the living and ghosts. Passion ignites fires that burn down buildings; unconsummated longings cause starfish to proliferate all over Paris; a hallucinatory dreamworld is created, which has its own random logic.

However, the most significant and influential development of Surrealism in the theatre came with Antonin Artaud, who rejected everything ethereal in pursuit of "the truthful precipitate of dreams . . . imprinted with terror and cruelty." Artaud's principles are essentially modernist – his aim being specifically "to return to the theatre that total liberty which exists in [contemporary] music, poetry, or painting, and of which it has been curiously bereft up till now"[17] – but the visionary path he took in realizing modernist aims led in strikingly new directions.

Like many of his contemporaries in the 1920s and earlier, Artaud was hypersensitive to the destabilizing effect of modern conditions, of being faced with a period "when the world . . . sees its old values crumble. Our calcined life is dissolving at its base." His theatre was both a response, and a reflection in being designed to function metaphorically like "the plague" that ushers in "spiritual freedom" by causing "all social forms to disintegrate." He attacked realism, and all traditional European forms of representation – going so far indeed as to junk all "masterpieces" as irrelevant – and instead sought "images that spring uniquely from themselves, which do not derive their meaning from the situation . . . but from a kind of internal necessity." Indeed, his underlying premise epitomizes the imagist position: "what is important is not the objective drama of images, but the subjective drama of souls." He worked for direct communication (in which the theatrical spectacle would affect the audience in the same way as acupuncture), and explored irrationality. He constantly stressed the significance of myths, being in his view "precipitates of the universal dream," but valued them solely as a mode of experience, envisaging "a drama which, without resorting to the defunct images of the old Myths, shows it can extract the forces which struggle within them."[18]

At the same time, in Artaud's hands all these typically modernist qualities were transmuted into elements of a unique vision that only became realized in the counterculture avant-garde theatre of the late 1960s. Even the conclusions drawn from the sense of social breakdown and individual fragmentation that motivates the whole modernist search were more extreme: "If confusion is a sign of the times," Artaud declared, then at its root was "a rupture between things and words, between things and the ideas and signs that are their representation."[19] The ideal of direct communication that he developed in response was not subliminal, but intensely physical, with the audience surrounded by the action, their senses bombarded into overload, and all barriers between stage and spectator demolished. Instead of an ordering principle (as, say for Eliot), myth offered Artaud a reservoir of anarchic extremity, in which the darkest forces of the human psyche were exteriorized. His primitivism was qualitatively different to the Oriental borrowings of Yeats, Craig, or Strindberg. Those were stylistic or philosophical. Artaud's model was the Balinese dance troupe that he witnessed at a colonial exhibition performing a Barong drama, which involved a mythical beast and trance states (during which at a similar performance filmed by Margaret Mead the dancers become invulnerable to the swords they turn against their naked chests). The Balinese ritual, with its archaic incantation and hieratic gestures, leading to mass hypnosis through contagious delirium, became his ideal for performance. Achieving "the automatism of the liberated unconscious," actors would be "signalling through the flames" using a "concrete language, intended for the sense and independent of speech" in which "everything is . . . regulated and impersonal; not a movement of the muscles, not the rolling of an eye but seem to belong to a kind of reflective mathematics which controls everything."[20] Following on his belief that "the images of thought can be identified with a dream which will be efficacious [i.e. induce a trance state in the spectators] to the degree that it can be projected with the necessary violence," he adopted "Theatre of Cruelty" as his title, declaring "Everything that acts is a cruelty. It is upon this idea of extreme action, pushed beyond all limits, that the theatre must be rebuilt."[21]

Such ideas led to a theatre of passionate excess, dealing with "great crimes" as the most powerful emotional catalyst, embodied in hallucinatory images that were communicated through physical action. The only one of his own plays that Artaud produced was *The Cenci* (an exaggerated version of Shelley's pseudo-Jacobean tragedy of a tyrannical father who rapes, and is murdered by his own daughter), although perhaps the clearest example of his drama is the short *Jet of Blood*. In this piece, Artaud completely discards cause-and-effect narrative along with even chronological consistency, to create a dreamworld where modern figures mingle with divine apparitions, and with historical archetypes and grotesques such as a medieval Knight in a vast oversized suit of armor, who is in constant pursuit of a Nurse with immensely swollen breasts. The play also combines the breaking of primal taboos – incest and blasphemy – with surrealistic shock effects. A Whore and a Young Man eat each other's eyes; the Young Girl (the Young Man's sister/wife) is *"crushed flat as a pancake,"* but revives to cry out "The virgin! Ah, that's what he was looking for." The huge hand of God seizes the Whore's hair, which *"bursts into ever-widening flames"*; and when she bites God's wrist, the blood that spurts across the stage kills almost all the characters. The Knight stands transfixed as *"An army of scorpions comes out from under the Nurse's dress and swarms over his sex, which swells up and bursts, becoming glassy and shining like the sun."* Physical action overwhelms the scarcely 300 words of dialogue, as when the statement "how well ordered this world is" provokes a long sequence in which fragments of human bodies and the detritus of Western civilization (colonnades, temples) rain down *"with a vomit-inducing slowness."*[22] Such visceral effects were intended to short-circuit rational responses and liberate the audience's subconscious.

Jet of Blood is the dramatic equivalent of the surrealist Dalí/Buñuel film, *Un Chien Andalou*; and it is worth noting that Artaud himself wrote several screenplays. In 1928 he declared that his theatrical ideas could only be realized through the cinema – and indeed other Modernists were also clearly reaching towards effects that had become newly available through film, the most obvious example being Wyndham Lewis's *The Enemy of the Stars* over a decade earlier. Perhaps as a result, even though it had been announced for the 1927 programme of Artaud's theatre, *Jet of Blood* remained unperformed until 1964. After a bare handful of productions between 1927 and 1935, Artaud abandoned the stage; and the most effective part of his work became his incendiary essays and manifestos.

In some ways T. S. Eliot's first play, *Sweeney Agonistes* (written in 1925–6 and first performed in America in 1933), is comparable to the Surrealists. Unlike his other drama, this deals with unsavory lower-class, even underworld "furnished flat sort of people." An explicit attack on "the conven-

tionalities of modern behaviour with its empty code and heartiness –
immoral, but never immoral enough – decaying, but so long in dying," the
vestigial action is presented as a nightmare dream. All the other characters
are seen as projections of the title figure's agonized consciousness, and
indeed an early title had been *The Marriage of Life and Death: A Dream*.[23]
Specifically Sweeney's dream is a grotesque nightmare of murder, with
Sweeney himself as the notorious wife-murderer Dr. Crippen (with whom
Eliot might have identified, since Crippen was an American from St. Louis
– Eliot's birthplace – transplanted to England, like Eliot, who had buried
his wife's dismembered body in his London basement). In the text Sweeney,
for whom "life is death," merely expresses the desire to "do a girl in,"
telling the story of a man – perhaps himself – who kept his butchered
female victim's body for months in a bathtub, preserved in lysol, while he
goes about his daily routine. But in the London production of 1934, with
which Eliot was directly involved, this became more than fantasy. The
performance ended with Sweeney brandishing a cut-throat razor as he
chases a prostitute, a police whistle, then pounding on the door, and a girl's
scream in the final blackout: a gruesome dance of death. As blind (in moral
terms) as Sampson Agonistes, Sweeney is the modern equivalent of Milton's
heroic biblical avenger, who has been degraded to Jack the Ripper under
the corrosive pressures of the twentieth-century world. In this production
too, the gap between performers and audience was broken down, by setting
the acting area – distinguished only by a pool of light – in the middle of the
spectators who, with the actors seated among them when "off-stage," were
implicitly cast as a chorus of accomplices.

Eliot was possibly the greatest of the modernist poets; and the figure of
"apeneck Sweeney" surfaces recurrently in his poems, representing degraded and aggressive sexuality. Found "Among the Nightingales" (a slang
term for prostitutes), in "Sweeney Erect" he is reduced to little more than a
phallus, as the title of the poem indicates. He reappears in *The Waste
Land*, perverting the lifegiving urges of spring by resorting to a brothel,
while one of the whores from the play also carries over into the poetry,
giving her name to "Doris's Dream Songs" (published in 1924, with one of
the poems becoming part III of "The Hollow Men"). Eliot recognized
drama as the logical development of his poetic aims, since in his view "The
most useful poetry, socially, would be one which could cut across all the
present stratifications of public taste – stratifications which are perhaps a
sign of social disintegration. The ideal medium for poetry . . . and the most
direct means of social "usefulness' for poetry, is the theatre."[24] And the
continuum between his poetry and his plays is nowhere clearer than in
Sweeney Agonistes.

Sweeney Agonistes is a literal transcription of Eliot's principle that "the music of poetry . . . must be a music latent in the common speech of its time," using jazz rhythms in the dialogue and including a parody of a Bob Coles' hit *Under the Bamboo Tree*. In addition, one of the gangster figures is ironically characterized as a traditional role in the Negro minstrel show – "Snow as Bones" (a double death figure) – and, in his notes for the director of the 1933 American production, Eliot suggested that the chorus should sound like a street drill. *Sweeney Agonistes* is also the most unequivocally modernist of his plays. An accompaniment of drumbeats (paralleling O'Neill's use of a drum in *The Emperor Jones*) emphasizes its ritualistic basis, which is also implicit in the music-hall elements: the music hall being in Eliot's eyes "one of the few surviving rituals in modern life."[25] Following Yeats, he wanted performances of the play stylized like a Noh drama; and the actors were to be masked. Narrative structure was consciously avoided, with the play being arbitrarily split into two halves, both incomplete and explicitly composed as a "Fragment of a Prologue" and a "Fragment of an Agon": an expressionistic montage which the London production of 1934 emphasized by blackouts between each small segment of the action.

Yeats saw the performance – as did Bertolt Brecht, who was greatly impressed – and *Sweeney Agonistes* was picked up by the avant-garde after the Second World War in an early Living Theater production that also featured Picasso's *Desire* and Gertrude Stein's *Ladies' Voices*. This grouping confirms the position of *Sweeney Agonistes* as a key example of modernist drama. But it was an experiment Eliot never repeated. With *Murder in the Cathedral* in 1935, religious themes and traditionalist perspectives became dominant; and from *The Family Reunion* in 1939 to his last play, *The Elder Statesman*, in 1958, his work came increasingly to resemble the domestic comedy that was the standard commercial fare of the time. The substructure of Greek myth that Eliot used to frame the dramatic action of these plays – also pointed to in one of the epigraphs to *Sweeney Agonistes*, which was taken from Aeschylus – is progressively more deeply buried and obscure. Even the poetic quality of the verse dialogue diminishes to the point that, as Eliot himself acknowledged, referring to one of the later comedies, "it is perhaps an open question whether there is any poetry in the play at all."[26]

Where Yeats sacrificed theatre to his poetry, Eliot might be said to have sacrificed Modernism to the theatre. *Sweeney Agonistes* was certainly dramatically viable. Indeed, with the exception of *Murder in the Cathedral* (which as church drama falls into a special category), it has been revived more often than any of Eliot's other plays, even though they were consciously written in a more accessible form. But in almost every one of the cases examined so far, the theatrical life of each attempt to transpose the modernist vision to the stage was extremely brief or limited. Even Expressionism, the most widespread aspect of the movement, only flourished in its ecstatic form for about five years from 1919, when Strindberg's concepts became adopted in Germany, to 1924. Only two of O'Neill's plays are fully expressionistic; and when O'Casey adopted the approach in 1928, his work was rejected by the Abbey. Artaud's drama had little influence when it was staged, although some of his techniques were picked up by Jean Louis Barrault, who became a central figure in French theatre. After only four years as a director, Craig retreated into pure theory, finding it impossible to get his ideas accepted by the turn-of-the-century theatre, while Wyndham Lewis never attempted to get his drama staged at all. Some of their plays and ideas were to be the basis for avant-garde performances thirty to forty years later. Yet, apart from Strindberg, in their own time they had little influence. Extremism marginalized their work.

Compromises had to be made if viable work was to be produced for the stage; and in drama the most influential practitioners of Modernism are defined by the infusion of a modernist spirit into standard theatrical forms. This had been begun by George Bernard Shaw, whose refurbishing of traditional melodrama and romance offers a basic example. All Shaw's plays have standard narrative structures and retain the semblance of a naturalistic surface, as well as being (notoriously) intellectual. Yet Shaw uses the intellectual qualities of inversion and paradox to an extent that undermines their apparent rationalism, and conceived his plays as "musical performances" in which the "long rhetorical speeches" were consciously written "like operatic solos." Thus in *Man and Superman* (1903), although the plot as such is a standard three-act marriage comedy – doubly reversed in that it is the woman who pursues, and the object of pursuit is not emotional fulfillment but an idea of existence – the essence of the play is an interpolated Dream sequence. This comprises well over half the length of the total script, and takes place outside space and time where the Devil appears along with figures from the Don Juan legend. While unlike other modernist dream plays since there is no attempt to reproduce the illogic or symbolism of the unconscious, this Hell scene has a significant degree of abstraction. The figures are archetypal projections of the characters in the outer play (implicitly exposing their individualized personalities as illusory), inhabiting "the void" and corresponding to motifs from Mozart's operas (*The Magic Flute* as well as *Don Giovanni*).[27] Emphasizing the musical quality of the Dream, Shaw annotated the speeches with different musical keys, crotchets, and crescendos, as a guide for the actor playing Don Juan.

Other plays by Shaw reveal equally modernist concerns. For instance, in *Misalliance* (1910) the destabilizing effect of technological advance and cultural disintegration is given concrete shape in the aeroplane piloted – incongruously – by an elegant female Polish acrobat, which crashes through the glass roof of the conservatory of an English country mansion, literally shattering both commonplace realities and established social structures. Though the tone is comic, this rupture of normalcy exposes the fragility of the twentieth-century psyche as a timid clerk, representing the completely conditioned personality, turns revolutionary, leaping out of a portable Turkish bath with the cry "Rome fell. Babylon fell. Hindhead's turn will come." Here the pistol-waving revolutionary is easily disarmed and the social order – however tenuously – reimposed, although in *Heartbreak House* the inevitable Armageddon occurs. Writing in the depths of the First World War, Shaw envisages the self-destruction of England, and by extension the whole of Western civilization, since this "fantasia in the Russian manner" is modeled on Chekhov's *The Cherry Orchard*. The characters are the social elite, who have abdicated responsibility. They exist in a hell of unreality where, as the disillusioned heroine discovers, all intellectual, economic and political power are illusory:

ELLIE. Marcus's tigers are false; Mr. Mangan's millions are false . . .
The one thing that was left to me was the Captain's seventh degree of concentration: and that turns out to be –
CAPTAIN SHOTOVER. Rum.

For these "heartbroken imbeciles," the only hope of escaping the lunatic society they inhabit is through the destruction of the "madhouse" – "This soul's prison we call England" – and at the end, after German bombs have killed the tycoon and a burglar ("the two practical men of business"), the survivors turn on all the lights in the house as a beacon for the bombers.[28]

At the same time, *Heartbreak House* is the most poetic of Shaw's plays, with the dialogue progressing along nonlogical, musical lines and at times breaking into pure stream of consciousness or verse. Insistent Symbolism fragments the naturalistic surface, and the structure is openly symphonic. Indeed, a "fantasia" (the genre indicated by Shaw's subtitle) is a musical composition in which form is subservient to fancy, a dream vision. The play is designed as the theatrical equivalent, with Shaw affirming that it "has more of the miracle, more of the mystic belief in it than any of my others."[29]

None of Shaw's other work moves as far from standard dramatic forms, but the same elements are present in most of his later plays. Beneath his social polemics lies an awareness of irrationality, even mysticism, together with a tendency to abstraction. However, it was his claim of a direct social influence for theatre, together with the naturalistic elements of his drama of ideas, that had the most influence – and simply through longevity and the sheer volume of his work Shaw dominated the British stage from the opening of the modern period up to his death in 1950 – with the result that the main stream of "serious" drama in England is still political and largely naturalistic.

Not all compromises were as traditional as Shaw's. When linked with Marxist ideology, Futurism proved a vital catalyst; and the theatrical styles developed during the 1920s by Vsevolod Meyerhold in Russia and Erwin Piscator in Germany each represent different applications of futurist principles. Meyerhold's system of "biomechanics" applied industrial technology directly to performance, based on the analysis of production-line workers by Frederick Taylor (the inventor of time-and-motion studies) and Pavlov's behaviorist psychology. This was combined with "constructivist," nonrepresentational scenery. On Meyerhold's stage figures became types, and the actor's role was turned into a construct of movements, while the action became a montage of independent images. Following his colleague Eisenstein – who intriguingly had planned to film *Ulysses* even before Joyce found a publisher – Meyerhold isolated each beat in a production, every "episode" being played as an independent "turn," which produced highly exciting performances that emphasized "theatricality." But although on one level the equivalent of Pound's dislocated syntax and Imagism, these abstract qualities were translated into the physical, performative aspects of presentation. "Theatricality" in itself could be seen as the equivalent of the formalism that characterizes more literary expressions of Modernism, but in the theatre this led to the foregrounding of technology, not to abstraction, as Piscator's "documentary" drama demonstrates. Piscator used modern technology and mechanization as the controlling image for contemporary existence. For instance, in his 1927 production of *Rasputin, the Romanoffs, the War, and the People who Rose Up Against Them*, Piscator's staging (as his choice of title indicates) was the outline of an era, "condensing reality" and giving concrete shape to such sociological abstractions as "Capitalism" or "the class struggle" through the integration of film with acted scenes and a mechanized stage construct. A metallic half-globe that almost filled the stage, divided into multiple acting spaces behind hinged flaps, rotated or opened up into segments. Film could be projected on to its curving surface as well as surrounding screens, which together with a mobile "calendar" screen at one side of the stage juxtaposed different levels of reality. The fluidity and movement of the "globe" made a panoramic treatment of the epic sweep of events possible; swiveling like a tank turret from scene to scene, it served as a graphic image of the modern technology that gave the First World War its scope and intensity.[30] However, both "biomechanics" and "documentary drama" were short-lived. Piscator was only able to sustain his own theatre for two years before the exorbitant cost of such technological productions forced it into bankruptcy, while Meyerhold fell victim to Stalin and his censored work only started to become known over thirty years after his murder.

Even so, their ideas were carried forward – in a very changed shape – by the most influential dramatist of the century, Bertolt Brecht. It was while Brecht was working with Piscator that he developed his concept of an "epic theatre"; and in many ways his unrepresentational form of staging, which broke down characterization by emphasizing the act of acting and separated out the various elements of presentation, echoed Meyerhold. Brecht had also admired Eliot's *Sweeney Agonistes*, and since his first plays were expressionist, his work effectively gathered together the major streams of theatrical Modernism.

Brecht dismissed both "Aristotelian" dramatic forms and "culinary" commercial entertainment, and in 1929 posed a question that remains the fundamental challenge for contemporary theatre: "Can we speak of money in iambics? . . . Petroleum resists the five-act form; today's catastrophes do not progress in a straight line but in cyclical crises . . . Even to dramatize a simple newspaper report one needs something much more than the dramatic technique of a Hebbel or an Ibsen." It is a typically modernist question; and for Brecht the only solution was political: to represent the world "as being capable of transformation."[31] That formed the thesis of *Man is Man* in 1926, which demonstrates that personality is completely changeable, indeed interchangeable, being the product of social conditioning. Carried into the dualistic, even schizoid figures of his mature plays, where instinct conflicts with the dictates of class or wealth, this creates a radically different type of dramatic character from the coherent individual of naturalism. Thus, in *The Good Person of Setzuan*, the kind-natured, but poor and helpless female protagonist takes on the persona and appearance of a ruthless male capitalist to protect her unborn child. Brecht's actors were also trained to present their roles objectively: for instance, through rehearsing speeches replacing the first-person "I" with "s/he said . . ." Frequently masked, his actors were required to demonstrate the act of acting instead of pretending to "be" the characters, an approach derived partly from Chinese theatre. The aim of such techniques was to prevent empathy, although the effect was a precise theatrical rendering of the fragmented and dissociated personality that preoccupied modernist poets and painters.

The type of structure that Brecht developed was just as much a departure from the naturalistic norm. In deliberate contrast to the linear plots of standard "dramatic" theatre, Brecht used techniques to present events as narrative – hence his label of "epic theatre" – creating discontinuous action from a montage of scenes. Linked primarily by their illustrative relationship to a central political theme (though in practice Brecht's plays also provide other through-lines, with the same central figures occupying each scene, and developing situations), the sequences proceed "in curves / jumps".[32] Thus in *The Caucasian Chalk Circle* each half of the play starts at the same point, and covers the same time-frame from completely opposed perspectives. The double action then fuses together in the final scene to provide a solution to the apparently very different type of problem raised in the preface, which is not only set in another century but presented in a radically different style. With the exception of his first play, *Baal* (an expressionistic exploration of a poet's vision) Brecht's approach is the opposite of stream-of-consciousness. Yet his "epic" play-construction echoes the "curvilinear" forms of modernist painting, as well as the discontinuity and montage of modernist literature.

In addition to fragmenting traditional plot lines and characterization, the various elements of theatre were to be separated: speech from gesture, voice from music. Again, although explicitly designed as an antidote to the Wagnerian synthesis that included the audience in an emotional unity (which Brecht saw as inherently reactionary), such disconnection and diffraction have identifiable correlatives in other modernist art. This complication of the actor's function was accompanied by extreme simplification in staging. Brecht's settings are stripped down, and placards indicate the scene or give information to remove suspense. Machinery and lights are exposed to prevent illusion; stagehands work in full view and instrumentalists playing the music for the songs that punctuate Brecht's plays are visible to the audience. A "half-curtain" replaces the solid drapes that customarily close the proscenium arch, to emphasize that the stage is not a special or magical space, but part of the everyday world. However, removing pretended illusion has the effect of emphasizing performance. Rather than "metatheatre" – a traditional technique where theatre is used as a metaphor through references to the stage in a play text (for instance the appearance of actors and the "mousetrap" play-within-a-play in *Hamlet*) – Brecht's overt theatricality highlights the form of presentation purely as a means of communication. The few metatheatrical moments that occur in his work are parodistic – as with the mounted messenger bringing the Queen's pardon just as Macheath is about to be hung at the close of *The Threepenny Opera* – and in general the exposure of stage mechanisms and of the actor behind each character carries no added signification. It is the theatrical equivalent of modernist formalism.

At the same time, for all the extreme positions taken in his theory – and in the number of manifestos and essays accompanying his plays too, Brecht is typically modernist – Brecht's work mediates between antitraditional form and conventional dramatic content almost to the same degree as Shaw (whom Brecht in fact saw as sharing many of his own aims). Despite all the avoidance of empathy through "distancing" techniques, objectification, and "clinical" lighting, Brecht's theatre is by no means purely rational, as he continually claimed. On the stage, his plays have an exceptionally strong emotional charge, which is actually intensified by "factual" presentation. Spectators fainted in 1929 when a giant clown was sawn apart limb from limb in the *Baden-Baden Cantata of Acquiescence*, even though the dismemberment was clearly unrealistic, being carried out by other clowns on a grotesque figure with obviously wooden arms and legs. Later plays like *Mother Courage* or *The Caucasian Chalk Circle* contain moments of tear-jerking melodrama or nail-biting suspense. A dumb girl sacrifices herself to save the children of a besieged town, beating a drum despite the rifles of the assaulting troops leveled at her. A desperate flight, babe in arms and brutal pursuers at heels, over a rickety bridge, rivals such spectacularly melodramatic sequences as the escape over the ice in the nineteenth-century classic of melodrama, *Uncle Tom's Cabin*. Even Brecht's principle of montage has an inherent effect of intensification, since in practice it focuses exclusively on the "high points" of an action. Indeed, corresponding to the distinction McLuhan pointed out between "cool" and "hot" mediums of expression (where the less emotion in the way an image is presented, the more powerfully it affects the spectators who read in their own feelings), the restraint of Brecht's techniques and the purely denotative quality of presentation make for more audience involvement than the most rhetorical and emotive of traditional performances.[33]

Perhaps as a result, Brecht is the only dramatist to translate the principles of Modernism to the stage and at the same time create strikingly successful theatre. His plays almost immediately attained the status of modern classics, and unlike most modernist experiments, have become as much a part of the theatrical mainstream as Shaw's work. However, in contrast to all other Modernists, Brecht gained his own, state-supported theatre where for the last decade of his life he was able to set the style of presentation for his plays. Even in the 1920s he had gathered a group of actors committed to his ideas, and at the Berliner Ensemble with a whole troupe trained specifically in his method as well as complete control of productions, Brecht created definitive performances of his major works. Where the other

Modernists were relegated to the theatrical fringes, or (like Shaw) found that the commercial theatre distorted their work, Brecht was unique in having the ability to set his own artistic agenda.

As one novelist and poet put it, the key quality defining modernist art was the "unflinching aim – to register my own times in terms of my own time"; and in their very different ways each of the playwrights and directors in the movement follow this underlying principle. Given the public and social nature of stage performances, however, almost all had strong and overt political motivation. Practically the only exceptions are the early Imagists, Yeats and Craig – although Yeats, too, was highly political in the Irish nationalism of a play like *Cathleen ni Houlihan*, and together with Eliot has been accused of fascist tendencies. Shaw embraced Fabianism; Brecht and Meyerhold were committed Marxists. Even Dada and the Surrealists adopted Communism – despite the fundamental contradiction between their aims and the materialist ideology of Marxism – while many of the Futurists turned to fascism, with Marinetti becoming Mussolini's minister for culture. Artaud, too, declared that "our present social state is iniquitous and should be destroyed. If this fact is a preoccupation for theatre, it is even more of a matter for machine-guns," and this anarchic extremism also led to fascist tendencies, with Artaud dedicating a poem to Hitler.[34] Even O'Neill, who in one early poem had compared himself to a submarine with his words as torpedoes that would explode the American social structure, writes as a revolutionary socialist in his early modernist plays. In the first draft of *The Hairy Ape*, for instance, his eponymous hero Yank ends by joining the IWW (International Workers of the World) – and it is noticeable that this political commitment vanishes as his drama moved away from Modernism.

By contrast, there was no such open ideological commitment among Modernists writing in other forms. However political Eliot's views or the implications of the theories expounded in his essays, his poetry speaks in universal and religious terms. The singular exception is Ezra Pound, with his embrace of fascism. In general the principles of Modernism, as expressed in poetry and painting, deny the validity of politics. But in drama, stylistic and social revolution went together.

Drama is also distinct from other forms of Modernism in that modernist principles are still active. Although the main creative period of modernist theatre occupied the first thirty years of the century, arguably it has not yet been completely superseded by postmodernism in drama. In a sense, Samuel Beckett's plays represent a decisive new breakthrough, as does Robert Wilson's work. Yet Brecht's theatre gained fresh influence in the late fifties and through the 1960s, while Artaud became the ideal of American radicals in the late sixties and through the 1970s, as well as conditioning the work of Peter Brook. An example of the way in which Modernism continues to inform contemporary developments can be seen in the work of Harold Pinter, who is usually seen as a follower of Beckett. Pinter not only subverts realistic sets and rational structures. Particularly in his "memory plays" of the 1970s, he creates a drama of the mind, which directly corresponds with Walter Pater's principle in aspiring to the condition of music through the emotionally evocative, rhythmic patterning of the dialogue and the associative repetition of images. Indeed Pinter openly acknowledges a relationship to one of the leading Modernists in *Old Times* (1971). All his "memory plays" build on Eliot's lines, "Time present and time past / Are both perhaps present in time future . . . And all time is unredeemable" from *The Four Quartets*; and in *Old Times* one of the soliloquies is full of allusions to Eliot's poetry, in particular *The Love Song of J. Alfred Prufrock*.

Pinter has become a standard feature on the commercial stage as well as in the National Theatre; and his example demonstrates the degree to which Modernism has become the norm for drama. The inherently conservative nature of the stage may have meant that the adoption of modernist principles were delayed in mainstream drama. However, these are now diffused everywhere, even if the modernist enterprise is no longer clearly identifiable, and in the theatre Modernism has become merged with other approaches.

NOTES

1 For example, Peter Faulkner's *Modernism* (London: Methuen, 1977), glances at drama in one brief paragraph, but only to disqualify the genre from the movement as tending "towards the direct representation of social experience rather than the complexities of Modernism" (p. 21).

2 T. S. Eliot, "*Ulysses*, Order and Myth," *Dial* (November 1923): 483; Wassily Kandinsky, *Concerning the Spiritual in Art* (1912; New York: Morgan Press, 1972), p. 71.

3 Wyndham Lewis, *Blast*, 1 (June 1914): 141; Henri Gaudier-Brzeska, "Vortex. Gaudier-Brzeska," *Blast*, 1 (June 1914): 155.

4 Wyndham Lewis, *Blasting and Bombadiering* (London: Eyre and Spottiswoode, 1937), p. 285; and *A Soldier of Humour and Selected Writings*, ed. Raymond Rosenthal (New York: Signet, 1966), pp. 86, 83, 101, 105, 104, 74, 76 and 84.

5 *A Soldier of Humour and Selected Writings*, pp. 118, 121, 122, 129; *Blasting and Bombadiering*, p. 49.

6 Ezra Pound, "Fenellosa on the Noh" in *The Translations of Ezra Pound* (New York: New Directions, 1953), pp. 279–80, and W. B. Yeats, *Explorations* (London: Macmillan, 1962), p. 178.

7 *The Variorum Edition of the Plays of W. B. Yeats* ed. Russell K. Alspach (London: Macmillan, 1966), p. 400, and W. B. Yeats, *Essays and Introductions* (London: Macmillan, 1961), p. 230.

8 *W. B. Yeats and T. Sturge Moore: Their Correspondence, 1901–1937*, ed. Ursula Bridge (New York: Oxford University Press, 1953), p. 156.

9 W. B. Yeats, *Saturday Review*, 8 March 1902, Max Beerbohm, *Saturday Review*, 5 April 1902.

10 Ezra Pound, *Gaudier-Brzeska* (New York: New Directions, 1970), p. 98, and E. G. Craig, patent application AD 24 January 1910, no. 1771, pp. 1 and 2.

11 E. G. Craig, cited in Maurice Magnus, unpublished typescript, 1907 (Humanities Research Center, Austin, Texas). For a full discussion of Craig's art, see Christopher Innes, *Edward Gordon Craig* (Cambridge: Cambridge University Press, 1983).

12 W. B. Yeats, in the *Irish Statesman*, 29 November 1919, and E. G. Craig, *On the Art of the Theatre* (London: Mercury Books, 1962), pp. 46–7 (Craig's italics).

13 Erwin Kalser, programme note to *Von Morgens bis Mitternacht*, Lessingtheater, Berlin, 1916, and Stefan Zweig, in *Das Neue Pathos*, 1 (Berlin, 1913): 2.

14 *Six Plays of Strindberg*, trans. Elizabeth Sprigge (Garden City, NY: Doubleday, 1955), pp. 193, 199.

15 Oskar Kokoschka, *My Life* (London: Thames and Hudson, 1974), pp. 26–7.

16 André Breton, *Manifestes du Surréalisme* (Paris: Pauvert, 1962), p. 40.

17 Antonin Artaud, *The Theatre and Its Double* (Paris, 1938), trans. Mary Caroline Richards (New York: Grove Press, 1958), p. 92.

18 Ibid., pp. 115, 23 and 85; Antonin Artaud, *Oeuvres complétes* (Paris: Gallimard, 1961–74), vol. II, p. 37 and vol. III, pp. 22–3; and Antonin Artaud in *Cinémagazine* (9 September 1927).

19 Antonin Artaud, *The Theatre and Its Double*, p. 7.

20 Ibid., pp. 13, 87, 54, 57–8.

21 Ibid., pp. 86 and 85.

22 Michael Benedikt, *Modern French Theatre*, trans. Michael Benedikt and George Wellwarth (New York: Dutton, 1966), pp. 223–6. For a full discussion of Artaud's drama, see Christopher Innes, *Avant Garde Theatre* (London: Routledge, 1993), pp. 59ff.

23 T. S. Eliot, cited in *The Journals of Arnold Bennett, 1921–1929* (London: Cassell, 1933), p. 52, and Richard Doone, producer's note in the programme for the Westminster Theatre production, 1 October 1935.

24 T. S. Eliot, *The Use of Poetry and the Use of Criticism* (London: Faber and Faber, 1933), pp. 152–3.

25 T. S. Eliot, *On Poetry and Poets* (London: Faber and Faber, 1957), p. 31, and in *Dial* (December 1922): 659. For a full description of the 1934 and 1935 Group Theatre productions of *Sweeney Agonistes*, see Michael Sidnell, *Dances of Death* (London: Faber and Faber, 1984), pp. 100ff.

26 Eliot, *On Poetry and Poets*, p. 85.

27 George Bernard Shaw, *Shaw on Theatre*, ed. E. J. West (New York: Hill and Wang, 1958), p. 220, George Bernard Shaw, *Letters*, ed. Clifford Bax (New York: Dodd, Mead, 1942), p. 43.

28 *Misalliance*, p. 7; *Heartbreak House*, pp. 106, 96, 90 (in *The Works of George Bernard Shaw* [London: Constable, 1930–50]).

29 *George Bernard Shaw: A Critical Heritage*, ed. L. Kronenberger (New York: World, 1953). For a fuller discussion of *Heartbreak House*, and an alternative view of Shaw's "Modernism," see Christopher Innes, *Modern British Drama: 1890–1990* (Cambridge: Cambridge University Press, 1992), pp. 14ff.

30 For a full treatment of Piscator's work and a discussion of Brecht's involvement, see Christopher Innes, *Erwin Piscator's Political Theatre* (Cambridge: Cambridge University Press, 1972).

31 Bertolt Brecht, *Brecht On Theatre: the Development of an Aesthetic*, ed. and trans. John Willett (New York: Hill and Wang, 1964), pp. 30, 275.

32 Ibid., p. 37.

33 Although this has all too frequently not been the case when directors approach Brecht's plays through his theoretical writings, his own productions created a high degree of emotional involvement. Indeed, at the climax of a 1989 Berliner Ensemble performance of *Chalk Circle* in North America, many of the spectators actually wept at the small boy's cry as he is torn from the arms of the loving peasant girl to be given to the biological but unnatural mother who abandoned him as a baby.

34 Ford Madox Ford, preface (1911) in *Collected Poems* (Oxford: Oxford University Press, 1936), p. 327, and Autouin Artaud, *The Theatre and Its Double*, p. 42.

6

SARA BLAIR

Modernism and the politics of culture

Since its inception as a category of literary study during the 1930s, Modernism has been notoriously inhospitable to definition. Nowhere is this inhospitability more pronounced than in the fraught issue of the relations of art to politics. How does aesthetic activity categorized as modernist stand in relation to forms of power? And how to the experiential realities that constitute the charged political dimensions of social life? With respect to these questions, Anglo-American Modernism has been both celebrated and derided; it has been praised for its richness in negotiating historically new forms of experience, and it has equally been censured for a defensive fear and loathing of precisely those forms. To complicate matters even more, we find the makers of Modernism spread all over the political map of twentieth-century Western Europe, England, and America: running with Reds; making political broadcasts for Mussolini; militating against the Ku Klux Klan; arguing for free speech and free love as well as free verse. How are we, then, as latter-day readers, to evaluate the political meaning of Modernism, especially when we are taught that its most notable – indeed, perhaps *only* – unifying feature was the attempt to transcend the political altogether?

W. H. Auden sums up this common literary historical wisdom in the admonition that "Art is not life and cannot be / A midwife to society." This way of reading – indeed, of *constituting* – literature, as a hermetically distinct sphere of activity willfully set apart from the rough-and-tumble of everyday social life, is a useful point of origin for our purposes. But even this vision of art, it must be noted, amounts to a political stance, albeit one of willed withdrawal. And historically speaking it neglects the busy two-way traffic making up what the bracing American critic Lionel Trilling would call "the dark and bloody crossroads" of politics and art in this era.[1] What Auden's lines obscure are the ways in which modernist texts, writers, and institutions not only reflect (in the mimetic sense) but in turn contribute to social experience, shaping ideals being forged in the name of culture.

These include, but are not limited to, the wide range of political operations and events in which Anglo-American Modernists self-consciously assist, from militarist right-wing movements to progressive labor, feminist, and race struggles, mounted from Paris to Paterson, New Jersey. How can we most productively read the politics of Modernism, from right to left, across that enormous range of commitments? Indeed, how might our reading of the political change or newly inform an understanding of the problems of constituting a literary field such as Modernism itself?

I want to address these questions by mapping the fields of modernist activity in the following way. Rather than rely on traditional political and social markers – the death of Victoria in 1901, the war of 1914–18, the inauguration of Prohibition and the Jazz Age in 1919 – I want to examine the engagements of Anglo-American Modernists with explicitly political activity, both on the right and the left, with an eye toward the range of commitments exercised under the banner of art, culture, the literary. This kind of summary will not only help us reconsider the political aspirations of modernist texts long canonized as hermetic literary machines, indifferent to contemporary experience; it will also allow us to recover fierce contests over the social meaning of the literary that themselves, I argue, constitute the real politics of Modernism – understood not only as engagement in particular movements but as a set of ongoing activities. In the moment of Modernism, "culture" itself – what constitutes it, whose property it is, how it identifies or informs national or racial bodies – is a deeply political issue. And this fact, it can be argued, is Modernism's most important contribution to the politics of its moment, and to those of our own.

Modernism on the right

I begin with the most often-noted, most problematic version of Modernism and politics: its notorious engagements with Fascism. What kind of sense can we make – or do we want to make – of Modernism's flirtations and fascinations with militarism, xenophobia, racism, and anti-Semitism, in all their shifting forms? How should we read the engagement with fascist ideology and leadership of such canonical figures as Ezra Pound, Wyndham Lewis, and other Anglo-American "men of 1914"? And to what extent is it possible or desirable to distinguish "aesthetics" from "politics" in a reading of Pound's *Cantos*, or of T. S. Eliot's pronouncements on Christian order and Christian society? Although numerous studies have been made of Modernism's alliances with an extreme political right, it is worth rehearsing here briefly some of the most infamous episodes, with a view to the way in which literary ideology – notions of tradition, poetic value, and form – are knottily entangled with more narrowly political ideologies of culture, nation, modernization, and race.

For a baseline sense of the political designs of modernist aesthetics we have only to recall the titles of some of the projects associated with its traditionalist wing: *Blast*, the aptly named journal produced by Wyndham Lewis and Ezra Pound; *Ripostes*, the title of Pound's 1912 collection of verse; *The Enemy*, a review of art and literature edited by Lewis. In these texts, as in the agenda-defining polemics of T. E. Hulme, the energy of formal and narrative experimentation is clearly understood as a political force. In particular, that energy is a salvo directed against Victorian humanist social ideals and the contemporary versions of populism, individualism, and liberalism they were thought to inform. Hulme, the movement's most effective advance man and influential formulator of modernist ideology in such essays as "Romanticism and Classicism" (1913), pungently dismissed liberal conceptions of human nature and the literary practices of romanticism alike as "spilt religion"; the only cure for these linked ills, he argued, was a return to managed social orders and to "har[d]," "dry," "definite" forms of literary expression that would delineate them.[2] These kinds of social commitments, it must be noted, are continuous with Pound's well-known imagist, or aesthetic, dicta (brevity, precision, anti-sentimentality) – and they bear more than a family resemblance to idioms of militant nationalism emerging in Anglo-American politics. In a kind of cultural militancy, both Hulme and Lewis cultivated relations with fascist movements: for Hulme, the prewar *Action française*, a cadre of French right-wing intellectuals led by Charles Maurras, committed to guerrilla action against so-called "degenerate" cultures and thereby to the "salvation" of European cultural institutions for their rightful (white) inheritors; for Lewis, Nazi Berlin and Hitler, whom he celebrated in a 1930 study for the power to unify "white Europe" and provide an "antidote" to both corporate capitalism and Soviet socialism.[3] If Hulme and Lewis directed their considerable intellectual and narrative energies to proselytizing for aesthetics as a distinct realm of human activity, those energies derived powerfully from the radicalism of the contemporary right, and they promoted versions of culture that were – at least in their moment of inception – securely linked to ideals of racial fitness and purity.[4]

The acknowledged master of this high modernist milieu, T. S. Eliot, likewise fashioned his poetics in increasingly conversative if less militant lineaments. He labeled himself – only partly in jest – "'classicist in literature, royalist in politics, and Anglo-Catholic in religion," and his landmark essay "Tradition and the Individual Talent" (1917) would make a cultural politics of tradition central to the canons of English-language poetry for decades to come.⁵ Eliot became increasingly preoccupied with what he would call the idea of a Christian society (the title of a collection of essays appearing in 1939); after his formal conversion to Anglicanism in 1927, he became fully invested in the church as the premier source of political and social authority. By 1933 he would infamously pronounce in the published (but never republished) version of his lectures at the University of Virginia, *After Strange Gods*, on the dangers of "free-thinking Jews" – a virtual trope for Eliot for "adulterat[ion]" and Europe's "inva[sion] by foreign races" – to the continuity of that Western cultural tradition.⁶

Eliot alone of this group had no formal ties to English or European Fascist groups. But as Anthony Julius has recently argued, his poetry and poetics during the 1920s turn on some of the least apologetic, most virulently anti-Semitic images in all of that same Western tradition.⁷ In "Burbank with a Baedeker, Bleistein with Cigar," Eliot's signature preoccupation with the decadence and enervation of modernity takes the form of a Jew-baiting all too common to right-wing critiques of modernity's social forms. The ubiquitous Bleistein – "Chicago Semite Viennese" – "Stares from the protozoic slime" at monuments of Western civilization, whose talismanic power fails to protect against the ravages of retrogression and "Declin[e]": "The rats are underneath the pile. / The jew is underneath the lot." Here, as in fascist propaganda in Germany, England, France, and the US, the Jew could conveniently be invoked to signify all the worst excesses of modernity: capitalism, spurious production divorced from a realm of value, sexual degeneracy or impotence, the perversion of "true" cultural (or racial) characters, histories, ideals.

If such figures for the corruption of an ostensibly unified, authentic, organically Western culture are themselves "underneath the lot" of Eliot's œuvre, critics have felt able to bracket or excise them in readings of individual texts.⁸ (Indeed, such poems as "Burbank" rarely appear in anthologies of Eliot, Modernism, or twentieth-century poetry.) But the same gesture is virtually impossible to make in the case of Ezra Pound. Tireless promoter, literary midwife, editor extraordinaire, apologist for Italian Fascism, he would be described by *Time* magazine in a suitably flippant homage as "part despot, part poet, part press agent."⁹ His *Cantos* began appearing in 1917; by the mid-1920s they already smack of the strange stew of Chinese ideograms, Jeffersonian agrarianism, and populist poetics – a mishmash of political, economic, and aesthetic theories and pseudo-theories – that would be more elaborately recorded in his *A B C of Economics* (1933) and *Fifth Decade of Cantos* (1937). The result was political notoriety: to date, Pound is the only author entrenched in the American canon – and indeed, one of only very few US citizens ever – to have been indicted for treason. Throughout the Second World War, he inveighed live on Rome Radio against then-president Franklin Roosevelt, the US, and Jews (whose extermination he publicly approved), preaching the fascist social order installed by Mussolini and Hitler.[10] Excoriating "twenty years of Judaic propaganda, Lenin and Trotsky stuff," Pound attempted to rally "real" Americans under the banner of militant racial purity and cultural authenticity.[11] His appeals to extremist anxieties of "liberty" are all too familiar in historical context:

> And how much liberty have you got, anyhow? And as to the arsenal – are you the arsenal of democracy or of judeocracy? And who rules your rulers? Where does public responsibility end and what races can mix in America without ruin of the American stock, the American brain? Who is organized? What say have you in the choice of your rulers? What control of their policy? And who does own most of your press and your radio? E.P. asking you.[12]

Based on these performances, Pound was indicted for treason in 1943 and confined in a US Army stockade in Pisa, where he wrote some of his most technically accomplished, emotionally complex verse. In 1945 he was flown to Washington, DC for legal proceedings, but judged unfit to stand trial by court-appointed psychologists, who testifed that Pound suffered from "delusions of grandeur."[13] The unofficial poet laureate of Modernism was confined to St. Elizabeth's Hospital for the Criminally Insane until 1958, when such influential writers as Robert Frost, Ernest Hemingway, and Archibald MacLeish successfully lobbied for dismissal of the charges. In the interim Pound's literary reputation grew stronger; in 1949 he was awarded the Library of Congress's highly prestigious Bollingen Prize. The result was a political firestorm, raging not only in elite cultural circles but throughout the popular press. Supporters contended that the choice valorized the value of "pure" poetry, while protestors deplored the racism and political intolerance of his anti-"usury" gospel.

What makes this episode emblematic for our purposes is precisely the questions it raises about what has been taken to be Modernism's definitive ideology: the belief that art is, and should be, radically distinct from life; that aesthetics and politics constitute entirely separate spheres of action, value, and consequence. There are some serious questions to be raised about the relation between that ideology and modernist texts, and some equally serious questions about how that ideology continues to inflect our notions of what literature is and how it makes sense, makes ideals, for its readers. In the case of Pound, scholars still hotly debate the relative *aesthetic* merits of those moments in *The Cantos* that blast false monetary systems, the reign of "Rothschild," and the "Eunited States uv America," and perversely exalt ancient Greek rites, the highly dubious "social credit" theories of contemporary economist C. H. Douglas, and images of natural fertility.[14] But is there any way of considering Pound's famous "ideogrammatic method" – what he himself would call the "*kinema*" or movement of his art, with its charged energy of presentation and critique – in isolation from its venomous images of racial and cultural threat? Do we read such towering poems rightly if we insist on their status as merely poetic documents, whose investments in political and social experience can be justifiably ignored? In such moments, in such texts, can aesthetic intention or effect be distinguished from politics at all?

To ignore the problem, as some critics have done, with respect to Pound or Eliot – or indeed any of Modernism's right-leaning writers – is hardly satisfactory. Any attempt to read modernist texts "neutrally," as *purely* aesthetic objects, itself constitutes a political act, not least in that it valorizes formal expression over social commitment. Nor is the out-of-hand dismissal of such texts as politically corrupt or offensive a sufficient gesture, since it forecloses possibilities for closer thinking about how literature, in its distinctive forms, ideals, and performances, means variously in contexts beyond its immediate ones. Literary theorists Fredric Jameson and Julia Kristeva, writing respectively on the fascist engagements of Wyndham Lewis and of the French writer Céline, have powerfully argued that specific literary performances undercut, exceed, or problematize the explicit commitments of their authors.[15] In so doing, these critics tend to minimize the problem posed for latter-day readers by Modernism's vigorous flirtations with Fascism. But they productively point the way toward recognition of the much more varied political and social work being done in the early twentieth century by literature, and by modernist formalism in particular.

For high Anglo-American Modernism, with its embrace of ideals of cultural unity and organicism, hierarchy, and social order, is only one of many Modernisms – only one, that is, of many historically linked attempts to reformulate the conditions under which literature was being produced. The vaunted energy, formal experimentation, and psychic shock of modernist texts in the moment of their appearance (much of which is lost to us through the force of familiarity and canonization) were hardly the sole property of culturally conservative writers, nor were their effects limited to the familiar circles associated with those figures. In a vast array of contexts and places, writers during the era of high Modernism and beyond adapted its formalism and techniques, even its defining idioms, often so as to contest its political commitments. This was especially true for certain women, African–American, and socialist writers – what we can cautiously, with qualification, term writers on the left – attempting to open new public spaces or spheres for the expression of varied responses to modernity, and various political and social claims on its realities.[16] By considering the broader political and social contexts of Modernism, and of literary production at large, we will gain a clearer view of these efforts, of their successes and their limits – and of the ways in which distinctly literary experimentation participated in the matrix (if not vortex) of modern social and political life.

The challenges of modernity

Why, the latter-day reader of Modernism might ask, has the circumference of politics been so narrowly drawn in our readings of the era? The traditional critical focus on Modernists as fascists – while certainly important, especially as an historical corrective – has obscured the much broader range of commitments to which modernist projects, polemics, and concerns were being harnessed. If the burden of modernist experimentation was the imperative to "make it new," as Pound's mantra would have it, the project of renewal encompassed a vast array of social traditions, norms, and gestures. Across numerous geographic and political divides, writers in the English-speaking world of 1900–1930 were participating not only in right-wing politics, or even politics in the usual narrow sense, but in the very grounds of their emergence: seismic shifts in the organization of cultural and political life, largely in the direction of increased mobility, technological complexity, and social heterogeneity. To grasp more fully how the concerns of high Modernism inform literary engagements on the left, we need to consider those shifts in some detail.

In Britain, the century's second decade ushered in the accession of George V to the throne (1910), increasingly visible public demonstrations mounted by militant suffragists and labor leaders, and the rise of the Labour party in national politics, culminating in the achievement of the first Labour government in 1923. All were evidence of a definitive break with Victorian norms of sobriety and social control. If that kind of break was at least partly threatening for cultural conservatives, it was celebrated as a felt turning point in the realm of everyday life by such differently committed writers as Virginia Woolf, who would describe the shift in characteristically domestic (and high bourgeois) terms:

> [O]n or about December 1910, human character changed . . . In life one can see the change, if I may use a homely illustration, in the character of one's cook. The Victorian cook lived like a leviathan in the lower depths, formidable, silent, obscure, inscrutable; the Georgian cook is a creature of sunshine

and fresh air; in and out of the drawing-room, now to borrow *The Daily Herald*, now to ask advice about a hat. Do you ask for more solemn instances of the power of the human race to change?[17]

Woolf's local image usefully suggests the entanglement of what we call politics and what we call culture as forms of experience; and it evidences the way in which writers committed to socialist, Fabian, feminist, and other left platforms insisted on that connection. Under the sway of new, mass cultural organs of entertainment and information (like the *Daily Herald*, founded in 1919 as the first mass daily "workers' paper"[18]), of the forms of fashion and style they promote (like the fetching new hat), and of consumer desire at large (promoted by mass-produced goods that held out promises of material fulfillment to all), traditional and rigidly hierarchical codes of class and national identity, social distinction, and cultural value were being rapidly broken. For all her vaunted aestheticism, Woolf – as well as English and Irish novelists as diverse as H. G. Wells, John Galsworthy, D. H. Lawrence, and James Joyce – would make the newly visible materiality of this everyday, middle- and working-class life-world central to her aesthetic.

To the process of social transformation, to be sure, other more narrowly political projects were also crucial. Some, it is worth pointing out, were explicitly concerned with the power of culture – and especially literature – to promote citizenship and civic pride. Progressive reformers in early twentieth-century Britain successfully campaigned for increased opportunities for public education for working men and women; in the same era, the elite universities grudgingly opened their doors more widely to women students (although the latter were still refused the benefits of substantial endowment support at Oxford and Cambridge throughout the 1920s). Both educational reform campaigns traded heavily on claims about the specific value of English *literature* and literary history for these social groups – unlike their male and upper-class opposite numbers, who were still expected to school themselves in the "higher" disciplines of classical studies and history.

More broadly, British political life would be altered by the extension of suffrage to women in 1919, after intense and decades-long political activism by such leaders as Sylvia and Christabel Pankhurst, and by the aftershocks of the General Strike of 1926, the culmination of a half-century of socialist, union, and other forms of protest against the traditional concentration of the country's wealth in the hands of an oligarchy.[19] Even the politically and culturally conservative project of Empire would contribute to the full-tilt modernization of British social life, as striving members of the bourgeoisie availed themselves of new opportunities for professional service and distinction opened up by Britain's military–bureaucratic missions in South Asia and Africa. (Among them was Virginia Woolf's husband Leonard, who served with distinction in the colonial mission in Sri Lanka, then Ceylon.) If what Woolf somewhat anachronistically called "human character" – not only consciousness *per se*, but the private self in social relations, implicated in forms of leisure and work – decisively "changed" in Britain in the moment of Modernism, that change registers as simultaneously political and cultural in its scope and effects.

An even more drastic reordination of cultural life was taking place during the teens and twenties in the US, and with decided consequences for the activities we call literary. By 1920, for the first time in US history, the majority of the country's 105 million citizens lived in urban centers. There, the effects of a new economic and social structure, monopoly capitalism, and of new technologies of leisure and entertainment, like radio, the movies, and sound recording, were being felt with an unstable mixture of enthusiasm and trepidation. If the American metropolis brought "the shock of the new" to bear on individuals with unprecedented power, it also served as a site for the eruption of anxieties about the social, psychic, and spiritual effects of modernity and modernization. Throughout the era of Modernism, the city symbolized the challenges of confronting not only the new but also the culturally other. Between 1880 and 1920 approximately 28,000,000 immigrants – mainly of southern and eastern European origin, and thus of the so-called "darker races" – entered the US, the vast majority settling in New York City, where by 1920 only one of every six inhabitants was white, US-born, and Protestant. The immigrants were joined by millions of African–Americans migrating from the rural South to industrial northern and midwestern centers, seeking economic and social opportunities attendant on the new status of the US as world industrial leader.

These kinds of cultural dislocation produced much of what we now count as American culture of the first decades of the century, including Tin Pan Alley, ragtime, jazz, and early Hollywood, and they contributed immeasurably to varied styles of avant-garde, bohemian, and high literary performance.[20] They also produced seething ethnic and racial tensions: white-on-black violence in cities as far flung as East St. Louis, Houston, and Chicago, which ultimately necessitated armed self-defense by African–Americans (termed "race riots") in 1919; the rise of black nationalism, promoted by such figures as Jamaican-born Marcus Garvey, whose Universal Negro Improvement Association advocated complete separation from white culture through return to Africa; the resurgence of the Ku Klux Klan, which reached its political apogee in the mid-1920s; and finally, and most ignominiously, such political *causes célèbres* as the 1914 lynching of Atlanta businessman Leo Frank, a Jew, for the supposed murder of an employee, the dubious conviction in 1921 of decidedly "foreign" anarchists Nicola Sacco and Bartolomeo Vanzetti for bank robbery and murder, and the 1931 incarceration in Alabama of nine African–American men, the Scottsboro "boys," on trumped-up charges of raping two white women.

No wonder then, that "making it new" could simultaneously mean the open embrace of modernity's opportunities and the defensive rejection of its challenges. For every figure of high anxiety, racial mastery, and loathing of modernity – the primal native woman in Conrad's *Heart of Darkness*, D. H. Lawrence's fetishized primitives, Eliot's Bleistein – we encounter equally assertive figures of curiosity, identification with the new aesthetic and social possibilities opened up by facts of mass production, urbanization, and cultural heterogeneity. If Eliot's *Four Quartets* (1943) seek a space in which time can be made static, present and eternal, Gertrude Stein's famously experimental prose playfully explores modernity's new "space of time that is filled always filled with moving."[21] Even as Pound blasted industrial, monopoly capitalism as a state of "botched civilization" and looked definitively elsewhere – to sixteenth-century Italian architecture, traditional Provençal lyrics, Confucian philosophy, and medieval economic history – for cultural and political models, William Carlos Williams would dismiss such anti-modernism as profoundly limiting. His own epic poem, *Paterson* (1946–58), concurs with Pound's modernist dictum of exhaustion, arguing that "The language is worn out," but works to renew it through commitment to the American now – the language of modernity, in which "noble has been / changed to no bull" and "things . . . lie under the direct scrutiny of the senses, close to the nose."[22] Even that arch-aesthete, Wallace Stevens, often taken in landmark poems like "The Idea of Order at Key West" and "Thirteen Ways of Looking at a Blackbird" to inscribe Modernism's most hermetic impulses, wrote privately in his journal that all his poetry ultimately concerns the shared realities of its moment: the hard facts of "What one reads in the papers."[23]

Modernism, in other words, can with qualification be understood as a unified movement promoting a distinct set of concerns, foremost among them a commitment to experimenting with the cultural power of literary traditions and forms. But to understand that commitment as necessarily linked with conservative, fascist, or right-wing political ideals is to miss the contestatory nature of Modernism's investments in form, technique, and literary value. If the landscape of modernity reads to Eliot and company as a symbolic wasteland, it appears for other writers to be a Mecca, a metropolis of multivalent possibilities. Against the powerful vision of the

Unreal City, we must accordingly counterpose actual sites of literary production and engagement in which writers, adopting modernist devices and concerns, relate themselves quite differently to the challenges of the modern. I thus want to conclude by considering briefly two such sites, and some of the writers and culture-makers who inhabited them: Greenwich Village and Harlem. Both emerged in New York, which we might justifiably call – after Walter Benjamin's famous description of Paris as the capital of the nineteenth century – the first city of the twentieth. And both fostered literary practices and engagements construed in continuing, sometimes tense dialogue with Modernism in the more restricted sense. The results – aesthetic, social, political – may have been uneven and short-lived, but they nonetheless remind us how variously the ideals of formalism, tradition, and literary commitment could be negotiated and deployed.

Literary spaces: Greenwich Village and Harlem, USA

Every self-respecting American bohemian knows Greenwich Village; for almost a century, the name has been a virtual synonym for poetry readings, Beat happenings, *literati*, the doings of the avant-garde. This association was especially resonant during the teens and twenties, when literary and social experimentation were explicitly conjoined with political activism. At the very heart of the Village's social life during these decades were flamboyant literary salons, sponsored by the likes of wealthy socialite-cum-radical Mabel Dodge. Such writers as Edmund Wilson and Malcolm Cowley – later extremely important critics of Modernism – Edna Millay, Theodore Dreiser, and Sinclair Lewis drank, opined, and recited poetry with the likes of radical labor organizer Big Bill Heywood, Communist John Reed (a classmate of Eliot's at Harvard, he was the only US citizen ever to be buried in the Kremlin), birth control pioneer Margaret Sanger, whose first clinic opened in 1916, and anarchist writer Emma Goldman, deported from the US during the anti-Communist Red Scare of 1919. This fluid interpenetration of literary and political avant-gardes within Village bohemia would produce several important cultural projects and artifacts. There were the energetic "little" magazines like the socialist *Masses* ("Bible of the radical"[24]), the Dada-inspired *Broom*, the urbane *Smart Set*, and the highly influential *Little Review*, housed in the Village during its glory years of 1917–22.[25] And there were such cognate mass-cultural spectacles as the 17 February 1913 Armory Show, which introduced post-impressionist art to an American public, and the 7 June 1913 Paterson Strike Pageant, lavishly staged by 1,500 striking textile workers in Madison Square Garden (at that time still an elite venue for leisure-class pleasures). Both exhibitions were organized by Village radicals for whom aesthetics and politics were virtually inseparable; if the shock for bourgeois viewers confronted with Marcel Duchamps' *Nude Descending a Staircase* involved very different cultural stakes than the battle for workers' rights, it nonetheless was felt to have the effect of "a political revolution," a "shattering even[t] . . . for the purpose of recreation."[26]

Such all-purpose radicalism, Daniel Aaron remarks in his landmark study of American left writers, reflected a generic "hostility of the artist to a world that . . . holds his [sic] values in contempt."[27] Emerging political realities – including the execution of Sacco and Vanzetti in 1927, the stock market crash of 1929, the uses of intimidation, terror, and state violence against striking mine workers in the early 1930s – would occasion a split among Village intelligentsia between "pink," or progressive, and deep-dyed Red. In a climate of increasingly bitter ideological opposition between liberal and radical, labor and management, white and "other" Americans, the porous boundaries between aesthetic and political agendas hardened; committed Communist Edmund Wilson would charge the young poets of the 1930s with adopting the "Gerontian pose" (after T. S. Eliot's elegantly attenuated persona in a poem of that name) and having "no stake in society."[28]

But even those writers most closely associated with hard-left politics of the obvious kind – including E. E. Cummings, whose flirtation with Communism waned after a 1931 pilgrimage to the USSR, Theodore Dreiser, who followed up his novelistic masterpiece, *An American Tragedy* (1925), with investigative trips to the Soviet Union and to Pittsburgh mining country, and John Dos Passos, who like Dreiser was charged with "criminal syndicalism" (labor agitation) for his investigative work on behalf of workers and Communists – remained indebted to many of the techniques and formal interests Wilson's comment was clearly meant to deride. In his *USA* trilogy, which included *The 42nd Parallel* (1930), *1919* (1932), and *The Big Money* (1936), Dos Passos renders urban life through the lens of "Camera Eye" and "newsreel," precisely by adapting the formal techniques of literary naturalism, Joycean impressionism, and the modernist collage. Malcolm Cowley, literary critic, novelist, poet, and the most important historian of the Village generation, would virtually define his cohort in such texts as *After the Genteel Tradition* (1937), *Books That Changed Our Mind* (1939), and *Exile's Return* (1951) against the cultural performances of Eliot, Joyce, and high Modernism – yet often with the same polemical energy and manipulation of *personae* he identifies as its signature formal characteristics. With respect to an evolving Village vanguard, then, the hard-and-fast distinction between Modernism and radicalism, between a self-reliant aesthetics and an active, engaged politics, looks deeply inadequate after all; in muckraking journalism and modernist blank verse, in experimental prose and in manifesto alike, we see a shared commitment to the value of literature and literary language as an active, and deeply social, power.

Above 125th Street in Manhattan, albeit worlds away, very different kinds of links between aesthetic activity and political activism were being forged during the same era. Like the Village, Harlem in its 1920s heyday boasted a spectacular salon life. Pacesetter A'Lelia Walker – nicknamed "the Great Black Empress," she had inherited a substantial fortune from her mother, who sold hair-straightening products to striving African–Americans – sponsored high society gatherings whose guest lists read "like a blue book of the seven arts."[29] Blacks and whites, royalty and racketeers alike, enjoyed extravagant hospitality in her Harlem mansion, dancing on the parquet floor or adjourning to the top-floor library, stocked with African–American literary achievements; she even had the verses of Langston Hughes's "Weary Blues" (1917) displayed on a wall. At novelist and critic Jessie Fauset's decidedly soberer salon, where conversations were often conducted in French, such political leaders as the quintessential black intellectual W. E. B. DuBois, Harlem Renaissance progenitor Alain Locke, and the charismatic labor activist A. Philip Randolph could be found engaging in such genteel activities as poetry recitation, oration, and book discussion. Indeed, for these self-styled "race men," this polite literary activity had heightened social force in the moment of modernity. "No race," the writer James Weldon Johnson would proclaim, "can ever become great that has not produced a literature."[30] Black aesthetic achievement – and particularly literary achievement – was understood by these culture builders as the clearest sign of black fitness for the demands of modernity; "pure" art would itself serve as a form of political activism, activity, propaganda. In the specific context of Harlem, and what has come to be called the Harlem or New Negro Renaissance, literary distinction served as a crucial index of political engagement and power.

This kind of ideology occasioned serious disagreement among the Renaissance's leading lights. If culture czar DuBois – progressive, elitist, and high bourgeois – would espouse an aesthetic of didacticism, by which the "Talented Tenth" (the leaders of the race) "rises and pulls all that are worthy of saving up to their vantage ground," younger writers like Langston Hughes and Zora Neale Hurston would vigorously oppose his ideology of uplift with an investment in the black vernacular and in such "low" forms as folktales, lying contests, and the blues.[31] In his most influential poems – "The Negro Speaks of Rivers," "The Weary Blues," and those collected in *Fine Clothes to the Jew* (1927) – Hughes wedded reigning formal conventions of Anglo-American verse to blues rhythms and idiom with remarkable results; Hurston's notoriously unclassifiable ethnographies, short stories, and prose works – including "The Eatonville Anthology" (1926), *Mules and Men* (1935), and *Their Eyes Were Watching God* (1937) – similarly insisted on the power of traditional orality to define and sustain African–American community in the face of ubiquitous threats to its health, empowerment, and survival. As ardently as DuBois, Locke, and other race leaders, Hurston vociferated for the power of aesthetic forms to enhance the self-imagination of black people – and to remake the larger culture they inhabited and shaped: "the world and America in particular," she argued, "need what this folk material holds."[32]

These *kinds* of investments, uptown and down-, in literature as resources for the renewal, transformation, or reanimation of collective life may seem naïve, misguided, in the retrospective light of the century's defining political realities: the Nazi Holocaust, bloody Stalinist purges of intellectuals and dissidents in the Soviet ranks, the rise of nativism and xenophobia during the 1920s and 1930s in the US, England, and throughout the West. But they nonetheless reveal how insufficient is our habitual mapping of literature in the early decades of the century as a self-enclosed activity, a defensive institution for warding off the new realities of the modern, urban metropole. In specific cultural locations, literary experimentation responsive to modernist ideals served as a social act, in and through which cultural value was constructed. In these places and ways, literature did extremely powerful political work, not (or not only) in the recognized mode of fascist or even liberal ideology, but by promoting collective activity, political enfranchisement, and increased access to cultural and civic institutions, especially for such hitherto unrepresented communities as African–Americans, immigrants, workers, and women. In this historically specific sense, Modernism has political ramifications far beyond those legible in conventional histories of its texts and forms. Reading with a heightened sense of these ligatures, we can productively cultivate a sense of how differently the aesthetic and the political *mean* earlier in the century. And we may also begin to understand the very distinction between aesthetics and politics – our felt sense of the incompatibility of these modes – as itself a product of modernist texts, history, and ideals.

NOTES

1 Lionel Trilling, "Reality in America" in *The Liberal Imagination: Essays on Literature and Society* (New York: Doubleday Anchor, 1957), p. 8.
2 T. E. Hulme, "Romanticism and Classicism" in *Speculations: Essays on*

Humanism and the Philosophy of Art (London: Routledge and Kegan Paul, 1949), pp. 118, 126, 132.

3 Wyndham Lewis, *Hitler* (1931) (New York: Gordon Press, 1972), p. 121. Lewis, it should be noted, withdrew his support of Hitler in a 1939 treatise ironically entitled *The Jews: Are They Human?* In *Fables of Aggression: Wyndham Lewis, the Modernist as Fascist* (Berkeley: University of California Press, 1979), Fredric Jameson has argued forcefully that Lewis is best understood not as fascist but as "proto-fascist"; see especially pp. 14–15 and pp. 180–2.

4 Feminist critic Janet Lyon has persuasively advanced the argument that male high Modernists – the "men of 1914" – appropriated the energy and form of suffragette discourse to create the rhetoric and high-art ideology of the avant-garde. See "Strange Bedfellows: Suffragettes and Vorticists before the War," *Differences*, 4.2 (Summer 1992): 100–32.

5 T. S. Eliot, preface to *For Lancelot Andrewes* (London: Faber and Faber, 1928), p. ix.

6 T. S. Eliot, *After Strange Gods* (New York: Harcourt Brace and Co., 1933), pp. 20, 17.

7 Anthony Julius, *T.S. Eliot, Anti-Semitism, and Literary Form* (Cambridge: Cambridge University Press, 1995).

8 Julius's "adversarial" readings of Eliot carefully outline arguments made by both detractors and defenders, noting that they have been equally misguided in attempting to bracket Eliot's anti-Semitic images and language: "Ignore the anti-Semitism," Julius argues, "and the poetry itself disappears" (ibid., p. 33).

9 "Treason," *Time*, 10 December 1945, reprinted in *A Casebook on Ezra Pound*, ed. William Van O'Connor and Edward Stone (New York: Thomas Y. Crowell and Co., 1959), p. 19.

10 On Pound's support for the extermination of Eastern European Jews, and his warnings to American Jews that "their turn was coming," see George Orwell, "The Question of the Pound Award," reprinted in O'Connor and Stone, *Casebook*, p. 61.

11 Pound, broadcast on Rome Radio, 26 February 1942 and 22 July 1942, reprinted ibid., pp. 163, 164.

12 Pound, Broadcast on Rome Radio, 22 July 1942, reprinted ibid., p. 164.

13 "Pound Foolish," *Newsweek*, 25 February 1946, reprinted ibid., p. 23.

14 Ezra Pound, "Canto XLVI," *The Cantos of Ezra Pound* (New York: New Directions, 1971), pp. 233, 235.

15 Fredric Jameson, *Fables of Aggression*; Julia Kristeva, *Powers of Horror: An Essay on Abjection*, trans. Leon S. Roudiez (New York: Columbia University Press, 1982).

16 My caution concerns the problematic move to equate women writers with feminism or progressivism, African–American and other minority writers with liberationist projects, solely on account of their subject positions. Such classic accounts of the Harlem Renaissance as David Levering Lewis's *When Harlem was in Vogue* (New York and Oxford: Oxford University Press, 1989) detail the complex range of political commitments – high and low, black nationalist, ameliorist, and assimilationist – made by its foremost writers; likewise, Rita Felski's recent study, *The Gender of Modernity* (Cambridge, MA: Harvard University Press, 1995), evidences the fitfully conservative and radical impulses

of women's cultures in the new social relations of modernity – and simultaneously suggests how difficult it is, in their moment, to distinguish adequately between "merely" consumerist, bourgeois pursuits of pleasure and "legitimately" intentioned forms of protest and self-affirmation.

In addition, there is the added difficulty of defining what counts as a "political" (vs. an aesthetic) avant-garde, particularly with respect to the context of the American 1920s and 1930s. Important treatments of writers' more narrowly political engagements and of the widening gap between high Modernism and socially engaged writing that purported to reject its tenets include Daniel Aaron's classic study, *Writers on the Left: Episodes in American Literary Communism* (New York: Harcourt Brace and World, 1961), Ralph F. Bogardus and Fred Hobson, eds., *Literature at the Barricades: The American Writer in the 1930s* (University, AL: University of Alabama Press, 1982), Alan Filreis, *Modernism from Right to Left: Wallace Stevens, the Thirties, and Literary Radicalism* (Cambridge: Cambridge University Press, 1994), and Cary Nelson, *Repression and Recovery: Modern American Poetry and the Politics of Cultural Memory, 1910–1945* (Madison: University of Wisconsin Press, 1989), which can be said to prove through its readings of left-wing aesthetics how deeply saturated they are with the formal concerns of Modernism. These accounts will help provide correctives for my necessarily schematic treatment of "left" commitments, which vary considerably in different cultural contexts, decades, and even moments of particular writers' careers.

17 Virginia Woolf, "Mr. Bennett and Mrs. Brown" in *The Essays of Virginia Woolf*, 4 vols., ed. Andrew McNeillie (London: Hogarth Press, 1986–94), vol. III, pp. 421–2.

18 Michael Bell, ed., *1900–1930* (London: Methuen, 1980), p. 111. Founding writers for the *Daily Herald* included Siegfried Sassoon, Osbert Sitwell, and W. J. Turner – middle-class intellectuals strongly associated with the literary world.

19 Historian A. J. P. Taylor points out that in the 1920s, by which time the traditionally agrarian capital of land had already been radically transformed by industrial development, 20 percent of Britain's population had claim to almost 90 percent of its lands. *English History, 1914–1945* (New York and Oxford: Oxford University Press, 1992), p. 167.

20 Michael North's recent study, the *Dialect of Modernism: Race, Language, and Twentieth-Century Literature* (Oxford and New York: Oxford University Press, 1994), explores in some detail the borrowings from African-American culture of Eliot, Stein, Pound, Picasso, and high Modernist poetics and ideology at large.

21 Gertrude Stein, "The Gradual Making of the Making of Americans" (1939), in *Selected Writings of Gertrude Stein*, ed. Carl Van Vechten (New York: Vintage/Random House, 1972), pp. 239–58.

22 William Carlos Williams, "A Poem for Norman Macleod"; William Carlos Williams, *The William Carlos Williams Reader*, ed. M. L. Rosenthal (New York: New Directions, 1966), p. 321.

23 Wallace Stevens, *Letters*, ed. Holly Stevens (New York: Knopf, 1966), p. 308.

24 Aaron, *Writers on the Left*, p. 18.

25 For extremely useful accounts of the histories and relations of such journals, see Frederick Hoffman, Charles Allen, and Carolyn Ulrich, *The Little Magazine: A History and A Bibliography* (Princeton: Princeton University Press, 1947).

26 Hutchins Hapgood, cited in Martin Green, *New York 1913: The Armory Show and the Paterson Strike* (New York: Macmillan, 1988), p. 184.
27 Aaron, *Writers on the Left*, p. 5.
28 Edmund Wilson, "The Muses Out of Work," *New Republic*, 50 (11 May 1927): 321.
29 "Royalty and Blue-Blooded Gentry Entertained by A'Lelia Walker . . .," *Amsterdam Daily News*, 26 August 1931. For a useful account of Harlem social life and sociality, see Steven Watson, *The Harlem Renaissance: Hub of African-American Culture, 1920–1930* (New York: Pantheon Books, 1995).
30 James Weldon Johnson, *Opportunity*, 3 (June 1925): 176.
31 DuBois, quoted in Arnold Rampersad, *The Art and Imagination of W. E. B. DuBois* (Cambridge, MA: Harvard University Press, 1976), p. 87.
32 Zora Neale Hurston, application for Rosenwald Foundation Fellowship, 14 December 1934, cited in Robert Hemenway, *Zora Neale Hurston: A Critical Biography* (Urbana, IL: University of Illinois Press, 1977), p. 207.

7

MARIANNE DEKOVEN

Modernism and gender

Shifts in gender relations at the turn of the century were a key factor in the emergence of Modernism. The period from 1880 to 1920, within which Modernism emerged and rose to preeminence as the dominant art form in the West (it remained dominant until the end of World War II), was also the heyday of the first wave of feminism, consolidated in the woman suffrage movement. The protagonist of this movement was known as the "New Woman": independent, educated, (relatively) sexually liberated, oriented more toward productive life in the public sphere than toward reproductive life in the home. The New Woman was dedicated, as Virginia Woolf passionately explained in "Professions for Women," to the murder of the "Angel in the House," Coventry Patmore's notorious poetic idealization of Victorian nurturant-domestic femininity. This New Woman inspired a great deal of ambivalent modernist characterization, from Hardy's Sue Bridehead and Ibsen's Hedda Gabler to Chopin's Edna Pontellier and Woolf's Lily Briscoe. But these famous characters, important as they are, constitute only the most obvious manifestation of turn-of-the-century feminism's formative influence on Modernism.

The radical implications of the social–cultural changes feminism advocated produced in modernist writing an unprecedented preoccupation with gender, both thematically and formally. Much of this preoccupation expressed a male modernist fear of women's new power, and resulted in the combination of misogyny and triumphal masculinism that many critics see as central, defining features of modernist work by men. This masculinist misogyny, however, was almost universally accompanied by its dialectical twin: a fascination and strong identification with the empowered feminine. The result was an irresolvable ambivalence toward powerful femininity that itself forged many of Modernism's most characteristic formal innovations. This ambivalence was felt by female as well as male modernist writers. While the male Modernists feared the destructive power of the radical cultural change they desired – egalitarian change often embodied in various figurations of empowered femininity – the female Modernists generally feared punishment for desiring that change.

Modernism, with its notoriously resistant complexity and its rarefied religion of art, is often thought of as the antithesis to representation of the threat/promise of radical political and cultural change: in fact, it is thought of as a retreat from, or rejection of, the failed, degraded, violent world of twentieth-century society and politics. Many Marxist critics, most importantly Lukács, have condemned Modernism not only as an evasion of the moral–political imperative of engagement with the life of society, but also as the ultimate representation of, or capitulation to, the alienation and dehumanization ("reification") resulting from capitalism's cultural distortions.[1] However, a closer look at Modernism through its complex deployments of gender reveals not only the centrality of femininity, but also, again, an irresolvable ambivalence toward radical cultural change at the heart of modernist formal innovation in the works of both male and female writers.

If we take a moment to define, briefly, the salient formal features of Modernism – the cluster of stylistic practices that, more than any of Modernism's other describable features, we use intuitively to identify literary works as modernist – it becomes clear that women writers were just as instrumental in developing these forms as the great male writers usually credited with inventing Modernism. In *Marxism and Modernism*, Eugene Lunn lists some of the most important of those features: aesthetic self-consciousness or self-reflexiveness; simultaneity, juxtaposition, or montage (I would add fragmentation); paradox, ambiguity and uncertainty; dehumanization and the demise of subjectivity conceived as unified, integrated, self-consistent. Bradbury and McFarlane, in their influential *Modernism*, using a different kind of rhetoric, attribute to modernist form "abstraction and highly conscious artifice, taking us behind familiar reality, breaking away from familiar functions of language and conventions of form . . . the shock, the violation of expected continuities, the element of de-creation and crisis."[2]

Using these formal descriptions as a neutral guide, we can displace the patrilineality of what, before second-wave feminist criticism's revisions, had been the exclusively masculine Anglo-American high modernist canon (James, Conrad, Yeats, Pound, Eliot, Lawrence, Joyce). Modernism had mothers as well as fathers. In texts crucial to the feminist canon such as Charlotte Perkins Gilman's "The Yellow Wallpaper" (1891), Kate Chopin's *The Awakening* (1899), Gertrude Stein's *Three Lives* (1903–6), and Virginia Woolf's *The Voyage Out* (1915), we can see that women writers produced modernist form concomitantly with the men generally credited with inventing Modernism. *Three Lives* was composed at the same time as early versions of Joyce's *A Portrait of the Artist as a Young Man* (*Stephen Hero*). With its fluid, obtuse narration, detached, ironic tone, impressionist as well as spatial or synchronic temporal structures, and disruptions of conventional diction and syntax, *Three Lives* has just as valid a claim to modernist "origination" as Joyce's *Portrait*. Though Virginia Woolf's first novel, *The Voyage Out*, was not published until 1915, she began working on it at about the same time as Stein was writing *Three Lives*. *The Voyage Out* initiates a number of modernist formal practices, particularly the predominance of symbolism as conveyer of the novel's central meanings, and an accompanying, pervasive sense of dreamlike irreality.

A decade earlier, "The Yellow Wallpaper" prefigures Kafka and the Surrealists, with its progressively deranged first-person narration and its use of dream structure as an ordering principle. *The Awakening* develops several modernist formal strategies, such as ambiguous, shifting narrative stance, density and foregrounding of imagery, and passages of repetitive, incantatory, "poetic" prose. Though Chopin and Gilman did not continue as modernist writers – Chopin died and Gilman turned almost exclusively to politics – Stein and Woolf must be central to any account of Modernism. Women writers continued, throughout the decades of Modernism's dominance of Anglo-American high literary art, to produce a large portion of its most important writing.

Despite the powerful presence of women writers at the founding of Modernism and throughout its history, and despite the near-obsessive preoccupation with femininity in all modernist writing, the reactive misogyny so apparent in much male-authored Modernism continues in many quarters to produce a sense of Modernism as a masculinist movement. Instances of modernist advocacy of firm, hard, dry, terse, classical masculinity, over against the messy, soft, vague, flowery, effusive, adjectival femininity of the late Victorians, abound, and instances of male modernist antifeminism and misogyny are legion. Some of the language of Ezra Pound's highly influential vorticist manifesto, for example, is characteristic of male Modernism's self-imagination as a mode of masculine domination:

> Mathematics is dull ditchwater until one reaches analytics. But in analytics we come upon a new way of dealing with form. It is in this way that art handles life . . . The statements of "analytics" are "lords" over fact. They are the thrones and dominations that rule over form and recurrence. And in like manner are great works of art lords over fact, over race-long recurrent moods, and over to-morrow.[3]

However, contrary instances of male modernist feminine identification, and support of the New Woman, are not difficult to find. The first issue of Wyndham Lewis's short-lived but influential vorticist journal *Blast* contains Rebecca West's powerful feminist story "Indissoluble Matrimony," as well as an encomium of feminism, precisely as a radical movement opposed to the gender conventionality for which Victorian femininity was a code or metonym. In the characteristically ironic but at the same time heartfelt brief unsigned exhortation "To Suffragettes," feminists are addressed as "brave comrades" (152), and told that "We make you a present of our votes," that "Nous vous aimons!" (we love you), that "We admire your energy. You and artists are the only things (you don't mind being called things?) left in England with a little life in them" (151). As the male Modernists intermittently realized, feminists were in fact just as committed to overthrowing the Victorian ideal of closeted, domesticated, desexualized, disenfranchised femininity as they were to overthrowing its attendant cultural ideal of high moral insipidity.

The œuvre of William Butler Yeats constitutes an exemplary instance of the undecidably contradictory juxtaposition of a fearful misogynist response to the New Woman with an identificatory admiration. As Elizabeth Butler Cullingford demonstrates in her admirable book on Yeats's love poetry, the well-known Yeatsian misogyny evident in "Prayer for my Daughter" or "Leda and the Swan" is counterbalanced by a feminine identification comparable to Eliot's and Lawrence's. Unlike Eliot's and Lawrence's association of feminine identification with self-loathing and sexual abjection, however, Yeats's feminine identification, buttressed by his positive involvement with a range of women in Irish politics, arts, and occult movements, produced empowering representations of women's presences and voices in the great body of love poetry inspired by Maud Gonne. As Cullingford argues, "Yeats loved, liked, collaborated with, and respected women – most of the time."[4]

Henry James's essay "The Future of the Novel," written in the pivotal year 1899, encapsulates in a single text this characteristic, irresolvably contradictory attitude of the male Modernists toward an empowered femininity. James begins with the standard modernist attack on femininity. He links it with the social and aesthetic deterioration of standards connected to a debased, feminine/feminized popular culture, by deploying the figure of flooding frequently used in modernist fiction to represent empowered femininity:

> The flood [of fiction] at present swells and swells, threatening the whole field of letters, as would often seem, with submersion. It . . . directly marches with the rapid increase of the multitude able to possess itself in one way and

another of the *book* . . . There is an immense public, if public be the name, inarticulate, but abysmally absorbent . . . The diffusion of the rudiments, the multiplication of common schools, has had more and more the effect of making readers of women and of the very young . . . the ladies and children – by whom I mean, in other words, the reader irreflective and uncritical.[5]

James appears here in the person of Modernist as misogynist, antidemocratic elitist, by now a wearyingly familiar figure.

As James proceeds in the essay to think about what he calls the "elasticity" of fiction, however – the way "it moves in a luxurious independence of rules and restrictions" (246), and "the immense variety of life" fiction must represent, that "will stretch away to right and to left" (247) – his tone and political stance shift markedly from the right to the left. The essay ends on a note diametrically opposite to that of its opening, expressing the endorsement of feminist aims, the desire for radical cultural "renewal," that coexists in unresolved contradiction with its opposite fear and loathing of such change:

> It would be curious – really a great comedy – if the renewal [of fiction] were to spring just from the satiety of the very readers for whom the sacrifices [to propriety] have hitherto been supposed to be made [i.e. to "the ladies"]. It bears on this that as nothing is more salient in English life today, to fresh eyes, than the revolution taking place in the position and outlook of women – and taking place much more deeply in the quiet than even the noise on the surface demonstrates – so we may very well yet see the female elbow itself, kept in increasing activity by the play of the pen, smash with final resonance the window all this time most superstitiously closed. (250)

Many literary texts by male Modernists contain the same kind of painfully misogynist writing with which James opens his essay. Among the most notorious instances are Pound's "Portrait d'une Femme" of 1912 – "'Your mind and you are our Sargasso Sea / . . . No! there is nothing! In the whole and all, / Nothing that's quite your own. / Yet this is you." – and of course his lines in *Hugh Selwyn Mauberley*'s epitaph for the Great War dead: "There died a myriad, / And of the best, among them, / For an old bitch gone in the teeth, / For a botched civilization." Eliot's misogyny is often expressed as a sexual disgust conflated with both anti-Semitism and class hatred, as for example in "Sweeney Among the Nightingales," whose "Rachel *née* Rabinovich / Tears at the grapes with murderous paws." The misogyny of the other great Anglo-American male Modernists has also been amply demonstrated by feminist criticism. Yet even in the most overtly misogynist literary texts, a more complex and ambiguous deployment of gender is often at the center of the work's modernist innovations.

In order to understand those complex deployments of gender, it is helpful to look briefly at the work of a quintessential male modernist gender theorist, Sigmund Freud, and of one of his most important contemporary feminist revisionists, Luce Irigaray.

In Freud's œuvre, the paradox of modernist femininity is most stark. Freud developed psychoanalysis largely by working with women – his observation of Charcot's treatment of female "hysterics" in the Salpêtrière Clinic in late nineteenth-century Paris initiated his theorizations of the unconscious, and these theories of the sexual etiology of the neuroses were then developed and articulated in large part through Freud's subsequent work with his own female patients (see for example *Dora: An Analysis of a Case of Hysteria* [1905]). However, the theorizations that emerged relegated women to an inferior status in every way: of secondary importance in the central Freudian Oedipal nuclear family drama of the psyche, which is dominated by the son as protagonist and the father as antagonist, with the mother as passive object of their conflicting desire, and the daughter as a near-invisible afterthought. Further, women are by Freudian definition "castrated," defined by and as "absence" and "lack," in the Lacanian–Freudian formulation; doomed to permanent moral immaturity, with a sexuality characterized, when "normal," as inherently masochistic.

Despite the founding role of female hysteria in psychoanalysis, and despite the extensive presence of female patients in his practice, Freud continued to find femininity a "mystery." In *Speculum of the Other Woman*, the French Lacanian psychoanalyst Luce Irigaray's groundbreaking work of feminist theory, this "mystery" is explained as a displacement of the central patriarchal suppression of the feminine.[6] For Irigaray, the "mystery" of man's role in reproduction (we always know who the mother is; paternity crucially is not self-evident) is reassigned to the "passive" woman. Her terrible power to engender life is repressed and reassigned to the man, who then appropriates all ownership of reproduction and powers of naming, and, therefore, of representation, under what Lacan calls the Name-of-the-Father. The vigilant repression and exclusion of the feminine "origin" of life results in the starkness of the familiar normative gendered self/other dualisms of Western culture: masculine/feminine, white/black, higher/lower, culture/nature are only the most rife with political implications of these pervasive dualisms. In Freud, as in Modernism in general, the power of the maternal feminine comes closest to erupting into representation, and therefore is met by an even more cruelly powerful act of re-repression.

It is in modernist forms themselves that the repressed maternal feminine unconscious of Western culture actually emerges into representation. Irigaray, and other psychoanalytically oriented theorists of gender in language, usually known as "French feminists," such as Julia Kristeva and Hélène Cixous, find the inscription of the de-repressed maternal feminine in non- or anti-realist deployments of language and literary form, which are, precisely, the defining formal features of Modernism. Irigaray describes the feminine attributes of language, linked to its embeddedness in the maternal unconscious, as its "effects of deferred action, its subterranean dreams and fantasies, its convulsive quakes, its paradoxes and contradictions" (*Speculum*, 141). These are precisely the aspects of language, and potentialities of literary structure, foregrounded in modernist form.

For Irigaray, Freudian Modernism represented at once the greatest potential for de-repression of the feminine and also the harshest denial of that potential de-repression – a reinstitution of the founding patriarchal repression in even more rigid terms. This dialectic of embrace of the empowered feminine along with violent repudiation of it is precisely the structure we find underlying male modernist misogyny, where the harshest vituperation against women, or the loftiest superiority to them, often occurs in works in which an empowered femininity governs the most radical modernist elements of the text.

Joseph Conrad is a Modernist founding father whose oeuvre is profoundly masculine. He works primarily off the masculine tradition of adventure fiction. There are few women characters in his novels and stories, major or minor, and those who do appear are consistently flatter, more stereotypical, less fully realized than Conrad's great masculine characters.[7]

Nonetheless, the empowered maternal feminine is at the heart of Conrad's invention of Modernism. In *The Nigger of the "Narcissus"* (1897), in many ways Conrad's first real step into the twentieth century (as Stein will describe "Melanctha" in *The Autobiography of Alice B. Toklas*), the dying black sailor James Wait is the figure of moral and narrative undecidability who pushes the text beyond the boundaries of realism. The rescue of Wait in the storm, which is at the center of this story, is figured very explicitly in childbirth imagery: "he [Wait] pressed his head to it [a hole in the bulkhead beneath which he is trapped in a tiny room], trying madly to get out through that opening one inch wide and three inches long" (54; he is "crowning").[8] Finally, after much struggle, "suddenly Jimmy's head and shoulders appeared. He stuck halfway, and with rolling eyes foamed at our feet . . . all at once he came away in our hands as though somebody had let go his legs. With the same movement, without a pause, we swung him up. His breath whistled, he kicked our upturned faces" (55).[9] The text as maternal womb gives birth to James Wait, the embodiment of the powerful, dark complexities of Modernism. As black and working class, he also embodies the central conflation in modernist figuration of the maternal with the "darker" races and "lower" classes implied by the crucially symbolic positioning of the womb, darker and lower down (Irigaray brilliantly elaborates the masculinist Platonic parable of the cave as repudiated maternal womb in her *Speculum* chapter "Plato's Hystera"). This conflation of erupting, newly empowered femininity, "darker" races and "lower classes," precisely the conflation suggested by the political contiguity of socialism and feminism in turn-of-the-century radicalism, reappears throughout modernist figuration.

In *Heart of Darkness*, it is Africa itself that becomes the undecidable locus of empowerment of the maternal feminine as racially and geographically darker and lower down (the birth sequence in *The Nigger of the "Narcissus"* occurs as the ship passes through a gale in the Cape of Good Hope, at the southern tip of Africa). Conrad's figuration of Africa is rife with maternal imagery. The "dark continent" is notoriously a figural conflation of racial and female–maternal otherness for white Western masculinity. In Conrad's upriver journey into Modernism, the dark continent begins stereotypically as terrifying, death-dealing, devouring, the locus of illusion. But as Marlow gradually shifts his allegiance from the "civilized" (actually cruelly barbaric) European imperialism of "the Company" and its "faithless pilgrims," to what becomes the "truth" of the African wilderness itself, the heart of moral darkness shifts in the text from Africa to Kurtz, embodiment of the monstrous failure of Europe's "civilizing" mission. The deepest informing "truth" of the novella, a truth associated with the modernist forms of symbolism and the dream, and with the "unreliable" first-person narration that, more than anything else, marks this text as a founding work of Modernism, resides in the undecidable (at once deathly and empowering) maternal African jungle.

The racially "primitive" is also conflated with the empowered working-class feminine in Picasso's iconic modernist work *Les demoiselles d'Avignon* of 1907. *Les demoiselles* is a painting of nude female bathers, prostitutes, whose nudity is explicitly sexualized; that sexuality is marked simultaneously by degradation and by accessibility to the male viewer/voyeur/customer. It is, for 1907, a radically stylized painting, not only in the harsh discord of its treatment of the women (a harshness that still now strikes the viewer powerfully), but in its invention of the vocabulary of Cubism: the overall composition organized by, and the contours of the figures broken into, angular geometric shapes, the three-dimensionality or depth illusion of traditional pictorial representation flattened, the figures radically stylized and distorted so as to seem splayed against the surface of the canvas, and the overtly nonrealistic conventions, influenced by African tribal masks, in the drawing of the faces.

Les demoiselles fuses the invention of these modernist formal practices with representation of an empowered sexual femininity. The female bathers are degraded within dominant convention (nude prostitutes), but are transformed here *by modernist form*, including alliance with racial blackness as well as with the working class, into a powerful force, which, like Modernism in general, retains its great strength now. It was in the process of painting and repainting these women that Picasso invented his version of modernist art. By means of that modernist art, these women become awesome, frightening, magnificent, powerful figures. They are figures of modernist art as the release into new form of the empowered sexual feminine; of the new form as release into representation of the power and terror of the sexual feminine; of the irresolvable ambiguity – the figures are just as hideous and distorted as they are powerful and riveting – of that femininity.

Feminist modernist criticism had a great amount of work to do, in its initial phases, before this male modernist ambivalence could become visible. In order to open a space for the study of gender and Modernism, it was necessary to contest and counteract a well-established New Critical tradition that both placed male modernist writers at the center of a rigorously exclusive canon, and also celebrated those features of modernist writing associated with masculinity: hardness, toughness, a terse, cerebral economy. This early phase of feminist modernist criticism was therefore preoccupied primarily with establishing the importance of women modernist writers, both by opening the canon to include them and by broadening our understanding of what constitutes Modernism so that it is not so exclusively defined by the valorization of formal as well as thematic characteristics (vast, unifying mythic themes) associated with masculinity. Most of the work done in this phase focused on women Modernists, both individually and as constructors of a separate women's tradition of Modernism. The attention feminist critics paid to male Modernists in this phase was on the whole negative, focused on delineating, in derogatory terms, their differences from women Modernists, and on claiming misogyny as the foundation of their modernist practice.

Once the tradition of women's modernist writing, and the importance of the major female Modernists, became better established, and concomitant developments in feminist theory enabled broader discussions of femininity and the feminine in literary texts, the kind of attention feminist critics paid to the male Modernists shifted. The focus changed from stark denunciations of misogyny to more complex, theoretically nuanced, historically oriented investigations of the contradictory presence of the feminine, in its variegated manifestations, in the writing of male Modernists. This shift also brought a decline in the emphasis on viewing male and female Modernists as members of divergent literary species, and a concomitant interest in seeing Modernism as a broadly diverse movement, crossing not only gender and national but also racial, class, and sexual boundaries. Current feminist modernist criticism is just as likely to focus on questions of race, class, sexuality, and nation as on questions of gender. In any case, the interconnectedness in historical situation between male and female Modernists has become much more important than it was when the category "female Modernists" had not yet been established.

One of the key points of interconnection, again, is an irresolvable ambivalence, shared by male and female Modernists, toward the threat/ promise of revolutionary cultural and political change, embodied in the figure of the empowered feminine, at the turn of the century. The same ambivalence, differently inflected, characterizes the work of women Modernists as that which characterizes the work of the men. In "The Yellow Wallpaper," an originary work of feminist Modernism, the unnamed protagonist, trapped postpartum in a dungeon-like attic nursery by her domineering doctor-husband, projects – literally, writes – her unallowable desire for freedom, autonomy, and sexual fulfillment on to her wallpaper, only to divide the wallpaper against itself so that the figuration associated with freedom and empowerment becomes linked to an imprisoning masculinity. At the same time, femininity reveals itself as fully abjected – a creeping, skulking figure imprisoned behind the bars of the protagonist's erstwhile hopeful desire. All the protagonist can do, by the end of the story, is tear down those "bars," destroying the wallpaper, her own creation, and releasing the creeping woman she has become into full-blown madness. The story ends with the protagonist, having tied herself to the symbolically nailed-down marriage bed in her nursery prison chamber, crawling repeatedly around the perimeter of the room. She crawls over the prostrated, fainted body of her husband, who had all but imprisoned her in this room, but this is a pyrrhic victory, because her madness precludes any meaningful emancipation. The desire for freedom invents the modernist wallpaper (modernist in its heightened, dreamlike, shifting, and overdetermined uses of figuration); the fear of that desire destroys it.

Similar structures of desire for freedom in unresolved dialectic with fear of punishment inform other founding early modernist works by women. In Kate Chopin's *The Awakening*, Edna Pontellier, like the "Yellow Wallpaper" protagonist, gains a pyrric victory over the strictures of her patriarchal marriage: her freedom "to swim far out where no woman has swum before" comes at the cost of her death. The complex oscillations in narrative point of view that make this a founding work of Modernism are very similar to Conrad's in *Lord Jim* (1899–1900): both narratives oscillate undecidably between approval and disapproval of their protagonists. Conrad's ambivalence (via Marlow) toward Jim reflects his ambivalence concerning the traditional Western masculine code of honor, with its attendant modern nexus of imperialism and misogyny, that Jim first abrogates and then dies in order to uphold. For Chopin, each feminist assertion on Edna's behalf is immediately countered by a fearful withdrawal of approval. This modernist form is, therefore, directly produced, for both Conrad and Chopin, by irresolvable ambivalence toward what Perry Anderson calls the "revolutionary horizon" of the twentieth century: for Conrad, the possibility of the overthrow of traditional masculinity; for Chopin, the possibility of the emancipation of women.[10]

Gertrude Stein's revolutionary "Melanctha" goes well beyond earlier fiction's development of modernist forms. Stein initiates, in all three parts of *Three Lives* but particularly in "Melanctha," an unprecedented stylization of the prose surface. (The other two novellas are "The Good Anna," written and placed first, and "The Gentle Lena," written second but placed last. Both have working-class German immigrant protagonists. The characters in "Melanctha" are all black.) Stein uses a flattened, reduced, simplified vocabulary, much the way Picasso and the cubists, her collaborators in the production of Modernism, use a palette reduced to a few tones of gray and brown, in order to intensify the nuance and effect of slight variations of color and of the complex geometric shapings and light–dark modelings on which cubism was founded. For Stein, this reduced vocabulary allows key, repeated words, phrases, and motifs to acquire an openended richness of accumulated meaning, that shifts and grows as the narrative develops, so that in reinventing familiar words and phrases, Stein, through formal means, defamiliarizes and reinvents the familiar or ordinary world.

Each of Stein's key words or phrases increases in significance as it passes through successive contexts, as its familiar, everyday meanings are gradually replaced by a large complex or cluster of undefined meanings. There are many such thematically central words and phrases in "Melanctha": "wisdom," "understanding," "experience," "excitement," being "quiet together." "Wisdom" becomes emblematic of everything in life that is desirable but difficult to attain; "excitement" of everything that is alluring but dangerous. These are the unanchored, refunctioned words that Stein uses to describe the dangerous, powerful fascination of Melanctha's working-class, black, sexually experimental unconventionality – the dangerous allure, that, precisely like James Wait's for Conrad in *The Nigger of the "Narcissus,"* led Stein to invent Modernism.

Stein's reduced vocabulary is accompanied by an incantatory mode of repetition she called "insistence," in order to distinguish it from mere mechanical reiteration. In "insistence," repetition is never verbatim; rather, the narrative moves forward in incremental shifts through what Stein called a "continuous present": meaning is steadily reformulated in each present moment, with no reference to previous formulations, therefore inevitably repeating (because unaware of) them, though in modified form.

Jefferson Campbell, coprotagonist of "Melanctha," is a transformation of the autobiographical protagonist of Stein's earlier, formally conventional, lesbian novel Q.E.D. (1903), which she put away in a drawer; it was not published until after her death. Stein's lesbianism, and her long-term relationship with Alice B. Toklas, were common knowledge among the large, famous, "charmed" circle of their avant-garde, bohemian, modernist acquaintance in Paris and beyond, but no reference was made in print to this knowledge until after Alice B. Toklas's death in 1967. Q.E.D. narrates the deadlocked erotic triangle Stein was involved in as a medical student at Johns Hopkins University in Baltimore.

The white, upper-middle-class, highly educated Adele of the conventional realist novel Q.E.D., virtually indistinguishable from Gertrude Stein, becomes, in the radical modernist "Melanctha," a heterosexual black male doctor. Jeff is bourgeois, restrained, "regular" in his habits where Melanctha is "reckless" and irregular, given to "wandering" in search of "wisdom." The race and class of Melanctha enable Stein, as Wait's race and class enable Conrad in The Nigger of the "Narcissus," simultaneously to undo her own naturalist narrative (Melanctha as hapless victim of cruel societal circumstances beyond her control) and to explore dangerous thematic possibilities. Again, it is the conflation of nonwhite race and the working class, embodied in the undecidable (dangerous, fascinating) feminine, that produces modernist form: it is in following her lesbian desire for Melanctha, and therefore for Melanctha's sexual and intellectual "wandering," that Stein is able to take her text out into its formal terra incognita.

Once there, Stein, for the next three decades, went further than any other twentieth-century writer in English (perhaps in any language) in reinventing literary language and form, undoing conventional, hierarchical, sense-making modes of signification – modes that privilege the signified over the signifier in a way that can be considered characteristically patriarchal – substituting, in diverse stylistic modes, a rich, complex, open-ended, antipatriarchal syntactical and semantic polysemy. Generally, Stein was one of the most prolific, important, and influential writers of this century, in any formal mode, with twenty-five books published in her lifetime and approximately the same number, including anthologies, published posthumously. However, until, in the past decade, feminist and postmodernist criticism began to take Stein's writing seriously, most studies of her were biographical, focusing on her influence on other writers and her life in the Parisian bohemian–modernist art world rather than on this remarkable productivity, or on the unparalleled diversity and originality of her work.

Stein was well aware of what she was doing as a groundbreaking experimental writer; she was eminently a literary theorist as well as a practitioner. (She launched her intellectual life as a star pupil of William James at Harvard.) Her essays and extended meditations of the 1930s, theorizing the radical innovative writing she had done in the teens and twenties, do a great deal more than explain her own literary practice – they treat standard preoccupations of literary theory, such as definitions of genre, accounts of periodization, and literary nationality, as well as general philosophical–aesthetic questions of the nature of representation and of literary time. While Stein seldom deals directly with the question of gender in these essays, the unpretentiousness and whimsical informality of her style, and the simplicity of her diction, "do theory" in a way that is welcoming and suggestive for theoretically oriented feminists who find inimical the overbearing, obfuscating language of so much masculine theoretical discourse. At the same time, the quality and structures of her thought are profound, challenging, complex. As she says in "A Transatlantic Interview, 1946," one of the last of her pieces, "After all, my only thought is a complicated simplicity. I like a thing simple, but it must be simple through complication."

Stein was at the center of three major modernist/avant-garde Parisian groups: the lesbian Left Bank documented by Shari Benstock, the bohemian Montmartre of Picasso and modernist painting described by Stein herself in vivid detail in *The Autobiography of Alice B. Toklas* (1932), and the postwar scene of younger American expatriate Modernists, most notably Hemingway, Fitzgerald, Anderson, and Wilder, who sat at Stein's feet at 27 rue de Fleurus. But it was not until the avant-garde gained wider currency as precursor of postmodernism, poststructuralism, and French feminism, and effected a general shift in our sense of the possible in literature, that the revolutionary character of Stein's work was rendered visible.

Fortunately, that is not the case for Virginia Woolf. Partly because of her key position in the "Bloomsbury Group," the nodal center of British Modernism, and partly because her fiction is at least superficially closer to recognizable convention than Stein's genre-bending experimentalism, Woolf's nine major novels, her two great works of feminist theory, *A Room of One's Own* (1928), and *Three Guineas* (1938), and her multivolume stories, essays, diaries, and letters, have long been readily available and widely read. Even when academic New Critical Modernism was virtually entirely white and male, as it was even into the late 1960s, when I was in college, Virginia Woolf was taught. She was not, however, taught in relation to questions of gender, except insofar as her femininity was a code or metonym for inferior status: her preoccupations were viewed as "domestic," "personal," "private," and therefore of lesser value and significance than the classical–mythical themes of the male modernists; her writing, though clearly modernist, was seen as lightweight, insubstantial compared to theirs. No writer, perhaps not even Charlotte Brontë, has benefited more from feminist criticism than Virginia Woolf. She has become, with solid justification, one of the great literary "mothers" we "think back through if we are women," as she herself said in *A Room of One's Own*.

Woolf revised the association of Modernism with masculinity by associating it with femininity instead. Her arguments for the subversiveness of modernist form, its ability to penetrate and represent the underlying, multiplicitous truths of consciousness and psyche beneath the outward, unitary, coherent appearances of social, and realist fictional, convention, most notably in "Modern Fiction" (1919), and in "Mr. Bennett and Mrs. Brown" (1924), as well as in *A Room of One's Own*, connect with Irigaray's linkage of repressed maternal femininity to the Freudian unconscious, and also with Stein's invention of antipatriarchal, polysemous literary and linguistic forms. Beginning with her first novel, *A Voyage Out*, with its New-Woman-inspired heroine Rachel Vinrace attempting to "voyage out" of Europe and thereby of its patriarchal–imperialist gender relations, but ultimately defeated by the community's translation of heterosexual love into patriarchal marriage, and throughout her career, Woolf used literary form to explore the possibility of releasing into representation the subversiveness of a culturally suppressed and repressed femininity. At the same time, in ways that the New Critics miraculously entirely missed, Woolf wrote directly about the great social and political issues of this century. A socialist, she always aligned herself with democratic egalitarian hope, even if she was not always in control of the upper-middle-class British ideologies of her upbringing.

A Room of One's Own makes a materialist argument for financial freedom for women from dependence on the support and approval of men: women will not be able to achieve intellectual independence, thereby realizing their potential as writers, until they have that freedom. *A Room* also argues for a separate tradition of women's writing, a history and future of literary forms and preoccupations particular to women's minds and bodies, and, at the same time, contradictorily, for the "androgyny" of great literature. *Three Guineas*, written in the shadow of fascism and impending world war, makes a powerful case, with a burning but controlled rage, for egalitarian, antihierarchical femininity as antidote to the masculinism underlying fascism and war as life modes. Women should not collaborate; women should form "societies of outsiders" to resist and reconfigure the militarist authoritarian state from within.

All of these preoccupations and motifs work in complex, interwoven ways throughout Woolf's major fiction. In novel after novel, Woolf's female and gender-ambiguous protagonists try to reform (literally, re-form) their worlds according to their enlightened ideas, their fidelity to the complex truths of their perceptions, and their connectedness to the culturally alternative truths of the psyche. At the same time, Woolf pushed fiction as far formally as any of the other major Modernists, using fragmentation, collage-like juxtaposition, densely poetic language, episte-mological and therefore narrative multiplicity and indeterminacy, temporal dislocations, heavy reliance on symbolism, fluidity, and dedefinition of characterization, and an utterly destabilizing, pervasive irony, to realize her vision of a transcendently truth-revealing art – like all the Modernists, she saw art as the only remaining avenue to truth, meaning, value, and transcendence in the otherwise bankrupt twentieth century. Writing for Woolf could embody a subversive feminine consciousness by penetrating the mind of Mrs. Brown, the anonymous, humble, marginal everywoman, and showing how the world looks when viewed through her eyes.

Woolf was not alone in these ambitions. She was joined by a wide range of other women Modernists, many of whose works and even names have only recently been revived, made available, and studied by feminist criticism. A recent volume entitled *The Gender of Modernism* has chapters on (in addition to Stein and Woolf, and also Eliot, Joyce, Lawrence, Hugh MacDiarmid, and Pound) the following, all of whom made vital contribu-tions to Anglo-American Modernism: Djuna Barnes, Willa Cather, Nancy Cunard, H.D. (Hilda Doolittle), Jessie Redmon Fauset, Zora Neale Hurston, Nella Larsen, Mina Loy, Rose Macaulay, Katherine Mansfield, Charlotte Mew, Marianne Moore, Jean Rhys, Dorothy Richardson, May Sinclair, Sylvia Townsend Warner, Rebecca West, Antonia White, Anna Wickham. It would be impossible to survey here, in any meaningful way, the major contributions, let alone the œuvres, of such a large and diverse range of writers, or even of a few of the most important of them; I recommend *The Gender of Modernism* as an invaluable resource for further study of the richness of the legacy of modernist writing by women.[11]

Instead, we might look closely at works by two of the most important writers in the above list: H.D. (Hilda Doolittle), one of the great poets of Modernism, and Zora Neale Hurston, novelist, anthropologist, and towering figure of the Harlem Renaissance. H.D.'s œuvre includes the great, mythological–historical–political–visionary, late modernist long poems *Trilogy* (1944–6), which is comprised of *The Walls Do Not Fall*, *Tribute to the Angels*, and *The Flowering of the Rod*, and *Helen in Egypt* (1961). These poems are premised generally on a revisionary feminist mythology, and a utopian belief in, or prophecy of, a regeneration of the world based on the power of female creativity. Before she had, in the company of her lover and lifelong companion Bryher (the writer Winifred Ellerman; H.D., like Woolf, was bisexual) the revelatory post-World War I psychic–visionary experiences on which these poems were based, H.D. had been cofounder with Pound of Imagism (it was Pound who invented the pen name "H.D. Imagiste"). H.D.'s role in and version of Imagism stand in the same subversive relation to Poundian masculinism as do Woolf's feminist–modernist manifestos, *A Room of One's Own* and *Three Guineas*.

H.D.'s *Sea Garden* (1916), her first collection of poems, was a crucial imagist book. "Sea Rose," one of the best known, most widely anthologized poems in that volume, is usually discussed in relation to its fulfillment of the Poundian dicta of Imagism: allowing images to do the poetic work of making meaning; also brevity and concision, "direct treatment" of the material, no inessential words, and rhythms based on musical phrasing rather than the regular, metronome beats of poetic tradition in English. "Sea Rose" is in fact also a powerful and radical work of feminist Modernism.

The title itself is jarring in its linkage of the small, perfect, fragile, traditional feminine beauty of which the rose is the most standard poetic representation, with the vast power of the sea. The poem opens with an even more jarring invocation:

> Rose, harsh rose,
> marred and with stint of petals,
> meagre flower, thin,
> sparse of leaf

"Harsh" releases the rose of female sexuality from its imprisonment in a gentle, perfected beauty, allowing it its raw power, as does the title's conjunction of "rose" with "sea." "Marred" insists on the vitality of the rose's *im*perfection, in a cultural tradition that links its perfection to its reification. "Marred" also insists on the poem's rejection of the conventions of female beauty. "Stint," "meagre," "thin," "sparse" all contradict the opulence, the concupiscent lushness, of conventional images of the rose. At the same time, subversive though they are, these adjectives do not cancel their own negative connotations. Rejection of gender stereotype always comes at a cost. (One thinks of Woolf's "puckered-up" Lily Briscoe of *To the Lighthouse*, whose name enacts a similar association of a flower with the "brisk" – very close to "crisp" – that is her nickname.)

The second stanza makes the speaker's polemic position clear:

> more precious
> than a wet rose
> single on a stem –
> you are caught in the drift.

This harsh, marred, meagre sea rose is "*more precious* / than a wet rose, / single on a stem" – not only the conventional rose, but the sexually available flower perched on the phallic stem. The sea rose, unlike the stem's single monogamous possession, is "caught in the drift": the power of the maternal ocean, of the urban crowds of modernity, of modernist sea-change itself. Again, while it is better to be caught in the drift than to be single on a stem, the negative connotations of "caught in the drift" are allowed to stand, in this modernist poem of irresolvable ambivalence toward the feminist–modernist "revolutionary horizon."

In the final stanza, the sexuality of the sea rose itself is redeemed and made superior to that of the "wet rose, / single on a stem":

> Can the spice-rose
> drip such acrid fragrance
> hardened in a leaf?

The "spice-rose" may or may not be equivalent to that wet rose, single on a stem, but it is certainly suggestive of the rose's sexuality, here seemingly released ("drip") by its association with the sea rose. But the sea rose itself is superior to the "spice-rose" in the dripping (manifest) acridness of its fragrance: a wonderfully ambiguous choice of adjectives for the sea rose's sexuality, clearly presented as desirable by the syntax of the sentence, but nonetheless carrying negative connotations. The "hardened" "leaf" reminds us again of the sea rose's empowered difference from the soft rose petals of feminine subservience.

Two decades later and in another country, Zora Neale Hurston published her greatest novel, *Their Eyes Were Watching God* (1937) (her other novels are *Jonah's Gourd Vine* [1934], *Moses, Man of the Mountain* [1939], and *Seraph on the Suwanee* [1948]; she also wrote the autobiography *Dust Tracks on a Road* [1942], and the anthropological works on

African–American and Caribbean folklore, *Mules and Men* [1935], and *Tell My Horse* [1938]). *Their Eyes*, while affirming the autonomy and strength of black culture in general, of black women in particular, and of the feminine narrative voice, in the face of murderous racism and sexism, refuses, in its modernist complexity – its undecidable ambivalence toward radical egalitarian change – to choose black conclusively over white, or female over male.

In the courtroom scene that is the climax of the novel, Janey, the protagonist, who is on trial for shooting her literally rabid lover, Tea Cake, is surrounded by a sympathetic group of white women, protected from the black men who, in an eruption of male bonding, despise her for shooting Tea Cake in self-defense, insisting on believing her guilty of murder: "And the white women cried and stood around her like a protecting wall and the Negroes, with heads hung down, shuffled out and away" (279–80).[12]

The painful implications of this scene (particularly evident in the bowed heads and shuffling) are quickly undercut. The narrator, Janey's surrogate in this free-indirect narrative, provides Janey with a rationalization of the behavior of Tea Cake's friends – "she knew it was because they loved Tea Cake and didn't understand" (281) – and in fact it turns out they do understand. It is Janey who makes the first gesture of reconciliation, but the men relent easily and apologize to her, drawing her back within the warm circle of black community at Tea Cake's funeral.

That circle is not always a reliable defense against racism, however, any more than either Tea Cake's relatively egalitarian love for Janey, or Janey's nurturing friendships with other women (her closeness to Pheoby Watson – "'mah tongue is in mah friend's mouf'" (17) – is the narrative's condition of possibility), are a reliable defense against sexism. Earlier in the novel, Tea Cake beats Janey in a fit of jealousy of Mrs. Turner's brother. Janey is innocent. Mrs. Turner is a racist, light-skinned black woman who identifies with whites and hates Tea Cake for his dark skin. Mrs. Turner's racism, which Hurston develops in episodes of her attempts at sisterly bonding with Janey, is repellent, but Tea Cake's violently macho response to it is equally so, to the reader if not (consciously) to Janey. Tea Cake's friends come to blame his death on Mrs. Turner's brother, and Janey, on the witness stand, says "Tea Cake couldn't come back to himself until he had got rid of that mad dog that was in him and he couldn't get rid of the dog and live. He had to die to get rid of the dog" (278). Tea Cake literally has rabies, having been bitten by a mad dog, and he is trying to kill Janey when she shoots him in self-defense. He dies with his teeth buried in her forearm. But the "mad dog" is also symbolic, I would argue, of Tea Cake's violent response to his unfounded jealousy, and his death is a (rather extreme) punishment for it.

Tea Cake is certainly better than Janey's other, oppressive husbands, and is as close as any male character in this novel to being the "New Man" suitable for the New Woman. But even Tea Cake cannot kill that very strong patriarchal dog before it manages to bite him fatally. The new order of empowered femininity both preserves women like Mrs. Turner and still carries on its back that rabid dog.

Woolf's *To the Lighthouse* (1927), ends as the New Woman and modernist artist Lily Briscoe finishes her painting, with a "line there, in the centre" (310).[13] The closing "line" of Lily's, and the novel's, final "vision" is a line of simultaneous separation and union: separation and union of the (devastated/freed) postwar modernist present and the (murderous/fructifying) Victorian–Edwardian realist past; separation and union of disillusioned but freer adulthood and idealized but oppressed childhood; separation and union of empowered/enchained, inspiring/inhibiting Victorian mother, Mrs. Ramsay, and cramped/autonomous modernist daughter, Lily; separation and union of tyrannical/visionary patriarchal male, Mr. Ramsay, and fecund/murdered patriarchal female, Mrs. Ramsay.

It would be impossible, and a serious distortion of the text, to claim that Woolf resolves any of those myriad interconnected gendered dualisms in favor of one term over the other. Instead, the text represents more clearly perhaps than any other the modernist moment of unresolved contradiction, unsynthesized dialectic: of dualism that seeks neither unitary resolution in the dominance of one term over the other or in the third term of dialectical synthesis, but rather the two-way passage, difference without hierarchy.

Feminist modernist criticism has in many ways achieved greater success than its practitioners would have thought possible when we began this work twenty-five years ago. The tradition of women's modernist writing is established, not just as separate and (at least) equal, but also as a crucial part of the complex, multifaceted historical phenomenon of Modernism. Writers such as Woolf, Richardson, Mansfield, West, Rhys, Gilman, Chopin, Stein, Cather, H.D., Moore, Larsen, Hurston, and Barnes are widely read, taught, and written about; their work is not only taken seriously but also admired. Scores of less well known women modernists are also being rediscovered, reissued, and generally given their critical due.

Moreover, it is no longer necessary to think exclusively about women in the feminist study of gender and Modernism. Questions of sexuality, of masculinity in dialectic with femininity, as well as of male and female writers, are regularly raised now along with a range of historical and theoretical questions relating to race, ethnicity, class, nation, location, and empire. But those critics attuned to the quarter-century history of feminist work on Modernism remain committed to the importance of keeping both women writers, and the related questions of woman and the feminine, centrally in view.

NOTES

1 For Lukács's argument, and various Marxist responses to it, see *Aesthetics and Politics*, ed. Perry Anderson, Rodney Livingstone and Francis Mulhern (London: New Left Books, 1977). For an extended discussion of Lukács's relation to Modernism, see Fredric Jameson, *The Political Unconscious: Narrative as a Socially Symbolic Act* (Ithaca, NY: Cornell University Press, 1981).

2 Eugene Lunn, *Marxism and Modernism: A Historical Study of Lukács, Brecht, Benjamin and Adorno* (Berkeley: University of California Press, 1982), pp. 34–7; Malcolm Bradbury and Robert McFarlane, *Modernism* (Harmondsworth: Penguin, 1976), pp. 24–5.

3 Ezra Pound, "Vorticism," *Gaudier-Brzeska*, 1916; reprinted in Richard Ellmann and Charles Feidelson, eds., *The Modern Tradition* (New York and Oxford: Oxford University Press, 1965), pp. 145–52, p. 152.

4 Elizabeth Butler Cullingford, *Gender and History in Yeats's Love Poetry* (Cambridge: Cambridge University Press, 1993), p. 9.

5 Henry James, "The Future of the Novel," 1899, reprinted in *The Act of Criticism: Henry James on the Theory and the Practice of Fiction*, ed. William Veeder and Susan M. Griffin (Chicago and London: University of Chicago Press, 1986), pp. 242–51, pp. 242–5.

6 Luce Irigaray, *Speculum of the Other Woman*, trans. Gillian C. Gill (Ithaca, NY: Cornell University Press, 1985).

7 See Thomas Moser, *Joseph Conrad: Achievement and Decline* (Cambridge, MA: Harvard University Press, 1957), for an analysis of heterosexuality as Conrad's "uncongenial subject."

8 Joseph Conrad, *The Nigger of the Narcissus*, in *Three Great Tales* (New York: Vintage–Random House, n.d.).

9 See Albert J. Guerard, *Conrad the Novelist* (Cambridge, MA: Harvard University Press, 1958; New York: Atheneum, 1970): "The actual rescue is presented as a difficult childbirth" (112).

10 See Perry Anderson, "Modernity and Revolution," *New Left Review*, 144 (March/April 1984): 96–113.

11 *The Gender of Modernism*, ed. Bonnie Kime Scott (Bloomington: Indiana University Press, 1990).

12 Zora Neale Hurston, *Their Eyes Were Watching God* (Urbana and Chicago: University of Illinois Press, 1978).

13 Virginia Woolf, *To the Lighthouse* (New York: Harcourt Brace and World, 1927).

8

GLEN MACLEOD

The visual arts

The ancient parallel between literature and the visual arts – i.e. painting, sculpture, and architecture – becomes newly relevant in the twentieth century. Painters were the first to explore the revolutionary possibilities of Modernism, so that painting became the leading art form. Modernist writers often patterned their literary experiments on parallels drawn from the visual arts. It is impossible to understand fully the development of literary Modernism, therefore, without at least a rudimentary knowledge of modern art. This chapter is intended to provide a brief history of modern art for those whose primary interest is modern British and American literature. It follows the version of Modernism that was endorsed by the Museum of Modern Art in the 1930s and that has served as the standard for most of this century. Literary parallels will be drawn primarily from poetry, since there the influence of the visual arts is deepest and most direct.

The great progenitor of modernist revolt was the impressionist movement in the second half of the nineteenth century. The first official exhibition devoted to artists rejected by the established Academy was the "Salon des Refusés" (1863), famous for the scandal it caused by showing Manet's *Le déjeuner sur l'herbe*. That painting's offense both against bourgeois morality (showing a nude woman with two fully clothed men at a picnic) and against academic standards (the flatness of his technique, the lack of careful modeling) anticipates the uncompromising posture of modernist paintings to come. The Impressionists, whose name was first applied to them as a term of derision, established the pattern of the avant-garde: an elite group of artists, scorned but heroic, leading humanity into the future through their prophetic vision. The foundation in 1884 of the Société des Artistes Indépendents, whose exhibitions had no jury and were open to anyone, marked the coming-of-age of this anti-academic tradition that was essential to the development of modern art.

The history of that development is conveniently illustrated by a chart made in 1936 by Alfred Barr, director of the Museum of Modern Art. In that year, the Museum mounted two landmark exhibitions, "Cubism and Abstract Art" and "Fantastic Art, Dada, Surrealism," which were meant to survey, between them, the entire field of modern art. This version of the history of modern art sees two clearly defined lines of development: from Cubism to purely abstract art on the one hand, and from Dada to Surrealism on the other. This is still a useful way to make sense of the welter of isms that comprise modern art.

Barr's chart (figure 1), which appeared on the cover of the catalog for the "Cubism and Abstract Art" exhibition, conveys at a glance both the great number of movements contributing to the development of abstract art and their complex interrelations.[1] Yet it also shows one clear, central current amidst these diverse tributaries. The mainstream begins with Post-Impressionism in the 1890s (Van Gogh, Gauguin, Cézanne, and Seurat), climaxes in Cubism (the largest lettering on the chart), and proceeds inevitably to abstract art (whither all arrows point at the bottom of the page). The development from Cubism to abstract art parallels the contemporaneous line of development from Dada to Surrealism (for which Barr did not make another chart). That these two movements sometimes overlap is suggested by the inclusion of two in-between categories in the lower left quadrant: "(Abstract) Dadaism" and "(Abstract) Surrealism."

The tradition of abstract art begins most importantly with the post-impressionist Cézanne (1839–1906). Cézanne was associated with the Impressionists, who were concerned primarily with light and color. But he was not satisfied with their focus on surface effects, which made their canvases appear formless and shallow – decorative in the pejorative sense. He longed to create an art that would "make of Impressionism something as solid and durable as the art of the Museums." Retaining the Impressionists' broken brushstrokes and their use of pure color, Cézanne added weight and volume by emphasizing the underlying geometric structure of objects (figure 2). He advised painters to "deal with nature in terms of the cylinder, the sphere, the cone." His parallel strokes of color called attention to his painterly technique and to the flat surface of the canvas, as did the art of the Impressionists. But his new method also, paradoxically, created a solid architecture of interlocking planes, making possible a monumentality beyond the reach of Impressionism. Yet the method could be applied as well to a teacup as to a mountain. Indeed, many of Cézanne's greatest canvases are still lifes. His elevation of this formerly lowly subject overturned the traditional hierarchy of genres and pointed the way (though this was hardly Cézanne's intention) to the ultimate disappearance of objects altogether in purely abstract art.

Cézanne was the major influence on both Matisse and Picasso, the two

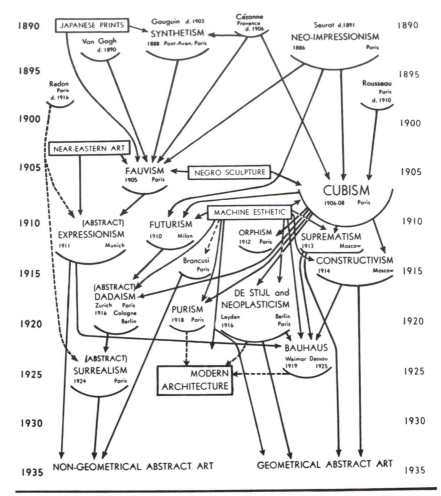

1890 · 1895 · 1900 · 1905 · 1910 · 1915 · 1920 · 1925 · 1930 · 1935

JAPANESE PRINTS

Gauguin d. 1903
SYNTHETISM
1888 Pont-Aven, Paris

Cézanne
Provence
d. 1906

Seurat d.1891
NEO-IMPRESSIONISM
1886 · Paris

Van Gogh
d. 1890

Redon
Paris
d. 1916

Rousseau
Paris
d. 1910

NEAR-EASTERN ART

FAUVISM
1905 · Paris

NEGRO SCULPTURE

CUBISM
1906-08 · Paris

(ABSTRACT)
EXPRESSIONISM
1911 · Munich

MACHINE ESTHETIC

FUTURISM
1910 · Milan

ORPHISM
1912 · Paris

SUPREMATISM
1913 · Moscow

CONSTRUCTIVISM
1914 · Moscow

Brancusi
Paris

(ABSTRACT)
DADAISM
Zurich · Paris
1916 Cologne
Berlin

PURISM
1918 Paris

DE STIJL and
NEOPLASTICISM
Leyden · Berlin
1916 · Paris

BAUHAUS
Weimar Dessau
1919 · 1925

(ABSTRACT)
SURREALISM
1924 · Paris

MODERN
ARCHITECTURE

NON-GEOMETRICAL ABSTRACT ART

GEOMETRICAL ABSTRACT ART

REPRODUCED FROM THE JACKET OF THE ORIGINAL
EDITION

Figure 1 Chart prepared by Alfred H. Barr, Jr. for the dust jacket of the exhibition catalog
Cubism and Abstract Art, Museum of Modern Art, New York (1936).

leading artists of the early twentieth century. Matisse (1869–1954) was the
dominant figure of the "Fauves" (or "Wild Beasts") who, at the turn of the
century, borrowed Cézanne's use of pure color to define space and
developed it in a more freely expressive manner. The mysteries of color
occupied Matisse for the rest of his career. Picasso (1881–1973) developed
in a very different direction. Beginning with Cézanne's interest in geometric
form, Picasso – together with Georges Braque (1882–1963) – invented

Figure 2 Paul Cézanne, *View of L'Estaque and the Chateau d'If*, 1883–1885

Figure 3 Pablo Picasso, *Houses on the Hill, Horta de Ebro* (1909)

Cubism, the chief break with the Western tradition of representational art and the most influential art movement of this century. Between 1907 and 1914, these two artists developed the possibilities of Cubism in three stages.[2]

Cubism

Picasso's *Les demoiselles d'Avignon* (1907) marks the beginning of Cubism, with its depiction of the female nude in terms of a few simplified, flattened shapes. Obviously inspired by Cézanne's *Bathers*, this painting disturbed even the most advanced painters because of its deliberately "primitive" distortions and because of its utter disregard for conventional standards of beauty. Cézanne's influence is perhaps even more evident in Picasso's landscapes of this period. A painting like *Houses on the Hill, Horta de Ebro* (1909) (figure 3) reflects the influence of Cezanne's landscapes not only in its method of composing a scene in terms of geometrical planes, but also in its simplified palette of green and ocher.

Cubism's second stage, known as Analytical Cubism, occurs from about

Figure 4 Georges Braque, *Man with a Guitar* (1911–12)

1910 to 1912. During this period Braque and Picasso so thoroughly analyzed (or broke into smaller parts) objects that they became hardly recognizable (figure 4). This is one respect in which Cubism points the way to purely abstract art. At the same time, the two artists banned almost all color from their canvases. Their pictures became nearly monochromatic, usually restricted to a small range of browns and greys, so that the viewer's attention is focused exclusively on matters of form. This was a particularly bold step for Braque, who had recently been painting in a Fauvist manner, and it clearly marks the Cubists' distance from Matisse, whose dismissal of their efforts as "little cubes" gave the new movement its name.

Analytical Cubism is a watershed in the development of modern painting primarily because it invents a new kind of pictorial space. The centuries-old tradition of deep perspective is replaced by a shallow space in which there is little distance between figure and background. The eye is not led back into an imaginary distance, but is held on the painting's surface. In this respect, Cubism anticipates the central concerns of later abstract artists with flatness and the two-dimensionality of the picture plane. At the same time, Cubism introduces a new way of representing three-dimensional objects. Instead of reproducing the object according to realistic conventions dating from the Renaissance, the painter is free to break apart the object and distribute its pieces about the canvas as the composition requires. The painter can show the back and the front of a chair at the same time, for instance, or paint a face with one eye viewed frontally and the other in profile.

The third stage, Synthetic Cubism (1912–14), set off in a new direction. Having stripped the object of virtually all color and recognizable shape, Picasso and Braque now began adding elements back into their canvases. Color reappears, then letters and words are introduced, inviting the viewer to compare and contrast verbal and visual signs. Finally, the two artists started putting real objects into their artworks: a cigarette wrapper, a piece of fabric or wallpaper or rope, a sheet of music or a newspaper article (figure 5). This technique, known as *collage*, is a revolutionary invention because it breaks down the boundaries between art and life, causing the viewer to ponder various kinds and degrees of artifice.

The literary implications of Cubism are vast. Probably the first writer in English to appreciate them was Gertrude Stein who (with her brothers Leo and Michael) lived in Paris and was an early patron of Picasso. She consciously thought of her own literary experiments as parallels to modern painting. Her book *Three Lives* (1909) was written in response to a portrait by Cézanne, and her own literary "portraits" were modeled on the cubist paintings by Picasso, Braque, and Juan Gris that she collected.[3] Few

Figure 5 Pablo Picasso, *La Suze* (1912)

cases of cubist influence are as direct as this, but it is certainly true that a great deal of modernist experimentation in both prose and poetry was inspired to some extent by Cubism. The cubist techniques of fragmentation, multiple perspectives, and juxtaposition are part of the standard modernist repertoire, from Eliot's *The Waste Land* to Stevens's "The Man with the Blue Guitar." Marianne Moore's famous definition of poetry as "imaginary gardens with real toads in them" conceives of imaginative activity in terms that call to mind cubist collage, a technique which also underlies her idiosyncratic method of splicing direct quotations into her poems. Without the invention of Cubism, Pound's *Cantos* and Williams's *Paterson* probably would not exist as we know them.[4] Wendy Steiner is surely right to call Cubism "the master-current of our age in painting and literature."[5]

London, 1910–14

From the point of view of modern art, Paris is the vital center. During the modernist period, the major artists converged there, and the rest of the world looked to Paris for the latest artistic developments. The way these Parisian innovations were introduced to Britain and the United States helped to determine the way modern literature developed in those countries. The first major showing of modern art in London was the exhibition "Manet and the Post-Impressionists" at the Grafton Galleries in 1910.[6] This was the first of two exhibitions devoted to "Post-Impressionism" that were organized by Roger Fry (who invented the term). It is some measure of the insularity of London at the time that the press and public found this show shocking, even though it was, in fact, an historical survey of painting done in Paris about a quarter of a century before. (It focused mainly on Gauguin, Van Gogh, and Cézanne, with a few more recent works in the fauvist or neo-impressionist styles.) The stunning impact of the first post-impressionist show marks the beginning of the British modernist movement; it was what Virginia Woolf had in mind when she wrote that "In or about December 1910 human character changed."[7]

There were no cubist paintings in the first post-impressionist exhibition. The second exhibition in 1912 did include cubist works, but it is clear that Roger Fry had little sympathy with Cubism or the radical experiments that followed in its wake. Fry's chief interest was Cézanne. But he most admired those qualities in Cézanne that aligned him with Matisse – his sensuous use of color combined with his intuitive feeling for form – rather than the rational geometry that attracted Picasso and the Cubists. Fry's taste for Cézanne and Matisse is reflected in his own paintings as well as in those of

Vanessa Bell, Duncan Grant, and other artists of the Bloomsbury group with which Fry was associated.

It is as an art critic that Roger Fry has had the greatest influence. In trying to explain the innovations of Cézanne and the other Post-Impressionists, he came to the conclusion that the essential aesthetic quality has to do with pure form. He soon developed (along with his disciple Clive Bell) a method of analyzing art solely according to its formal characteristics. In this view, subject matter is irrelevant to aesthetic considerations. Fry's formalist art theory was attractive because it could be applied democratically to any work, from any period or culture, no matter what the subject and no matter how abstractly it was treated. The influence of formalist criticism spread rapidly as modern art developed further and further away from the European tradition of representational art. A purely formalist interpretation of modern art history soon became (and remained, until recently) the orthodox version. Fry's critical emphasis on form in the visual arts has also had far-reaching influence in the realm of modern literature: in the ascendancy of the New Criticism from the 1930s through the 1950s, and in the formal experimentation that has characterized most avant-garde poetry in English since the 1910s.

The most important literary figure in London to be deeply influenced by modern art was the American Ezra Pound, who lived there from 1908 to 1920.[8] Pound dreamed of spearheading a poetic Renaissance and by 1913 his imagist movement had made modest progress in that direction. But his literary efforts were obviously overshadowed by events in the visual arts. Fry's two post-impressionist exhibitions had generated far more controversy and publicity. As Lawrence Rainey's chapter in this volume demonstrates in detail, Imagism was not nearly as well known in London as Futurism. Since 1910, F. T. Marinetti, leader and chief propagandist of the Italian Futurist movement, had been regularly provoking the English establishment with exhibitions, raucous lectures and press conferences, and aggressive manifestos. The Futurists advocated the complete destruction of the past, worshipped the sleekness and power of machinery, and sought to convey in their art the rapid pace of modern life. Their success in London provided Pound with a useful model for organizing and promoting his own movement.[9]

In 1914, Pound joined forces with Wyndham Lewis, Henri Gaudier-Brzeska, Jacob Epstein, Edward Wadsworth, David Bomberg, and others to form the movement he called Vorticism.[10] Like Futurism (and unlike Imagism), Vorticism was conceived as an interdisciplinary movement that included literature and music as well as the visual arts. With shameless bravado, in their publication *Blast* the Vorticists gleefully attacked Futurism (among many other targets) in the aggressive manner and in the inventive typography of the Futurists themselves.

In terms of the visual arts, Vorticism represented an original variant of elements borrowed from Cubism and Futurism. What Vorticism meant in terms of poetry is less clear. Pound's only obviously vorticist poem is "Dogmatic Statement on a Game of Chess: Theme for a Series of Pictures," whose angular shapes and abrupt movements could describe a vorticist painting. Pound's poetic principles remained essentially imagist: sharpness of observation, economy of phrasing, organic rhythm. Adopting the vorticist label allowed him to distinguish his own campaign for modernist reform from the debased form of "Imagism" popularized by Amy Lowell. And it allowed him to align poetry with other arts in a more broadly based movement.

Pound's excessive enthusiasm for his London artist friends – for instance, his praising Wyndham Lewis as a greater artist than Picasso – points up his obvious inadequacy as a guide to modern art. Nevertheless, the short-lived Vorticist movement – cut short, as it was, by World War I – played an important part in Pound's poetic development. His involvement with artists, and his thinking in terms of analogies with the visual arts, influenced both his poetry and his poetic theory. His own great influence in literary circles helped to disseminate the discoveries of modern art throughout modern literature in English.

Abstraction

Pound's thinking about modern art during his Vorticist period (c. 1913–15) was greatly influenced by the views of T. E. Hulme, a disciple of the German aesthetician Wilhelm Worringer. Worringer's *Abstraction and Empathy* (1908) analyzed the history of art according to two opposing impulses: (1) *empathy*, reflecting a secure, confident relation to the world and resulting in an organic, humanistic art like that of ancient Greece and Renaissance Italy; and (2) *abstraction*, reflecting an anxious, fearful relation to the world and resulting in a stylized, geometric art, as in African, Egyptian, and Byzantine art. Hulme borrowed Worringer's theory and used it to promote the geometric–abstract art of Lewis, Epstein, and others in the cubist tradition.[11] The modernist sensibility, according to Hulme, is fundamentally opposed to the Christian humanism of the Renaissance tradition; it is closer in spirit to more "primitive" cultures and expresses itself most fully in the hard, clean, geometric shapes characteristic of modern machinery. The vorticist painters and sculptors immediately adopted Hulme's rationale as their own, as is evident in their polemics in *Blast*. At the same time, Pound's prescriptions for poetry began to emphasize the "hardness" and "clarity of outline" typical of geometric–abstract art.

Another important influence on Pound during this early period was the painter Wassily Kandinsky (1866–1944). One of the pioneers of abstraction, Kandinsky painted his first purely abstract work in 1910 and was associated with the German Blaue Reiter group (represented on Barr's chart as "(Abstract) Expressionism"). His book *Concerning the Spiritual in Art*, one of the chief documents in the history of abstract art, was translated into English in 1914 and immediately circulated among avant-garde circles in both Britain and America. Kandinsky argued for the necessity of abstraction in the twentieth century, illustrating his points by drawing analogies with other art forms, particularly music. Pound admired Kandinsky's analogical method and asserted that his theory applied equally well to poetry: "The image is the poet's pigment; with that in mind you can go ahead and apply Kandinsky, you can transpose his chapter on the language of form and color and apply it to the writing of verse."[12]

Kandinsky thought of abstract art primarily in spiritual terms, as an attempt to discover a reality behind surface appearances. In this sense his aesthetics are at the opposite extreme from the pure formalism of Roger Fry. *Concerning the Spiritual in Art* argues that a great spiritual revolution is taking place and that the arts are leading the way, citing Madame Blavatsky's Theosophical Society as evidence. This view of art was typical of the founders of abstraction; Piet Mondrian and Kasimir Malevich also thought of it in these mystical, visionary terms.[13] Nor would Pound have found strange such an esoteric approach to Modernism. Recent scholarship has shown that Pound himself was interested in spiritualism, sharing in Yeats's occult studies at the very time he was working out his own theories of Imagism and Vorticism.[14] Kandinsky's faith that art can bring about the evolution of the human soul is hardly more grand than Pound's own project for *The Cantos*.

The spiritual basis of abstract art also informs Wallace Stevens's *Notes Towards a Supreme Fiction*, which explores the possibility of creating a modern substitute for God. The first section of that poem, subtitled "It Must Be Abstract," considers the supreme fiction as analogous to the spiritual content of Mondrian's pure geometric–abstract paintings.[15]

The term *abstract* can be applied to a bewildering variety of modern art. It can refer, on the one hand, to any form abstracted (to any degree) *from nature*; and, on the other, to purely abstract forms without any reference to nature. It can cover the full range of shapes from biomorphic (for example, Joan Miró) to geometric (for example, Piet Mondrian). In order to keep confusion at bay, it is helpful for the nonspecialist to bear in mind the clear organization of Alfred Barr's chart. There Cubism leads most directly to pure geometric abstraction. Picasso and Braque's analysis of objects into geometric shapes leads, with irresistible logic, to Mondrian's austere canvases that use only straight lines, right angles, and primary colors. The clarity of that development (from Cubism to pure geometric abstraction) provides a convenient standard by which to measure the many other kinds and degrees of abstract art.

New York, 1910s

There seemed little doubt in the 1910s that London was the heart of literary activity in the English-speaking world. In contrast with the portentous doings of Pound and Eliot in London, New York seemed relatively minor and provincial. From the perspective of the late twentieth century, however, the New York writers – especially the poets Wallace Stevens, William Carlos Williams, and Marianne Moore – assume an importance perhaps equal to that of their expatriate rivals.

The poetry of Stevens, Williams, and Moore owes much of its distinctive character to the preeminence of the visual arts in New York. Each of these poets wrote intensely visual poetry in which often the act or quality of looking is the central point. Moore's minute observations always showed a painter's eye, and when she edited the *Dial* in the 1920s, she made sure that it covered the visual as much as the literary arts.[16] Williams was friendly with New York painters such as Charles Demuth, Marsden Hartley, and Charles Sheeler; while he listened intently to Pound's bulletins from London, he developed his own poetic voice primarily by looking at modern paintings.[17] Stevens tended to visit art galleries rather than artists' studios but he, too, consciously modeled his poetry on analogies drawn from the contemporary art world.[18] This habit of mind is already well established in one of his earliest mature poems, "Disillusionment of Ten O'Clock" (1915), which expresses his delight in the imagination in terms of the bold shapes and colors of modern painting.

New York was, during the first two decades of this century, the only city in the United States where one could see with any regularity the latest art from Paris. Beginning in 1908, Alfred Stieglitz presented exhibitions of modern art in his small gallery called "291" (after its address on Fifth Avenue). There, adventurous spirits could encounter works by such European artists as Cézanne, Picasso, Brancusi, and Matisse, as well as by advanced American artists like Arthur Dove, John Marin, and Georgia O'Keeffe. Modern painting, sculpture, and architecture were reproduced often in Stieglitz's periodical *Camera Work*. It was not until 1913, however, that modern art really "arrived" in New York, with the legendary Armory Show.

The International Exhibition of Modern Art, held in the Sixth-Ninth Regiment Armory at Lexington Avenue and Twenty-Fifth Street in Manhattan, contained nearly 1,300 works by both European and American artists. It is remembered as the single most important exhibition in United States history because it first made the American public aware of Post-Impressionism and Cubism. From this show we can date the rise of Modernism in all the arts in America. Although versions of the Armory Show also traveled to Chicago and Boston, it had the biggest impact in New York. Aspiring Modernists were drawn there in the wake of the Armory Show, and New York soon became a thriving center of modernist activity. The close relation between poetry and painting that prevailed among the New York avant-garde is epitomized in the person of E. E. Cummings who, refusing to choose between the two art forms, always considered himself a "poetandpainter."[19]

A crucial ingredient in the formation of the New York avant-garde was the presence of foreign – primarily French – artists driven there by the outbreak of the First World War. Among these expatriates were Marcel Duchamp, Francis Picabia, Jean and Yvonne Crotti, Albert Gleizes and Juliette Roche, Edgar Varèse, and Henri-Pierre Roché. This concentration of French men and women established a New York–Paris axis that has characterized the mainstream of modern art for most of this century. Although London remained the center for poetry in English during the 1910s, as Pound never tired of reminding his New Jersey-bound friend Williams, the New York poets were actually in closer touch with the latest Parisian developments in the visual arts.

The leading figure among these French expatriates was Marcel Duchamp (1887–1968). When he first arrived in New York in 1915, Duchamp was already widely known there. His *Nude Descending a Staircase* (figure 6) had been the most notorious work in the Armory Show two years before. Critics singled out the *Nude* for ridicule – one called it "an explosion in a shingle factory" – and it quickly became a symbol in the American press for all modern art. A version of the *Nude* hung from 1915 to 1921 in the New York apartment of Walter Conrad Arensberg, a friend and patron of Duchamp, whose pioneering collection of modern art is now housed in the Philadelphia Museum of Art. Arensberg's apartment was a kind of salon where avant-garde writers and artists gathered to share their enthusiasm for modern art. Regular guests included (in addition to the French men and women named above), among writers, Williams, Stevens, Alfred Kreymborg, Carl Van Vechten, Djuna Barnes, and Mina Loy; and among artists,

Figure 6 Marcel Duchamp, *Nude Descending a Staircase, No. 2*

Demuth, Hartley, Sheeler, Joseph Stella, John Covert, Morton Schamberg, and Man Ray.

Dada

This loosely affiliated group is now known as the New York Dada movement.[20] The character of this movement differs significantly from that of Pound's circle in London. As an illustration, we may take Duchamp's *Nude*. Like the art of the Vorticists, this painting consciously combines elements of Cubism (the reduction of a nude body to an arrangement of geometrical planes) and Futurism (the kinetic motion of the figure). But these stylistic aspects are not enough to explain the notoriety of the *Nude*. What made the press and public single out this painting from among the many other cubist works in the Armory Show? The explanation lies in Duchamp's title, which promises a fairly racy spectacle but delivers, instead, a geometrical construction of planes and angles. The title arouses titillating expectations that the painting itself frustrates. The teasing humor in this conception – so different from the bombastic rhetoric of the Vorticists – is the defining quality of New York Dada.

A similar tendency toward ironic humor among the New York poets contrasts in the same way with the high seriousness of Pound and Eliot. Stevens's delight in puns, nonsense, and other kinds of wordplay, and Williams's often improvisational manner, for example, led early critics to dismiss them as minor. In hindsight, however, we can see these qualities as typical of Dada – an international movement that had great impact in both Europe and America but that seems to have bypassed London completely. As an official movement, Dada was founded in Zurich in 1916. Important Dada groups soon sprang up in Cologne, Hanover, Berlin, and Paris. Among the leading figures of the movement were Hugo Ball, Tristan Tzara, Jean Arp, Richard Huelsenbeck, Max Ernst, and Kurt Schwitters. Unlike Cubism, Dada is not an artistic style but an attitude or way of life. (There is, however, some overlapping of categories. A work may be cubist in style but Dada in spirit, for instance, like Schwitters's Dada collages.) Dada is a nose-thumbing challenge to all convention. It is the purest embodiment of the *destructive* element that is an essential part (though only a part) of Modernism. Outraged by the massive carnage of World War I, the Dadaists rebelled against all established institutions and traditional values – indeed, against reason itself since, as the guiding principle of Western civilization, rationalism had led directly (in their view) to the wholesale destruction of the war. The nonsense-term *Dada* was an appropriate name for this exuberantly anarchic movement. The Dadaists made artworks from found objects and chance occurrences; gave nonsense lectures and poetry readings, concerts of noise, and bizarre theatrical productions. If these events sometimes led to riots, so much the better.

New York Dada actually preceded European Dada and was less negative in character. Its leading figure was Duchamp, whose most notorious act while he lived in New York occurred in connection with the first annual exhibition of the Society for Independent Artists in 1917. Modeled on the famous French institution of the same name, the "Indeps" was to be thoroughly democratic, open to anyone, with no jury. In order to test the sincerity of the hanging committee (of which he was the head), Duchamp entered a work pseudonymously. Called *Fountain* and signed "R. Mutt," it was an ordinary porcelain urinal. The work was rejected and Duchamp resigned in protest from the committee.

Fountain is the most famous example of the art form Duchamp called the *readymade*. In creating a readymade, the artist selects an ordinary, mass-produced object and displays it as a work of art. His first readymade, *Bicycle Wheel* (1913), consisted of a bicycle wheel mounted upside-down on top of a four-legged stool. Over the next decade, the artist created a number of these works – a snow shovel, a bottle rack, a metal comb. The viewer's automatic first reaction, "Is it art?" cannot be answered without addressing the complex philosophical question, "What is art?" As Duchamp put it, "I was interested in ideas – not merely in visual products. I wanted to put [art] once again at the service of the mind."[21] In doing so, he laid the foundation for the later developments of Pop Art, minimalism, and conceptual art.

Traces of Duchamp's readymades can be discovered in some of the best-known works of the New York poets. Williams's "The Red Wheelbarrow" presents the object unadorned and without comment; his minimalist approach calls into question the very nature of poetry, as a readymade questions the very nature of art. Stevens's "Anecdote of the Jar" could describe the creation of a readymade: the speaker places a jar on a hilltop in Tennessee, thereby transforming both the object and its environment. Both of these poems reflect the combination of intellectual seriousness and deadpan humor that characterizes New York Dada.

After Duchamp, the most important Dada artist in New York was Francis Picabia (1879–1953) who first came there to see the Armory Show in 1913. He shuttled between Europe and America for the rest of the 1910s, participating in Dada activities on both continents. In New York, he exhibited paintings in exhibitions, became close to Duchamp and the Arensberg circle, and contributed to Stieglitz's magazine *291* and other publications. His paintings and drawings during this period are mainly

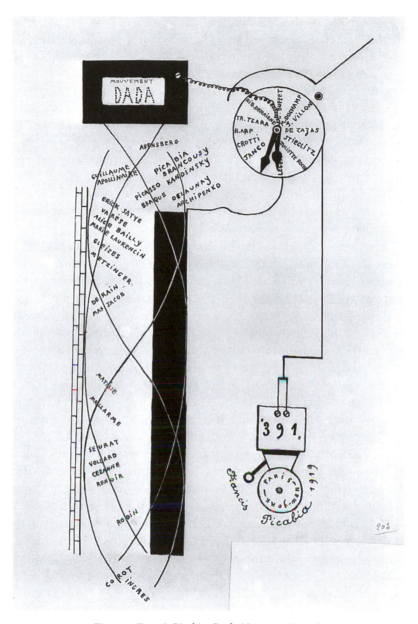

Figure 7 Francis Picabia, *Dada Movement* (1919)

based on machine forms, perhaps the best known of which are a series of mechanical portraits published in 291, including a portrait of the photographer Stieglitz (a modified camera) and *Portrait of a Young American Girl in a State of Nudity* (a spark plug). His drawing *Dada Movement* (figure 7) appeared in Tristan Tzara's *Anthologie Dada*, published in Zurich in 1919. It seems to show a kind of fire alarm system whose various parts display the names of Picabia's associates in Zurich, Paris, and New York (including Duchamp, Arensberg, and Stieglitz). The alarm bell announces the crucial "New York–Paris" axis. The irrational workings of this machine contrast appropriately with the geometrical and logical neatness of Barr's chart for *Cubism and Abstract Art*. The anarchic energy of Dada exists outside the rational development of the cubist tradition.

Critics have been slow to acknowledge the importance of Dada artists to modern writers in English, though Stevens's *Harmonium* (1923) records the very spirit of New York Dada, and though Williams remarked of his own work: "I didn't originate Dadaism but I had it in my soul to write it. *Spring and All* [1922] shows that."[22] Until recently it was not generally known that Pound, too, became interested in Dada when he lived in Paris from 1920 to 1924.[23] Disgusted by the violent spectacle of World War I, which he saw as the betrayal of all he valued, Pound shared wholeheartedly the Dadaists' desire to wipe the slate clean. In Paris, he took part in Dada activities; reported on them in letters to the *Little Review*, the *Dial*, and other literary journals; and contributed to Dada publications. He was most impressed with Picabia, praising him as the leading "intellect" of European Modernism and as "the man who ties knots in Picasso's tail." He recognized in Picabia's conversation, writings, and artworks the possibility of what we would now call conceptual art: "[Picabia works] in a definite medium, to which one may give an interim label of thought."[24] Pound's involvement with the Dadaists in Paris may well have been the catalyst that allowed him to renew his work on *The Cantos*. The "boisterousness and disorder" he sought to include in the "Malatesta Cantos," which mark such an artistic breakthrough in the compositional method of *The Cantos* as a whole, probably owe something to the anarchic energy of Dada.

Surrealism

Dada's commitment to anarchy and disorder contributed to its own demise. In 1924, most of its adherents became part of the newly formed surrealist movement, which had a more coherent theoretical foundation and a more positive agenda. The first *Surrealist Manifesto* (1924), written by André Breton, the high priest of the movement, declared: "I believe in the future resolution of these two states, dream and reality, which are seemingly so contradictory, in a sort of absolute reality, or surreality, if one may so speak."[25] To this revolutionary end, the Surrealists sought to free the irrational powers of the unconscious mind. One favorite method they used to disrupt conventional thinking was to create unexpected juxtapositions, as in the classic example from Lautréamont: "the chance encounter of a sewing machine and an umbrella on a dissection table." Although it began primarily as a literary movement (founding members Breton, Eluard, Soupault, and Aragon, for example, were poets), Surrealism has had the greatest impact in the visual arts. This is especially true in England and America where the language barrier has impeded the promulgation of surrealist texts.

Surrealist painting can be divided into two distinct kinds, veristic and absolute, to use Werner Haftmann's terminology.[26] Veristic surrealism is illusionistic; it distorts or oddly juxtaposes recognizable objects in order to create a kind of dream image or hallucinatory vision. The most extreme practitioner of veristic surrealism is Salvador Dalí, whose small canvas *The Persistence of Memory* (1931), with its melting watches in a barren land-scape, is one of the best-known images in modern painting. The opposite extreme – absolute surrealism – is represented by Joan Miró, whose strange, nearly abstract, biomorphic shapes were achieved through *automatism*: he used chance occurrences or spontaneous gestures as a way of starting a painting and gaining access to the unconscious. In one series of watercolors, for instance, Miró began by roughening the surface of the paper. "Painting over the roughened surface produced curious chance shapes" which he would then develop into a composition. "I would set out with no preconceived idea," he said. "A few forms suggested here would call for other forms elsewhere."[27] Miró's often flat, cartoon-like shapes contrast utterly with Dalí's conventionally modeled objects in deep Renaissance space. Between these two extremes stretches the full spectrum of surrealist art.

The chief impact of Surrealism on Anglo-American literature occurred among the New York-centered poets. Ezra Pound never showed any interest in the Surrealists, and in fact left Paris for Italy just as they came onstage.[28] William Carlos Williams, on the other hand, was quick to respond to the new movement. Williams's own experiments in automatic writing in *Kora in Hell: Improvisations* (1919) may actually have anticipated the first automatic surrealist text, *The Magnetic Fields* (1919) by André Breton and Philippe Soupault. When he visited Paris in 1924, Williams met and became friendly with Soupault; he later translated the Frenchman's surrealist novel *Last Nights of Paris* (1929). But Surrealism was not widely known in the United States until the 1930s, a decade during which Williams, Marianne Moore, and Wallace Stevens all frequently attended surrealist art exhibitions. The Museum of Modern Art's exhibition "Fantastic Art, Dada, Surrealism" (1936/7) stirred up nationwide interest in the Surrealists. Stevens had always been known for his surreal juxtapositions, such as the title image of "The Emperor of Ice-Cream." He had Surrealism in mind when he wrote his first prose essay, "The Irrational Element in Poetry" (1936), and in composing "The Man with the Blue Guitar" (1937).[29] Surrealist activity again swept through New York during the Second World War, when Breton and other Surrealists-in-exile were living there. Williams was at the heart of that activity.[30] Moore's interest in Surrealism is highlighted by her correspondence during the 1940s with the American surrealist Joseph Cornell, a kindred spirit, both of them fastidious hoarders of marvelous objects and curiosities.[31]

By the early 1930s, the Parisian art world was divided into two opposing camps: the Surrealists and the abstractionists. The rivalry between these two camps tended to make their theoretical positions more and more extreme, so that it became possible to consider them nearly absolute opposites. If Surrealism stood for the irrational, for literary content, and for figuration, then abstraction came to stand for utter rationalism, pure formalism, and non-objectivity. Between them, Surrealism and abstraction seemed to define the full range of possibilities for modern art. The two landmark exhibitions at the Museum of Modern Art in 1936 – "Fantastic Art, Dada, Surrealism" and "Cubism and Abstract Art" – officially codified this dualistic way of interpreting the development of modern art. For the non-specialist looking for a secure foothold in the complex field of modern art, it remains a useful paradigm.

NOTES

1 Alfred H. Barr, Jr., *Cubism and Abstract Art*, exhib. cat. (New York: Museum of Modern Art, 1936).

2 The standard history of Cubism is John Golding, *Cubism: A History and an Analysis, 1907–1914*, 3rd edn (1959; Cambridge, MA,: Harvard University Press, 1988). The most thorough study of Picasso and Braque's collaboration in the invention of Cubism, with the best illustrations, is William Rubin, *Picasso and Braque: Pioneering Cubism* (New York: Museum of Modern Art, 1989).

3 Wendy Steiner, *Exact Resemblance to Exact Resemblance: The Literary Portraiture of Gertrude Stein* (New Haven: Yale University Press, 1978).

4 Marjorie Perloff treats *The Cantos* as collage in *The Poetics of Indeterminacy: Rimbaud to Cage* (Princeton: Princeton University Press, 1981), ch. 5. Henry Sayre treats *Paterson* as collage in *The Visual Text of William Carlos Williams* (Urbana, IL: University of Illinois Press 1983).

5 Wendy Steiner, *The Colors of Rhetoric: Problems in the Relation Between*

Modern Literature and Painting (Chicago: University of Chicago Press, 1982), pp. 177–97. Jacqueline Vaught Brogan traces a cubist tradition in modern poetry in *Part of the Climate: American Cubist Poetry* (Berkeley: University of California Press, 1991).

6 See Richard Cork, *Vorticism and Abstract Art in the First Machine Age* (Berkeley: University of California Press, 1976), vol. I, pp. 16–18.

7 Virginia Woolf, *Collected Essays*, vol. I (New York: Harcourt Brace and World, 1967), p. 320.

8 For an overview of Pound's interest in the visual arts see *Pound's Artists: Ezra Pound and the Visual Arts in London, Paris, and Italy*, exhib. cat. (London: Tate Gallery, 1985).

9 For the influence of Futurism on Pound's poetry see Marjorie Perloff, *The Futurist Moment: Avant-Garde, Avant Guerre, and the Language of Rupture* (Chicago: University of Chicago Press, 1986), ch. 5.

10 On Pound and Vorticism see Cork, *Vorticism*; William C. Wees, *Vorticism and the English Avant-Garde* (Toronto: University of Toronto Press, 1972); Timothy Materer, *Vortex: Pound, Eliot, and Lewis* (Ithaca, NY: Cornell University Press 1979); and Reed Way Dasenbrock, *The Literary Vorticism of Ezra Pound and Wyndham Lewis: Toward the Condition of Painting* (Baltimore: Johns Hopkins University Press, 1985).

11 See "Modern Art and its Philosophy," in T. E. Hulme, *Speculations*, ed. Herbert Read (London: K. Paul, Trench, Trubner, 1924), pp. 75–109.

12 Ezra Pound, *Gaudier-Brzeska: A Memoir* (New York: New Directions, 1970), p. 86.

13 See Maurice Tuchman *et al.*, *The Spiritual in Art: Abstract Painting, 1890–1985* (New York: Abbeville, 1986); and Roger Lipsey, *An Art of Our Own: The Spiritual in Twentieth-Century Art* (Boston: Shambhala, 1988).

14 James Longenbach, *Stone Cottage: Pound, Yeats, and Modernism* (Oxford: Oxford University Press, 1988); Leon Surette, *The Birth of Modernism: Ezra Pound, T. S. Eliot, W. B. Yeats and the Occult* (Montreal: McGill – Queen's University Press, 1993); Timothy Materer, *Modernist Alchemy: Poetry and the Occult* (Ithaca, NY: Cornell University Press, 1995).

15 Glen MacLeod, *Wallace Stevens and Modern Art: From the Armory Show to Abstract Expressionism* (New Haven: Yale University Press, 1993), ch. 5.

16 For Moore's interest in the visual arts, see Bonnie Costello, *Marianne Moore: Imaginary Possessions* (Cambridge, MA: Harvard University Press, 1981), ch. 7; and Linda Leavell, *Marianne Moore and the Visual Arts: Prismatic Color* (Baton Rouge: Louisiana State University Press, 1995). Many visual sources of Moore's poetry (not only the visual arts) are discussed and reproduced in Patricia C. Willis, *Marianne Moore: Vision into Verse* (Philadelphia: Rosenbach Library, 1987).

17 The first major study of Williams and the visual arts was Bram Dijkstra, *The Hieroglyphics of a New Speech: Cubism, Stieglitz and the Early Poetry of William Carlos Williams* (Princeton: Princeton University Press, 1969). Since then other book-length studies have appeared by Dickran Tashjian (1978), William Marling (1982), Henry Sayre (1983), Christopher MacGowan (1984), Peter Schmidt (1988), Terence Diggory (1991), and Peter Halter (1994).

18 For Stevens's interest in the visual arts, see especially MacLeod, *Wallace Stevens*

and Modern Art, and Bonnie Costello, "Effects of an Analogy: Wallace Stevens and Painting" in Albert Gelpi, ed., *Wallace Stevens and the Poetics of Modernism* (Cambridge and New York: Cambridge University Press, 1985). See also Michel Benamou, *Wallace Stevens and the Symbolist Imagination* (Princeton: Princeton University Press, 1972), chs. 1 and 4; and Robert Buttel, *Wallace Stevens: The Making of "Harmonium"* (Princeton: Princeton University Press, 1967), ch. 6.

19 On Cummings and the visual arts see Milton A. Cohen, *Poet and Painter: The Aesthetics of E. E. Cummings's Early Work* (Detroit: Wayne State University Press, 1987).

20 The definitive history of the movement is Francis M. Naumann, *New York Dada, 1915–1923* (New York: Abrams, 1994). For a broader treatment of American responses to Dada, primarily from a literary perspective, see Dickran Tashjian, *Skyscraper Primitives: Dada and the American Avant-Garde, 1910–1925* (Middletown, CT: Wesleyan University Press, 1975).

21 Quoted in the introduction to Arturo Schwartz, *Marcel Duchamp* (New York: Abrams, 1975), n.p.

22 For Williams's interest in Dada, see Tashjian, *Skyscraper Primitives*, and Peter Schmidt, *William Carlos Williams, the Arts, and Literary Tradition* (Baton Rouge: Louisiana State University Press, 1988).

23 Vincent Sherry, *Ezra Pound, Wyndham Lewis, and Radical Modernism* (Oxford: Oxford University Press, 1993), pp. 142–3. Sherry summarizes recent work on Pound and Dada by Richard Sieburth, Andrew Clearfield, and Robert von Hallberg, with bibliographical information, on pp. 214n2 and 215n3.

24 Ezra Pound, "Parisian Literature," *Literary Review* [of the New York *Evening Post*], 13 August 1921, p. 7. Quoted in Richard Sieburth, "Dada Pound," *South Atlantic Quarterly*, 83.1 (Winter 1984), p. 50.

25 André Breton, *Manifestoes of Surrealism*, trans. Richard Seaver and Helen Lane (Ann Arbor: University of Michigan, 1972), p. 14.

26 Werner Haftmann, *Painting in the Twentieth Century* (1965; New York: Praeger, 1976).

27 Quoted in Herschel B. Chipp, *Theories of Modern Art: A Source Book by Artists and Critics* (Berkeley: University of California Press, 1968), p. 434.

28 Daniel Tiffany speculates on Pound's affinities with Surrealism in his *Radio Corpse: Imagism and the Cryptaesthetic of Ezra Pound* (Cambridge, MA: Harvard University Press, 1995), pp. 230–3, 280–1. There was a surrealist group in England that published the periodical *Contemporary Poetry and Prose* during the 1930s. Further surrealist influence is evident in the New Apocalypse movement of the 1940s that included poets David Gascoyne and Dylan Thomas.

29 MacLeod, *Wallace Stevens and Modern Art*, ch. 3.

30 For Williams's connection to Surrealism, see Mike Weaver, *William Carlos Williams: The American Background* (Cambridge: Cambridge University Press, 1971), ch. 8; and Dickran Tashjian, *A Boatload of Madmen: Surrealism and the American Avant-Garde, 1920–1950* (London and New York: Thames and Hudson, 1995).

31 Dickran Tashjian discusses Marianne Moore's correspondence with Joseph Cornell in *Joseph Cornell: Gifts of Desire* (Miami Beach: Grassfield Press, 1992), pp. 65–77.

9

MICHAEL WOOD

Modernism and film

I decided I liked Photography *in opposition* to the Cinema, from which I nonetheless failed to separate it.

Roland Barthes, *Camera Lucida*[1]

It is tempting to argue that all films are modernist, that the cinema itself is an accelerated image of modernity, like the railway and the telephone. But to do this is to miss the nostalgia inseparable from the way the medium has worked out historically, its (amply rewarded) yearning to become our century's version of last century's novel. There are modernist films, even outside the period we associate with Modernism; but the largest fact about the cinema over the hundred years since its birth is its comfortable embrace of ancient conventions of realism and narrative coherence.

When the German critic Walter Benjamin describes the strange mingling of artifice and illusion in the cinema – we know all about the tricky construction of the pictured world, which we nevertheless take as far more intimately actual than anything we could find in the live theatre – he says "the sight of immediate reality has become an orchid in the land of technology."[2] "In the theatre one is well aware of the place from which the play cannot immediately be detected as illusionary. There is no such place for the movie scene that is being shot. Its illusionary nature is that of the second degree, the result of cutting." Benjamin's inference is that the absence of illusion in the studio or on location is canceled by the sheer power and invisibility of the editing process. The result is (most often) more illusion, a modernist, distancing gesture swallowed up in denial; an orchid pretending to be a daisy or even a weed.

Still, technology is not always disavowed in the movies, and illusions are questioned as well as fostered, so we can ask what Modernism looks like when it does appear in the cinema; where it appears; and what this Modernism has to tell us about other modernisms. I have concentrated on particular films and ideas about films rather than attempt a survey, but I hope the reach of the questions will suggest something of the richness of the ground. My examples are chiefly German, Russian, French, and American films of the 1920s and early 1930s. A trawl which went on a little longer would pick up the work of Jean Renoir in France, and one which reached beyond the Second World War would find Modernism going strong in Italy, notably in the films of Federico Fellini and Luchino Visconti. But the range of modernist possibilities in the cinema was clearly outlined by the end of the 1920s; and the disavowal of modernist preoccupations was already proceeding apace.

In Christopher Isherwood's novel *Prater Violet* (1945), a brilliant and tormented Austrian film director defines his medium for us:

> The film is an infernal machine. Once it is ignited and set in motion, it revolves with an enormous dynamism. It cannot pause. It cannot apologize. It cannot retract anything. It cannot wait for you to understand it. It cannot explain itself. It simply ripens to its inevitable explosion. This explosion we have to prepare, like anarchists, with the utmost ingenuity and malice . . .[3]

We can scarcely miss this man's intricate pleasure in his contact with Hell, but the narrator also records a gesture for us: "Bergmann cupped his hands, lovingly, as if around an exquisite flower." A little later, the narrator explains to his mother and brother that Bergmann was talking about the fixed *speed* of film, the fact that it does not allow us to pause or go back, as a painting or a novel does, but this seems trite, a deliberate backing off from Bergmann's metaphor. The novel is set in 1933 and 1934, Austria is yielding to the National Socialists, we can think of other persons and inventions, apart from anarchists and movies, eminently incapable of pausing, apologizing, retracting, waiting or explaining. Bergmann is saying that film is not only an art of time but the art of his time, a modern, even a modernist art which cannot disentangle itself from the world it opposes, and which must describe its hopes in terms entirely appropriate also to its fears. His infernal machine recalls and looks forward to the factory worlds of Fritz Lang's *Metropolis* (Germany, 1926) and Charlie Chaplin's *Modern Times* (USA, 1936), as well as the ticking bombs of European politics. The irony is further complicated by the film Bergmann is making, a frothy operetta set in a Vienna which is all charm and unreality, impervious to the very notion of politics. Bergmann's infernal machine begins to look like a fancy cake.

Bergmann is working in an England where modernity is pictured as uncertainty, a kind of technological and commercial bewilderment. The "panic" is not the Wall Street Crash or the Depression, but the arrival of sound at Imperial Bulldog Pictures:

> At the time of the panic, when Sound first came to England and nobody's job was safe, Bulldog had carried through a hasty and rather hysterical recon- struction program. The whole place was torn down and rebuilt at top speed, most of it as cheaply as possible. No one knew what was coming next: Taste,

perhaps, or Smell, or Stereoscopy, or some device that climbed right down out of the screen and ran around in the audience. Nothing seemed impossible.[4]

I am sure this is an accurate enough picture of the British movie business in the 1930s – Isherwood would be the first to say he is writing from memory rather than invention – but as an image constructed in 1945 it means something rather different, just as the name of the movie company shifts in this light from broad comedy to rather subtler historical satire. This England is no more prepared for Hitler and war than the company was for sound. It is noticeably edgy, has lost all its old biting arrogance, but has found nothing to replace it. It is like an art form in transition; like a 1930s movie, or a movie studio. Later Isherwood describes a ghostly sound stage, with its multiple, partial sets: "a kind of Pompeii, but more desolate, more uncanny, because this is, literally, a half-world, a limbo of mirror-images, a town which has lost its third dimension. Only the tangle of heavy power cables is solid, apt to trip you as you cross the floor."[5] The unreality of the movie world is a trope as old as the movies themselves, so we must ask what produces its peculiar force in this context. The answer, I think, is history, and a form of double-take. We register the forlorn unreality of this half-world, because it is not like ours, then or now. Then we look at our world again, and are astonished at the resemblance. Emptied of what we thought was its reality, our world *is* the studio, frantically guessing at what it can not know. The Modernists kept frightening themselves with such thoughts, as if they were not quite ready for the implications of their insights.

Virginia Woolf's essay "The Cinema" (1926) does not seem to tell us a lot about the movies. She mentions only one film by name, glances at the contents or conceptions of a few others. Yet with characteristic shrewdness and indirection Woolf manages to evoke an essential feature of the cinema, an abstract, nonmimetic expressive possibility that the film industry, both before and after 1926, has devoted considerable amounts of time and money to refusing.

> For instance, at a performance of Dr. Caligari the other day a shadow shaped like a tadpole suddenly appeared at one corner of the screen. It swelled to an immense size, quivered, bulged, and sank back again into nonentity. For a moment it seemed to embody some monstrous diseased imagination of the lunatic's brain. For a moment it seemed as if thought could be conveyed by shape more effectively than by words. The monstrous quivering tadpole seemed to be fear itself, and not the statement "I am afraid."[6]

Woolf goes on to explain that the shadow was not part of the film but the effect of some sort of fault of projection or flaw in the print; but then implies that the unintentional quality of the image was also part of its magic – and a rebuke to the rather meager intentions of the cinema as Woolf understood it.

Yet if the shadow was an accident, an abstract shape rather than a scripted and performed human action, Woolf's interpretation of it as "fear itself" belongs very much to the world of this particular film. In another film the same shape would have meant something different, and Woolf through sheer mischievous intelligence appears to have stumbled on one of the fundamentals of film theory: the principle of montage.

The Cabinet of Dr. Caligari (directed by Robert Wiene, Germany, 1919) announces itself as old and new, in a way which is familiar to us from literary Modernism: "A tale of the modern re-appearance of an 11th century myth . . ." Later we are told that a monk called Caligari was practicing the dark arts of hypnotism in 1093; and that a modern psychiatrist has taken his name and turned showman, because his scientific interest in somnambulism has modulated into something more sinister: into the desire, as the doctor says, to get Cesare, his haunted, sleeping subject, to "perform deeds he would shrink from in his normal waking state." Cesare in his sleep kills the doctor's enemies, terrorizes the town, abducts a young woman. Then the doctor's part in these crimes is discovered, and he is pursued through a nightmarish landscape, only to disappear into the mental hospital of which he is, it turns out, the director. His assistants, quickly persuaded of his guilt, tie him up in a straitjacket: the fuming doctor is one of the great images of the film. A title card informs us that "Today he is raving under chains in his cell."

Except that he is not. The whole story we have seen has been told by one of the inmates of the doctor's hospital. The inmates, including the person who has been telling the story and someone who looks just like Cesare, walk dreamily around a courtyard, the doctor appears, unchained, reassuring – or even more sinister, if we are unable to shake off the effect of the story. His appearance, S. S. Prawer informs us, "was suggested to the script-writers by a photograph of the philosopher Arthur Schopenhauer in his old age";[7] but then this piece of information could lead us in several different directions. The common interpretation of the film, initiated by Siegfried Kracauer in his book *From Caligari to Hitler* (1947), is that a first, radical version of the story – the doctor is the criminal – was softened and commercialized by the frame story, which makes the bad doctor merely a patient's fantasy, and restores the threatened authority figure. This is no doubt true to the historical sequence of the film's creation, but I do not think viewers experience the alternatives in quite this way. The madman's story reveals the director of the asylum to be a villain, no doubt about it:

the doctor *is* Caligari. But the frame story does not and cannot show the unnamed director to be a benevolent authority. It can only show him in control, possibly benign, but probably not. The suggestion, I think, is that the madman's story, literally false, reports an important and irreducible truth: any person in authority could turn into Caligari, and some already have. When the doctor says at the end that he sees what the storytelling patient's problem is, the effect is not consoling.

The striking thing about this film, as a film, is that its most memorable moments actually come very close to the tadpole shadow Woolf saw. When the doctor turns himself into Caligari he devises a visiting card, which we see in close-up, heavy letters in ornate black script running across the screen like an announcement of death, a triumphantly squiggled flourish under the signature. How could a mere name seem so menacing? A minute or so earlier, when the doctor experienced his temptation to become Caligari, the name itself flashed at him from all corners of the screen, in lights, like the signs of nightclubs or theatres, as if his desire had been lit up like a city.

The other remarkable moment in the film is that of the awakening of Cesare from his supposed twenty-five years of sleep. Caligari as showman does his patter, we see the mask-like face of the young Conrad Veidt, the massive black makeup underneath the eyes. Are these eyes open yet, could we tell? Then suddenly they are open, there can be no mistake. The eyes are huge, otherworldly, back from the dead. They are otherness itself, to adapt Woolf's image, rather than the statement "I am other." This is the genuine, rational magic of the cinema, and we may think of a related movie moment: the birth of the monster in James Whale's *Frankenstein* (USA, 1931). Victor Frankenstein insists that he is not resurrecting the dead but making life. "And you really believe that you can bring life to the dead?" Frankenstein's former mentor asks. Frankenstein says, "That body is not dead. It has never lived. I created it. I made it with my own hands from the bodies I took from graves, from the gallows, anywhere." When the creature first comes to life, all we see is its hand, quite still, and then faintly moving, stirring into animation as Cesare's eyes open into sight. And what is truly spooky about the creature when we finally see it whole, as it backs into the room and turns towards the light, with its stiff legs, short-armed suit, heavy boots, bolt in its neck, is its unearthliness. It does not look as if it has come from the grave, it looks as if it has come from nowhere.

Something wakens in these scenes, and the movie camera is there to watch it. Paintings and photographs are, necessarily, always too early or too late for such a moment, and words have to approach it another way. But what is the moment, what is it that awakes, apart from Cesare or the monster? Is it far-fetched to see here a repetition of the original shock of the cinema, the arrival of the train at La Ciotat, in the Lumière Brothers' first film (France, 1895)? The traditional story, endlessly retold, is that the first audiences were terrified by the realism afforded by the new technology: they thought the arriving train was going to run them over. But audiences can also be terrified, even now, by the further and deeper effect of this realism: not the impression that the machines and creatures of this two-dimensional world can reach out into ours, but the conviction that in spite their incredibly lifelike motions and gestures they cannot. They are like the dead mother whom Odysseus failed to embrace in the underworld; they are shadows, the most perfect copies of animated life we are likely ever to see. And they make us conscious of our exclusion. Their world is complete without us, as Stanley Cavell says, and as Woolf had also suggested. The figures in moving pictures, she said, were not more beautiful than photographs, but they were perhaps "more real": "We behold them as they are when we are not there. We see life as it is when we have no part in it."[8] I am not suggesting that the awakening of Cesare or the monster, or the arrival of the train at La Ciotat, is an allegory of the cinema, or that the audience needs to be conscious of any question about reality as it watches a film; only that the sight of otherness, the unmistakable sight of actual alien existence, is one of the cinema's great gifts, and anyone meeting it would be right to be overwhelmed.

Life to those Shadows is the title of Noël Burch's remarkable book about the early cinema, but his argument is that commercial films have overwhelmingly attempted to deny that the shadows are shadows, to replace the expressive possibilities Woolf evoked with an old-fashioned and all-consuming illusion of life. Burch calls this practice the Institutional Mode of Representation, a system that has come to seem like nature to us, as if the movies had to become what they did become, and as if their development into the mode of realism still dominant in Hollywood and on television was only to be expected, a form of evolution. We can see things this way only by concentrating on the reality effect in movies, and denying the ghost effect which is its precise twin; and by thinking of the movies as mostly defined by the single shot, the watching camera, a moving picture which is also an impeccable picture of movement. The moment we put two shots together we have a syntax, and realism in this mode, as perhaps in any other, involves our thoroughly learning and thoroughly forgetting this syntax – or not even forgetting, since we usually learn it without even knowing we have. The syntax consists chiefly of the principle of montage, which I have already mentioned; and of another fundamental movie principle, that of the construction of imaginary space through the direction of the gaze. Both of these principles are so quintessentially modernist that their burial in Victorian narrative illusion makes for an all but unmanageable paradox. It is as if we were to read the broken images of *The Waste Land* as a smoothly written novella; not fragments shored against ruin but complete sentences connected by an invisible but quite unproblematic grammar.

"Montage is the organization of cinematic material," Lev Kuleshov wrote in 1929. "Separate shots . . . did not constitute cinema, but only the material for cinema."[9] Kuleshov conducted a famous experiment by alternating the same shot of the actor Mozhukin with "various other shots (a plate of soup, a girl, a child's coffin)." Depending on the cutting, the same face looked hungry, lascivious, grieving, and so on. Sergei Eisenstein reports an even more interesting historical case, a Russian version of a German film about Danton. Camille Desmoulins is sentenced to death, Danton rushes to meet Robespierre, who brushes away a tear. A title card says, "In the name of freedom I had to sacrifice a friend." "But who could have guessed," Eisenstein continues, "that in the German original Danton . . . ran to the evil Robespierre and . . . spat in his face? And that it was this spit that Robespierre wiped from his face with a handkerchief . . . Two tiny cuts reversed the entire significance of this scene."[10]

Montage, then, is not only the organization of cinematic material, it is the implication of meaning – of a meaning that can only be implied, since films, like dreams, have a syntax which functions chiefly by association and accumulation. They cannot say no, they compact every apparent contradiction into a metaphor, make every time into a version of the present. Title cards and dialogue and voice-over narrative or commentary work to disguise and mitigate these features, but nothing quite cancels the sight on the screen: we cannot *not* see what we are seeing, and much of what is not seen is not said either. The famous opening scene of Luis Buñuel's *Un Chien andalou* (France, 1928) shows us a man, a pair of hands, a razor, a young woman, an eye, the moon, clouds, another (animal) eye. Only a range of logical leaps and suppositions converts this sequence into narrative: "The man sharpens the razor and then he cuts the woman's eye." Film has no *and*, still less an *and then*, and in this case, no possessive apostrophe. Films replace grammar and causality by simple succession: *then, then, then, then*. We invent the missing syntax, supply all the connectives – or rather we invent and supply a good deal more than we usually recognize.

But then, Eisenstein and Kuleshov would say, films are made of images *and* implication: irrefutable images, ideally, and irresistible implication; not the illusion of life but the force of a passion or an argument. When Eisenstein's *Battleship Potemkin* (USSR, 1925) shows us the squirming maggots in the seamen's food, this *is* an argument against the men's terrible working conditions, and the ship's doctor's claim that these are just dead eggs seems extravagant and heartless in advance, a denial not only of justice but of the very idea of evidence. But Eisenstein does not oppose the literal to the metaphorical. This film, with its changes of light, ships in the mist, rocking spaces of gleaming water, is always photographically beautiful in ways that *The Cabinet of Dr. Caligari* is not, and no doubt could not be, since it sought not to reconstruct the historical world but to photograph a world of nightmare. Eisenstein called Caligari a "barbaric carnival." But then when Eisenstein, in *Potemkin*, shows the seamen off-duty, sleeping below decks, their hammocks are intricately strung across each other at all angles, like a cat's cradle, the camera lingers on the faces, the physical forms of the men. There is something similar to the *Caligari* effect here, in spite of all the differences. The resemblance has to do with complication and constriction, with the picture of reality as tangle; but even more fundamentally with the reaching for metaphor in the cinema. Montage *is* metaphor here, it is what makes the image into a story. Later in the film, in the famous massacre scene on the Odessa steps, the soldiers descend like automata, firing on the fleeing crowd. A child is shot, trampled. There is a close-up on the child's mother's face, then she is shot too. An abandoned baby carriage teeters on a step, then starts its amazing, solitary journey through the carnage. Another woman is seen in close-up, her eye slashed by a soldier. This is a modernist poem, we might say; but it is not a photograph album. We do not convert the images into simple protest or an exclamation of horror: there are too many of them, and they are too memorable, for that. But we do not just collect them. We *read* them, to use a term which is often problematic in talking about film, but carries the necessary intimation of interpretation here.

In a quite different register, Chaplin's *The Gold Rush* (USA 1925) is hugely and brilliantly dependent on montage. What is wonderfully funny about the great scene where the prospectors' cabin is tilted over an abyss is the alternation between different knowledges of the situation. It is because we have seen the cabin from a distance, hanging ridiculously over the cliff's edge, that we know what is happening in the cabin. Chaplin and Big Jim are merely mystified by the sudden tips and lurches of the place. When their random movements, their crossing over to either side of the cabin, for instance, maintain or restore the balance, we are delighted by the intersection of chance and physics. The two men stamp, jump up and down, proving to their own satisfaction, at least for a moment, that nothing is wrong. Then Chaplin's attack of hiccups disturbs this precarious order. They do get out alive, Big Jim discovers his lost claim (underneath the cabin, or rather where the cabin was), and they both become rich. What follows now is one of the most intricate moments in the movies. Chaplin and Big Jim are traveling ("Homeward bound on the good ship Success," a title card says). They get out of their old clothes, and Chaplin now looks not like the tramp Charlie but like a rich man – like the moviemaker Charles Chaplin, say. He is wearing a smart overcoat with an astrakhan collar (later taken off to reveal a fur coat underneath, and a very smart morning suit, with tails, under that). Boarding ship, he is asked by a photographer if he will pose in his old clothes. He agrees, goes into a room to change, a valet pulls a curtain. Then pulls back the curtain, as if Chaplin, now back in costume, was stepping on to a stage. He goes out on to the deck, poses for the photographer, cleans his finger nails with his cane, steps back, comes forward; steps back again and falls out of sight on to a lower deck behind him. This accident reunites him with the girl he had lost, but we can scarcely concentrate on the happy ending because of the astonishing pile-up of visual wit. Chaplin, having once turned himself into Charlie, now turns Charlie into Chaplin and back again into Charlie, before our very eyes. What do we see, when we see him posing for that photograph? The very image of the man we saw before, when he was not rich, just the endlessly unlucky (but resourceful) tramp. What's the difference? There is no difference, visually. Montage here is plot rather than metaphor, the story of the riches and the return to visual poverty for the photograph. But the interaction between image and implication is very similar to that in Eisenstein's Danton example, and everything depends on the fact that the image cannot simply be absorbed into an alibi or the plausibility of a narrative excuse, that it both lends itself to and resists interpretation.

Buñuel said that he had excluded all narrative sense, all logical association from Un Chien andalou. I have already mentioned the opening scene. A title card says, "Once upon a time," and a burly fellow, who happens to be Buñuel himself, appears in his shirtsleeves, smoking, sharpening a razor, testing it against his thumbnail. He steps out on to a balcony and takes a look at the moon. We see a young woman's face in close-up. A hand holds her left eye open, while another hand approaches the eye with a razor. A cloud passes across the moon, as though slicing through it, and in a very large close-up the razor cuts into an eye, which leaks matter immediately. A new title card says, "Eight years later."

People still gasp when this scene is shown. There is no way of reducing the intimacy of its violence. The fact that the same young woman appears soon after in the film, both eyes happily intact, and the fact that the sliced eye, on inspection, can be seen to be that of an animal – of one of the two dead donkeys, I take it, which are later draped over two grand pianos – are not as comforting as one might hope. Much has been written about this eye, but it is clear that however Buñuel and Dalí arrived at this image ("Dalí and I," Buñuel told François Truffaut, "rejected mercilessly all that could have signified something"[11]), there is nothing accidental about its place in the film. It assaults the very organ we are viewing with, blinds us by proxy, and our physical disgust and fright are complicated by an obscure sense that some sort of ugly justice has been done, that we have got what we deserve. Antonin Artaud had written earlier that a film should come as "a shock to the eye, drawn so to speak from the very substance of the eye,"[12] and *Un Chien andalou* renders this figure with horrible literality. The casual narrative adds to the effect. We did not think he was sharpening the razor for that, and the cards suggest an idiotic storyteller who just does not know what is in his tale.

I think it helps to see *Un Chien andalou*, and indeed much of Surrealism, as an exercise in nonsense, as nonsense was understood, for example, by Lewis Carroll, who fulfilled nearly every Surrealist prophecy before it was made. "What has been understood," Paul Eluard wrote in a poem, "no longer exists."[13] Buñuel told a friend that Surrealism was not to be confused with idiocy, although they "share something of the same quality"; and R. P. Blackmur's dubious definition of an idiot's exploit ("a dive beneath the syntactic mind"[14]) is a fine description of nonsense. Nonsense represents, in a broader and less mystified form, the freedom from meaning that the Surrealists sought in automatic writing, and it is similarly elusive, and short-lived. Lautréamont's "Nothing is incomprehensible"[15] is not opposed to Eluard's assertion; it merely marks a later stage in the game of meaning.

Much of the nonsense in *Un Chien andalou* has to do specifically with the cinema. It is true, as critics have often said, that in spite of its avant-garde reputation *Un Chien andalou* is not formally a very experimental film; does not, apart from a bit of slow motion and some dabbling with an iris, tinker much with technique. But it is because the work is conventional in so many respects that its questioning of convention is so interesting.

What makes us think, for example, that space in a movie is continuous and substantial? If a person leaves a room, we picture him or her arriving in another room, or in a corridor, or on a street; not merely in another frame of film, or off the set entirely; or as happens in *Un Chien andalou*, in the *same* room, or on a beach. The gags here concern not philosophers' space but moviemakers' space, the fabricated world we keep taking for a straightforward representation of the actual world. The cinematic rule Buñuel keeps breaking is that of shot–countershot, whereby an image of a face looking offscreen followed by an image of an object means the person is looking at the object. Or a face looking offscreen right followed by another face looking offscreen left means two people are in the same space and talking to each other. These are rules not in the sense that anyone is punished for breaking them, but in the sense that the very constitution of familiar film worlds depends on them. There is nothing natural about this rule, as Noel Burch says; although some theorists, notably David Bordwell, have argued that if it did not relate to the nature of human perception in some way it would not have established itself as it did. "It took some twenty years for this figure of editing to become the cornerstone of a narrative continuity in films," P. Adams Sitney writes. "By the end of the First World War, it was a firmly established convention."[16] When Alfred Hitchcock, cited by Sitney, describes Kuleshov's montage experiment – "Show a man looking at something, say a baby. Then show him smiling" – his first sentence, in this context, takes entirely for granted the grammar of shot–countershot, this just is one of the ways in which you "show a man looking at something." The figure is so extensive in the cinema that we scarcely need to illustrate it further; the important thing is that it *is* a figure, one of the principal ways in which films become worlds rather than sequences of flat images, and that its logic resembles not only that of dreams but that of modernist poetics as say Ezra Pound understood them.

In *Un Chien andalou*, Buñuel also plays with the idea that a film frame always excludes something; or rather seems to exclude a space that prolongs the scene that is viewed. We can get very anxious about what we are *not* seeing in a movie, even when we know there is nothing there, or only a studio, power-cables and boxes and arc lamps. We think we may be missing a piece of the heroes' universe, that a shift of the camera will reveal an essential truth, the crucial absent clue. When the protagonist of *Un Chien andalou* picks up two ends of rope and starts to drag on them, the film makes an implicit promise that it will let us know where the ropes lead; this is the sort of thing films do, part of their decorum. But then when the man's extraordinary cargo comes into view – cork mats, melons, two live priests, the grand pianos with the dead donkeys slung across them – we are being shown not only the repressed and displaced past of the character, as many critics have thought, but again, a certain provocative possibility of the cinema. *This is a film.* What is beyond the frame, what can be dragged into sight at any moment, may literally be *anything.*

Dziga Vertov's *Man with a Movie Camera* (USSR, 1928), a montage of events depicting the life of a city, is a celebration of film, shown as miraculously able to capture motion – as distinct from two forms of stillness, that of a sleeping world and that of frozen action, the world halted in a photograph. The first form is shown in the early part of the film:

machines idle, buses in their depot, streets unpeopled, a woman asleep, a tramp asleep. This is a world that could move, but is not moving – yet. The camera moves, the only live thing in sight. Then the machines are shown in whirring motion, the buses emerge, the streets fill up, the woman awakes, gets dressed, the tramp yawns, rolls over. But the camera is always alive in this film, and always in sight, here and later, because the man with the movie camera keeps showing up on the screen, trotting from location to location with his tripod over his shoulder, flat cap, checkered sweater, jodhpurs, what used to be the moviemaker's uniform – at least in the movies. The man and his camera are reflected in mirrors, in people's eyes; we see the camera perched on a high building, swiveling to catch another portion of the street below; the man clings dangerously to a moving train, cranking his camera furiously. But of course the camera is also not in sight – since there has to be another camera beside this one, an unseen apparatus photographing this one at work. As Stanley Cavell says, you can always feel a camera is left out of the picture, the one that is running now, and nowhere is this claim truer than for this movie. At one point, as if performing this truth, daring us to deny it, the camera on its tripod starts to work on its own, stalking about, stretching its legs, hauling itself up to its full height, looking very much like one of the long-limbed attack creatures in George Lucas's *Star Wars* (USA, 1977). So *Man with the Movie Camera* is a double, glancing title: it names the film's theme, and the visual image that connects scene to scene; and it names the invisible author, telling us that this is the actual world, collected with documentary enthusiasm, and also the world Dziga Vertov has made.

The second form of stillness is brusquely, bluntly introduced by a freeze-frame shot of a horse pulling a carriage. Racing along a moment ago, now the horse is stopped in mid-motion, just a photograph. Various other stills appear, a woman sewing, a baby, another woman's face, all intercut with moving pictures of a woman doing something else, looking at strips of . . . celluloid, slicing them with scissors. She is editing a film, and after a little more parallel montage (stills, woman editing) we see (we assume) what she has been editing, and these very stills come to life, fill the screen. The horse continues its career. There is a very strong sense of miracle. It does not seem strange that a film could be stopped; but it seems incredible that a photograph could be started, that these frozen figures spring to life, as if there had never been a photograph, as if they were simply there, alive, and film had registered their presence, the way an audiotape registers sound. What Vertov is suggesting, I take it, is that film neither invents the world nor simply records it. His term "cinema-eye," like Isherwood's famous phrase "I am a camera," insists on the documentary nature of the material to be seen; on the *seen* nature of the material. But eyes inhabit human heads, and are instructed by passions and prejudices as well as optics. Vertov thought the time was always the present in film, and did not like the simulation of historical scenes which Eisenstein (and many others) went in for. But his ideal was a cinema based on the "organization of camera-recorded documentary material,"[17] where the element of organization is at least as important as the element of record, and *Man with a Movie Camera* insists on the art of the filmmaker as a way, perhaps, of getting us to see historical reality more clearly – the way the Russian Formalists, in literature, saw the estrangement of the world as a path to the restoration of a world lost to automation and habit. There are several remarkable split-screen shots, for example, where the two halves of the screen dissolve into each other: two city scenes with criss-crossing crowds, the two halves of a theatre facade imploding on each other, like twin leaning towers colliding.

Man with a Movie Camera is all montage, a tribute to film as montage. Its narrative is that of the seeing eye, and it does not contain, as far as I can tell, a single instance of shot–countershot. Carl Theodore Dreyer's fabulous *Passion of Joan of Arc* (France, 1928), by contrast, takes this by now established, mainstream narrative figure and converts it into an art form of its own. The movie depicts Joan's trial, her stubborn resistance to her accusers, her recantation through fear, and her recantation of her recanta-tion. At the end she is burned, and the smoke-singed face of Maria Falconetti as Joan, intercut with Breughelesque faces in the crowd and among the soldiers, is one of the great moving icons of the cinema. What we see here is not so much her pain or terror, or even her heroism, as her helplessness, the agony of her loyalty to her simple ideas of goodness and justice. Before that we have seen what she sees, the rows of sympathetic and unsympathetic faces among her ecclesiastical judges, the hard mugs of the English soldiers, often shot from below in an angle which anticipates the directorial signature of Orson Welles. We see what she cannot see, the world outside her cell, a whole carnivalesque crowd of jugglers, acrobats, contortionists, a figure on a swing, another figure balancing a huge cartwheel on its head. And we see her as characters in the film can and cannot see her, a living person in the same room and a face in huge, long close-up, a map of the intimate, intricate sorrows of a simple soul. Buñuel wrote admiringly of the "pitiful geography" of all the faces in this film, as if flesh and blood were all a filmmaker needed for tragedy; but emphasized the delicacy of Dreyer's unsentimental attention to Joan's innocence: "Lit by tears, purified by flames, head shaved, grubby as a little girl, yet for a moment she stops crying to watch some pigeons settle on the spire of the church. Then, she dies."[18] The pigeons are probably larks, or pigeons cast as larks; but here as with Hitchcock's remark about the man and the baby, we note the ease of the syntax, the verb which slips into the space between frame and frame. "She stops crying to watch. . ." That is, a shot of her face is followed by a shot of some birds.

Dreyer later said he wished he could have made this film with sound, but the silence of this work has an extraordinary eerie quality, and tells us something about silent films in general. The French surrealist poet Robert Desnos once quoted an anonymous friend of his as saying that the old cinema was not silent (mute in French); it was the spectator who was deaf. "People say terrible things to each other, and like a sick person, he needs to have them written down."[19] In *The Passion of Joan of Arc*, we do indeed feel that the film is not silent, since it is full of talk, accusations, dialogue; and we guess at the dialogue, try to read lips, long before the title cards come to our assistance. The world of the film is complete, and sound could only help us to understand better what is already there without us. The same is true of all the great silent films: *Caligari*, Fritz Lang's *Dr. Mabuse the Gambler* (Germany, 1922), *Potemkin*, Erich von Stroheim's *Greed* (USA, 1924), many others. In other silent films, notably those of D. W. Griffith, like *Broken Blossoms* (USA, 1919) and *Intolerance* (USA, 1919), spectacular as they are, you feel the weight of prehistory: these lurid narratives are hampered by their silence, sound can only become a fulfillment for them.

Modernism in the movies was not always highbrow. Or, not only highbrow movies were modernist. One could argue (although I shall not just now) that animated cartoons are one of Modernism's most significant achievements, and certainly one of Modernism's most extravagant and brilliant appearances in the cinema occurs in the Marx Brothers' *Duck Soup* (Leo McCarey, USA, 1933). There is a scene here which makes the cinematic self-reference in Vertov or Chaplin seem very modest indeed. All three Marx Brothers, Groucho, Chico, and Harpo, look alike at this moment in the film. For the purposes of an elaborate secret-stealing plot, both Chico and Harpo are disguised as Groucho: all three are wearing a nightcap, a long white nightshirt, Groucho glasses and eyebrows and Groucho greasepaint moustache. After various misadventures, Harpo, pursued by Groucho, crashes through a full-length mirror. He pauses, and decides to simulate the mirror that is not there by imitating the gestures of Groucho as he faces it. Groucho scratches his chin, lifts an eyebrow, does a little dance; leaves the frame of the mirror and returns hopping; leaves the frame of the mirror and returns on his knees. Harpo copies all of these gestures with minute fidelity – or rather, since the gestures are simultaneous, he does not copy them, he intuits them and performs them. At one point, the point at which the routine reaches its funniest and also its most disturbing reach, Groucho spins full circle and spreads his arms, while Harpo stands quite still and spreads his arms.

Only the movie audience has seen that Harpo has not spun round, and the following implications and questions crowd upon us. The uncanny (and hilarious) imitation of a mirror gives way to a picture of the mirror's difference, not only what it can and cannot do, but what it does not have to do. When Harpo does not spin he asserts the reality of the mirror even more fully than in his other acts. If we were there, if we had spun around, we would not be able to see anything in the mirror except the moment of our turning away and the moment of our coming back. It is like missing the instant of Frankenstein's creature's birth, or Cesare's awakening. It is like a photograph, not a movie. It is only because this is a movie that we see what Groucho cannot see, what we ourselves would not see if we were there. You cannot see yourself in a mirror when you are looking away. Or more eerily, you cannot tell what is happening in a mirror when you close your eyes. And more subtly, if you are not looking at it, it does not matter whether the mirror is really a mirror or not.

Picturing a mirror, an empty space which becomes a mirror, the film pictures itself, and more than that. It pictures an anxiety of knowledge, comically drawn here, but desperate elsewhere, as in several of Welles's films, notably *Citizen Kane* (USA, 1941) and *Mr. Arkadin* (France/Spain, 1955), where the spectators' knowledge is fuller than that of the characters, but also useless. We know what "rosebud" means in the first of these two films – it refers to the sled taken away from Charles Foster Kane as a child, and therefore, sentimentally, to the child in him who got lost – but what good is that knowledge to him or us? Because films rely so much on our seeing things, on our watching a world, on the illusion of our being there, their richest effect is not like that of the great realist novels or plays, where our absence is what allows us to accept and rebuild and inhabit the offered worlds. In modernist cinema, or in any cinema which remembers its modernist possibilities, our absence, however much we are prepared for it, is a shock. How could a world so real get on so well without us? How could we not be able to reach into a world so meticulously resembling ours? Like the effect of immediate reality, this denied/recalled absence is "an orchid in the land of technology"; a false flower of the modernist waste land, desolate when it is not comic, but riotously comic, fortunately, when the infernal machine trusts us with its secrets. "We see life as it is when we have no part in it"; when it is not our face and body in the mirror. It is not just that we haunt the world of films, as Cavell memorably says. It is that a florid, blooming technology has taken our place there, and is living what used to be our life.

NOTES

1 Roland Barthes, *Camera Lucida: Reflections on Photography*. Trans. Richard Howard (New York: Hill and Wang, 1981), p. 3.
2 Walter Benjamin, *Illuminations*, trans. Harry Zohn (New York: Schocken, 1969), p. 233.
3 Christopher Isherwood, *Prater Violet* (New York: North Point Press, Farrar Straus & Giroux, 1996), pp. 30–1.
4 Ibid., p. 65.
5 Ibid., p. 71.
6 Virginia Woolf, *The Captain's Death-Bed and Other Essays* (New York and London: Harcourt Brace Jovanovich, 1978), p. 183.
7 S. S. Prawer, *Caligari's Children* (Oxford: Oxford University Press, 1980), p. 173.
8 Woolf, *The Captain's Death-Bed*, p. 181.
9 Lev Kuleshov, *Kuleshov on Film*, trans. Ronald Levaco (Berkeley, Los Angeles, and London: University of California Press, 1974), p. 48.
10 Sergei Eisenstein, *Film Form*, quoted in P. Adams Sitney, *Modernist Montage* (New York: Columbia University Press, 1990), p. 40.
11 Luis Buñuel, interview with Francois Truffaut, quoted in Steven Kovacs, *From Enchantment to Rage: the Story of Surrealist Cinema* (Rutherford, NJ: Fairleigh Dickinson University Press, 1980), p. 196.
12 Antonin Artaud, quoted in J. H. Matthews, *Surrealism and Film* (Ann Arbor: University of Michigan Press, 1971), p. 79.
13 Paul Eluard, *Capitale de la Douleur* (Oxford: Basil Blackwell, 1985), p. 77; my translation.
14 R. P. Blackmur, *Eleven Essays in the European Novel* (New York: Harcourt Brace and World, 1964), p. 144.
15 Lautréamont, quoted in Mary Ann Caws, *The Poetry of Dada and Surrealism* (Princeton: Princeton University Press, 1970), p. 175.
16 Sitney, *Modernist Montage*, p. 17.
17 Dziga Vertov, quoted in *Encylopedia Britannica*, entry on "Motion Pictures: Soviet Union."
18 Luis Buñuel, "Carl Dreyer's *Joan of Arc*" in Francisco Aranda, *Luis Buñuel* (New York: Da Capo, 1978), p. 268.
19 Robert Desnos, *Cinéma* (Paris: Gallimard, 1966), p. 99, my translation.

FURTHER READING

Intellectual and institutional contexts

Adorno, Theodor, and Max Horkheimer. *Dialectic of Enlightenment.* Trans. John Cumming. London and New York: Verso, 1986.

Altick, Richard. *The English Common Reader.* Chicago: University of Chicago Press, 1957.

Beach, Sylvia. *Shakespeare and Company.* Lincoln: University of Nebraska Press, 1980. First edition, 1956.

Bell, Michael. *Literature, Modernism and Myth: Belief and Responsibility in the Twentieth Century.* Cambridge: Cambridge University Press, 1997.

Bell, Michael, ed. *The Context of English Literature, 1900–1930.* London: Methuen, 1980.

Benjamin, Walter. "The Work of Art in the Age of Mechanical Reproduction." In Hannah Arendt, ed., *Walter Benjamin: Illuminations.* New York, Schocken Books: 1969, pp. 217–51.

Blumemberg, Hans. *The Legitimacy of the Modern Age.* Trans. Robert M. Wallace. Cambridge, MA and London: MIT Press, 1983.

Bohrer, Karl-Heinz, ed. *Mythos und Moderne.* Frankfurt: Suhrkamp, 1983.

Bradbury, Malcolm, and James McFarlane, eds. *Modernism 1890–1930.* Harmondsworth: Penguin, 1976.

Bürger, Peter. *Theory of the Avant-Garde.* Trans. Michael Shaw. Minneapolis: University of Minnesota Press, 1984.

Charvat, William. *The Profession of Authorship in America, 1800–1870.* Columbus: Ohio State University Press, 1968.

Collins, A. S. *Authorship in the Days of Johnson, Being a Study of the Relation Between Author, Patron, Publisher and Public, 1726–1780.* London: George Routledge, 1927.

Crow, Thomas. "Modernism and Mass Culture in the Visual Arts." In Benjamin H. D. Buchloh, Serge Guilbaut, and David Solkin, eds., *Modernism and Modernity* (Halifax: Nova Scotia College of Art and Design, 1983), pp. 215–64.

Dale, Peter Alan. *In Pursuit of a Scientific Culture.* Madison: University of Wisconsin Press, 1989.

Debord, Guy. *Society of the Spectacle.* Detroit: Black and Red, 1983. First edition, Paris: Editions Buchet-Chastel, 1967.

Delany, Paul. *Islands of Money: English Literature and the Financial Culture.* Andover: University of Massachusetts Press, 1998.

Eagleton, Terry. "Capitalism, Modernism and Postmodernism." In David Lodge, ed., *Modern Criticism and Theory: A Reader.* London: Longman, 1988, pp. 385–98.

Ellmann, Richard, and Charles Feidelson, eds. *The Modern Tradition.* Oxford: Oxford University Press, 1965.

Elsner, John, and Roger Cardinal, *The Cultures of Collecting.* London: Reaktion Books, 1994.

FitzGerald, Michael. *Making Modernism: Picasso and the Creation of the Market for Twentieth-Century Art.* New York: Farrar, Straus and Giroux, 1995.

Habermas, Jürgen. *The Structural Transformation of the Public Sphere: An Inquiry into a Category of Bourgeois Society.* Trans. Thomas Burger. Cambridge, MA: MIT Press, 1989.

"Further Reflections on the Public Sphere." In Craig Calhoun, ed., *Habermas and the Public Sphere.* Cambridge: MIT Press, 1992, pp. 421–61.

Hauser, Arnold. *The Social History of Art,* vol. IV, *Naturalism to the Film Age.* London: Routledge and Kegan Paul, 1962.

Heisenberg, Werner. *The Physicist's Conception of Nature.* London: Hutchinson, 1958.

Jensen, Robert. *Marketing Modernism in Fin de Siècle Europe.* Princeton: Princeton University Press, 1994.

Kaestle, Carl. *Literacy in the United States: Readers and Reading Since 1880.* New Haven and London: Yale University Press, 1991.

Kenner, Hugh. *The Pound Era.* Berkeley: University of California Press, 1971.

Kline, Morris. *Mathematical Thought from Ancient to Modern Times.* New York: Oxford University Press 1972.

Levenson, Michael. *A Genealogy of Modernism.* Cambridge: Cambridge University Press, 1984.

Lidderdale, Jane, and Mary Micholson. *Dear Miss Weaver: Harriet Shaw Weaver, 1876–1961.* New York: Viking Press, 1970.

Manganaro, Marc, ed. *Modernist Anthropology: from Fieldwork to Text.* Princeton: Princeton University Press, 1990.

McAleer, Joseph. *Popular Reading and Publishing in Britain, 1914–1950.* Oxford: Clarendon Press, 1992.

Naremore, James, and Patrick Brantlinger. *Modernity and Mass Culture.* Bloomington: Indiana University Press, 1991.

Nicholls, Peter. *Modernisms: A Literary Guide.* Berkeley: University of California Press, 1995.

Ohmann, Richard. *Selling Culture: Magazines, Markets, and Class at the Turn of the Century.* London and New York: Verso, 1996.

Pearson, Karl. *The Grammar of Science.* London: Walter Scott, 1892.

Rainey, Lawrence. *Institutions of Modernism: Literary Elites and Public Culture.* New Haven and London: Yale University Press, 1997.

Reid, B. L. *The Man from New York: John Quinn and His Friends.* (Oxford and New York: Oxford University Press, 1968.

Rowland, Jr., William G. *Literature and the Marketplace: Romantic Writers and*

Their Audiences in Great Britain and the United States. Lincoln: University of Nebraska Press, 1996.

Schwartz, Sanford. *The Matrix of Modernism: Pound, Eliot and Early Twentieth-Century Thought*. Princeton: Princeton University Press, 1985.

Sloterdijk, Peter. *Critique of Cynical Reason*. Trans. Michael Eldred. London and New York: Verso, 1985.

Sutherland, John. *Victorian Novelists and Publishers*. London: Athlone Press, 1976.

Taylor, Charles. *The Sources of the Self: the Making of Modern Identity*. Cambridge: Cambridge University Press, 1989.

Wexler, Joyce Piell. *Who Paid for Modernism? Art, Money, and the Fiction of Conrad, Joyce, and Lawrence*. Fayetteville: University of Arkansas Press, 1997.

White, Cynthia and Harrison. *Canvasses and Careers*. New York: Wiley, 1965.

Willison, Ian, Warwick Gould, and Warren Chernaik, eds. *Modernist Writers and the Marketplace*. London and New York: Macmillan and St. Martin's Press, 1996.

Wilson, Edmund. *Axel's Castle, a Study in the Imaginative Literature of 1870–1930*. New York: Scribner's, 1931.

Novel and poetry

Attridge Derek. *Peculiar Language: Literature as Difference from the Renaissance to James Joyce*. London: Methuen, 1988.

Baker, Houston A. *Modernism and the Harlem Renaissance*. Chicago: University of Chicago Press, 1987.

Bates, Milton. *Wallace Stevens: A Mythology of Self*. Berkeley: University of California Press, 1985.

Bell, Michael. *D. H. Lawrence: Language and Being*. Cambridge: Cambridge University Press, 1991.

Benstock, Shari. *Women of the Left Bank: Paris, 1900–1940*. London: Virago, 1987.

Bernstein, Michael. *The Tale of the Tribe: Ezra Pound and the Modern Verse Epic*. Princeton: Princeton University Press, 1980.

Blair, Sara. *Henry James and the Writing of Race and Nation*. Cambridge: Cambridge University Press, 1996.

Bloom, Harold. *Figures of Capable Imagination*. New York: Seabury Press, 1976.
  Wallace Stevens: The Poems of Our Climate. Ithaca, NY: Cornell University Press, 1977.
  Yeats. Oxford and New York: Oxford University Press, 1970.

Bradshaw, David. "The Novel in the 1920s." In Dodsworth, ed., pp. 195–224.

Breslin, James E. B. *From Modern to Contemporary*. Chicago: University of Chicago Press, 1984.
  William Carlos Williams. Oxford and New York: Oxford University Press, 1970.

Bromwich, David. *A Choice of Inheritance: Self and Community from Edmund Burke to Robert Frost*. Cambridge, MA: Harvard University Press, 1989.

Bush, Ronald. *T. S. Eliot: A Study in Character and Style*. Oxford and New York: Oxford University Press, 1984.

The Genesis of Ezra Pound's Cantos. Princeton: Princeton University Press, 1976.

Cave, Terence. *Recognitions: A Study in Poetics.* Oxford: Clarendon Press, 1990.

Costello, Bonnie. *Marianne Moore: Imaginary Possessions.* Cambridge, MA: Harvard University Press, 1981.

Elizabeth Bishop: Questions of Mastery. Cambridge, MA: Harvard University Press, 1991.

DeKoven, Marianne. *A Different Language: Gertrude Stein's Experimental Writing.* Madison: University of Wisconsin Press, 1983.

Dodsworth, Martin, ed. *The Penguin History of Literature: The Twentieth Century.* Harmondsworth: Penguin, 1994.

DuPlessis, Rachel Blau. *H.D.: The Career of that Struggle.* Brighton: Harvester, 1986.

Erkkila, Betsy. *The Wicked Sisters: Women Poets, Literary History and Discord.* Oxford: Oxford University Press, 1992.

Fussell, Paul. *The Great War and Modern Memory.* New York and London: Oxford University Press, 1975.

Gibson, Andrew, ed. *Reading Joyce's "Circe."* European Joyce Studies 3. Amsterdam: Rodopi, 1994.

Gordon, Lyndall. *Eliot's Early Years.* Oxford: Oxford University Press, 1977.

Eliot's New Life. Oxford: Oxford University Press, 1988.

Guest, Barbara. *Herself Defined: The Poet H.D. and Her World.* Garden City: Doubleday, 1984.

Hammer, Landon. *Janus-Faced Modernism: Hart Crane and Allen Tate.* Princeton: Princeton University Press, 1993.

Horne, Philip. "The Novel to 1914." In Dodsworth, ed., pp. 65–108.

Hynes, Samuel. *The Auden Generation.* London: Bodley Head, 1976.

The Pattern of Hardy's Poetry. Chapel Hill: University of North Carolina Press, 1961.

A War Imagined. London: Bodley Head, 1990.

Jarrell, Randall. *Poetry and the Age.* New York: Knopf, 1953.

Johnson, Barbara. "The Critical Difference: Balzac's *Sarrasine* and Barthes's *S/Z*." In Robert Young, ed. *Untying the Text: A Post-Structuralist Reader.* London: Routledge and Kegan Paul, 1981, pp. 162–74.

Kalstone, David. *Becoming a Poet: Elizabeth Bishop with Marianne Moore and Robert Lowell.* ed. Robert Hemenway. London: Hogarth Press, 1989.

Kenner, Hugh. *Ulysses.* London: Allen and Unwin, 1980.

Kermode, Frank. *The Sense of an Ending: Studies in the Theory of Fiction.* London: Oxford University Press, 1966.

Lawrence, Karen. *The Odyssey of Style in "Ulysses."* Princeton: Princeton University Press, 1981.

Lentricchia, Frank. *Ariel and the Police: Michel Foucault, William James, Wallace Stevens.* Brighton: Harvester Wheatsheaf, 1988.

Modernist Quartet. Cambridge: Cambridge University Press, 1994.

Levenson, Michael. *Modernism and the Fate of Individuality: Character and Novelistic Form from Conrad to Woolf.* Cambridge: Cambridge University Press, 1991.

Litz, A. Walton. *Introspective Voyager: The Poetic Development of Wallace Stevens.* Oxford and New York: Oxford University Press, 1972.

Litz, A. Walton, ed. *Eliot in His Time*. Princeton: Princeton University Press, 1973.

Longenbach, James. *Modernist Poetics of History*. Princeton: Princeton University Press, 1987.

    Stone Cottage: Pound, Yeats, and Modernism. Oxford: Oxford University Press, 1988.

    Wallace Stevens: The Plain Sense of Things. Oxford: Oxford University Press, 1991.

McDiarmid, Lucy. *Saving Civilization: Yeats, Eliot and Auden Between the Wars*. Cambridge: Cambridge University Press, 1984.

Mendelson, Edward. *Early Auden*. London: Faber and Faber, 1981.

Miller, J. Hillis. *The Linguistic Moment: From Wordsworth to Stevens*. Princeton: Princeton University Press, 1985.

    Poets of Reality. Cambridge, MA: Harvard University Press, 1966.

North, Michael. *The Dialect of Modernism: Race, Language and Twentieth-Century Literature*. Oxford: Oxford University Press, 1994.

Parisi, Joseph, ed. *Marianne Moore: The Art of a Modernist*. Ann Arbor: University of Michigan Research Press, 1990.

Perkins, David. *A History of Modern Poetry: From the 1890s to the High Modernist Mode*. Cambridge, MA: Harvard University Press, 1976.

    A History of Modern Poetry: Modernism and After. Cambridge, MA: Harvard University Press, 1987.

Perloff, Marjorie. *The Dance of the Intellect: Studies in the Pound Tradition*. Cambridge: Cambridge University Press, 1985.

    The Poetry of Indeterminacy: Rimbaud to Cage. Princeton: Princeton University Press, 1981.

Pinsky, Robert. *Poetry and the World*. New York: Ecco Press, 1988.

    The Situation of Poetry. Princeton: Princeton University Press, 1977.

Poirier, Richard. *Poetry and Pragmatism*. London: Faber and Faber, 1992.

    Robert Frost: The Work of Knowing. Oxford and New York: Oxford University Press, 1977.

Pritchard, William. *Randall Jarrell: A Literary Life*. New York: Farrar, Straus and Giroux, 1990.

    Robert Frost: A Literary Life. Oxford: Oxford University Press, 1984.

Rainey, Lawrence S. *Ezra Pound and the Monument of Culture: Text, History, and the Malatesta Cantos*. Chicago: University of Chicago Press, 1991.

Ramazani, Jahan. *Poetry of Mourning: The Modern Elegy from Hardy to Heaney*. Chicago: Chicago University Press, 1994.

Richardson, James. *Thomas Hardy: The Poetry of Necessity*. Chicago: University of Chicago Press, 1977.

Ricks, Christopher. *T. S. Eliot and Prejudice*. Berkeley: University of California Press, 1988.

Schweik, Susan. *A Gulf So Deeply Cut: American Poets and the Second World War*. Madison: University of Wisconsin Press, 1991.

Slatin, Myles. *The Savage's Romance: The Poetry of Marianne Moore*. University Park: Pennsylvania State University Press, 1986.

Trotter, David. *The English Novel in History*. London: Routledge, 1993.

Vendler, Helen. *On Extended Wings: Wallace Stevens' Longer Poems*. Cambridge, MA: Harvard University Press, 1969.

Part of Nature, Part of Us: Modern American Poets. Cambridge, MA: Harvard University Press, 1980.

Witmeyer, Hugh. *The Poetry of Ezra Pound*. Berkeley: University of California Press, 1981.

Yingling, Thomas. *Hart Crane and the Homosexual Text*. Chicago: University of Chicago Press, 1990.

Drama, film and the fine arts

Arnason, H. Harvard. *A History of Modern Art: Painting, Sculpture, Architecture, Photography*. Third edition. New York: Abrams, 1986.

Artaud, Antonin. *The Theatre and Its Double*. Trans. Mary Caroline Richards. New York: Grove Press, 1958.

Barthes, Roland. *Camera Lucida*. Trans. Richard Howard. New York: Hill and Wang, 1981.

Benjamin, Walter. *Illuminations*. Trans. Harry Zohn. New York: Harcourt Brace Jovanovich, 1968.

Bordwell, David, Janet Staiger, and Kristin Thompson. *The Classical Hollywood Cinema: Film Style and Mode of Production to 1960*. New York: Columbia University Press, 1985.

Bowser, Eileen. *The Transformation of Cinema, 1908–1915*. New York: Scribner's, 1990.

Brecht, Bertolt. *Brecht on Theatre: The Development of an Aesthetic*. Ed. and trans. John Willett. New York: Hill and Wang, 1964.

Brustein, Robert. *The Theater of Revolt: An Approach to the Modern Drama*. Boston: Little, Brown, 1964.

Burch, Noel. *Life to those Shadows*. Trans. Ben Brewster. Berkeley and Los Angeles: University of California Press, 1990.

Theory of Film Practice. Trans. Helen R. Lane. Princeton: Princeton University Press, 1981.

Butler, Christopher. *Early Modernism: Literature, Music, and Painting in Europe, 1900–1916*. Oxford: Clarendon Press, 1994.

Cavell, Stanley. *The World Viewed: Reflections on the Ontology of Film*. Enlarged edition. Cambridge, MA: Harvard University Press, 1979.

Charney, Leo, and Vanessa Schwartz, eds. *Cinema and the Invention of Modernity*. Berkeley, Los Angeles, London: University of California Press, 1995.

Chipp, Herschel B., compiler. *Theories of Modern Art: A Sourcebook by Artists and Critics*. Berkeley: University of California Press, 1994.

Coates, Paul. *Film at the Intersection of High and Mass Culture*. Cambridge: Cambridge University Press, 1994.

Gilman, Richard. *The Making of Modern Drama*. New York: Farrar, Straus and Giroux, 1974.

Desnos, Robert. *Cinema*. Paris: Gallimard, 1966.

Eisenstein, Sergei. *Film Form*. Trans. Jan Leyda. New York: Harcourt Brace Jovanovich, 1949.

Elsaesser, Thomas, ed. *Early Cinema: Space Frame Narrative*. London: British Film Institute Publishing, 1990.

Hollander, Anne. *Moving Pictures*. New York: Knopf, 1989.

Innes, C. D. *Avant-Garde Theatre*. London: Routledge, 1993.
  Edward Gordon Craig. Cambridge: Cambridge University Press, 1983.
  Erwin Piscator's Political Theatre. Cambridge: Cambridge University Press, 1972.
  Modern British Drama: 1890–1990. Cambridge: Cambridge University Press, 1992.
Jameson, Fredric. *Signatures of the Visible*. New York and London: Routledge, 1992.
Kennedy, Andrew K. *Six Dramatists in Search of a Language*. London and Cambridge: Cambridge University Press, 1975.
Kracauer, Siegried. *From Caligari to Hitler*. Princeton: Princeton University Press, 1947.
Kuleshov, Lev. *Kuleshov on Film*. Trans. Ronald Levaco. Berkeley, Los Angeles, London: University of California Press, 1974.
Lamm, Martin. *Modern Drama*. Trans. Karin Elliott. Oxford: Blackwell, 1952.
MacLeod, Glen G. *Wallace Stevens and Modern Art: From the Armory Show to Abstract Expressionism*. New Haven: Yale University Press, 1993.
Musser, Charles. *The Emergence of Cinema: The American Screen to 1907*. New York: Scribner's, 1990.
Perloff, Marjorie. *The Futurist Moment: Avant-Garde, Avant Guerre, and the Language Rupture*. Chicago: University of Chicago Press, 1986.
Prawer, S. S. *Caligari's Children*. Oxford and London: Oxford University Press, 1980.
Quigley, Austin E. *The Modern Stage and Other Worlds*. New York and London: Methuen, 1985.
Read, Herbert. *A Concise History of Modern Painting*. Revised edition. Preface by Benedict Read. Concluding chapter by Caroline Tisdale and William Feaver. London: Thames and Hudson, 1988.
Sidnell, Michael. *Dances of Death*. London: Faber and Faber, 1984.
Sitney, P. A. *Modernist Montage*. New York: Columbia University Press, 1990.
Steiner, Wendy. *The Colors of Rhetoric: Problems in the Relation Between Modern Literature and Painting*. Chicago: University of Chicago Press, 1982.
Styan, J. L. *Modern Drama in Theory and Practice*. 3 vols. Cambridge and New York: Cambridge University Press, 1981.
Szondi, Peter. *Theorie des Modernen Dramas*. Frankfurt-on-Main: Suhrkamp, 1966.
Williams, Alan Larson. *Republic of Images*. Cambridge, MA: Harvard University Press, 1992.
Wood, Michael. *America in the Movies: or, "Santa Maria, it had slipped my mind."* New York: Basic Books, 1975.

Gender and the politics of culture

Abraham, Julie. *Are Girls Necessary? Lesbian Writing and Modern Histories*. New York: Routledge, 1996.
Ardis, Ann. *New Women, New Novels: Feminism and Early Modernism*. New Brunswick, NJ: Rutgers University Press, 1990.
Benstock, Shari. *Women of the Left Bank: Paris, 1900–1940*. Austin: University of Texas Press, 1986.
Clark, Suzanne. *Sentimental Modernism: Women Writers and the Revolution of the Word*. Bloomington: Indiana University Press, 1991.

DeKoven, Marianne. *Rich and Strange: Gender, History, Modernism.* Princeton: Princeton University Press, 1991.

Denning, Michael. *Mechanic Accents: Dime Novels and Working-Class Culture in America.* London: Verso, 1987.

Dettmar, Kevin J. H., and Stephen Watt, eds. *Marketing Modernisms: Self-Promotion, Canonization, Rereading.* Ann Arbor: University of Michigan Press, 1996.

Douglas, Ann. *Terrible Honesty: Mongrel Manhattan in the 1920s.* New York: Farrar, Straus and Giroux, 1995.

DuPlessis, Rachel Blau. *Writing Beyond the Ending: Narrative Strategies of Twentieth-Century Women Writers.* Bloomington: Indiana University Press, 1985.

Elliott, Bridget, and Jo-Ann Wallace. *Women Artists and Writers: Modernist (Im)positionings.* New York: Routledge, 1994.

Felski, Rita, *The Gender of Modernity.* Cambridge, MA: Harvard University Press, 1996.

Friedman, Ellen, and Miriam Fuchs, eds. *Breaking the Sequence: Women's Experimental Fiction.* Princeton: Princeton University Press, 1989.

Gilbert, Sandra, and Susan Gubar. *No Man's Land*, vol. I, *The War of the Words.* New Haven: Yale University Press, 1988.

No Man's Land, vol. II, *Sexchanges.* New Haven: Yale University Press, 1989.

No Man's Land, vol. III, *Letters from the Front.* New Haven: Yale University Press, 1994.

Hanscombe, Gillian, and Virginia L. Smyers. *Writing for Their Lives: The Modernist Women, 1910–1940.* Boston: Northeastern University Press, 1987.

Hutchinson, George. *The Harlem Renaissance in Black and White.* Cambridge, MA: Belknap Press of Harvard University Press, 1995.

Huyssen, Andreas. *After the Great Divide: Modernism, Mass Culture, Postmodernism.* Bloomington: Indiana University Press, 1986.

Jardine, Alice. *Gynesis: Configurations of Woman and Modernity.* Ithaca, NY: Cornell University Press, 1985.

North, Michael. *The Political Aesthetic of Yeats, Eliot, and Pound.* Cambridge: Cambridge University Press, 1991.

Reed, Christopher, ed. *Not at Home: The Suppression of Domesticity in Modern Art and Architecture.* London and New York: Thames and Hudson, 1993.

Sante, Luc. *Low Life: Lures and Snares of Old New York.* New York: Vintage, 1992.

Scott, Bonnie K., ed. *The Gender of Modernism.* Bloomington: Indiana University Press, 1990.

Refiguring Modernism. Bloomington: Indiana University Press, 1995. Vol. I, *The Women of 1928.* Vol. II, *Postmodern Feminist Readings of Woolf, West and Barnes.*

Suleiman, Susan Rubin. *Subversive Intent: Gender Politics and the Avant-Garde.* Cambridge, MA: Harvard University Press, 1990.

Wall, Cheryl A. *Women of the Harlem Renaissance.* Bloomington: Indiana University Press, 1995

Williams, Raymond. *The Politics of Modernism: Against the New Conformists.* London: Verso, 1989.

INDEX

Index

CAMBRIDGE COMPANIONS TO LITERATURE

CAMBRIDGE COMPANIONS TO CULTURE